Tonality as Drama

Closure and Interruption in
Four Twentieth-Century American Operas

Edward D. Latham

University of North Texas Press
Denton, Texas

Printed in the United States of America.

10 9 8 7 6 5 4 3 2 1

Permissions:
University of North Texas Press
P.O. Box 311336
Denton, TX 76203-1336

The paper used in this book meets the minimum requirements of the American National Standard for Permanence of Paper for Printed Library Materials, z39.48.1984. Binding materials have been chosen for durability.

Latham, Edward David.
  Tonality as drama : closure and interruption in four twentieth-century American operas / Edward D. Latham.
        p. cm.
  Includes bibliographical references and index.
  ISBN 978-1-57441-249-9 (cloth : alk. paper)
  1. Operas—Analysis, appreciation. 2. Opera--United States--20th century. 3. Joplin, Scott, 1868-1917. Treemonisha. 4. Weill, Kurt, 1900-1950. Street scene. 5. Gershwin, George, 1898-1937. Porgy and Bess. 6. Copland, Aaron, 1900-1990. Tender land. I. Title.
  MT95.L37 2008
  782.10973--dc22

                         2008013679

To Cara—for the inspiration, and the perspiration.

Contents

Contents

List of Illustrations

Chapter 6

Chapter 7

Preface

I am a singer. My parents are both singers. I married a singer. My three children are all singers. Thus, although for a number of reasons I had to cut the sections explicitly devoted to performance implications from the four analytical chapters in this book, I approached the analyses with a singer's perspective in mind. It is my fond hope that they will eventually prove useful to those engaged in the ongoing production of opera—performers, conductors, and directors. Whether you are "in the business," or you are a music theorist, musicologist, or simply an opera enthusiast—read on! This is an analytical monograph by a Schenkerian music theorist, but it was also written by one performer and enthusiast for another.

My love for "dramatic vocal music"[1] began in high school, as I imagine it does for many high school students, with musical theater—in my case, with the musicals of Bernstein, Schwartz, Sondheim, Kander and Ebb, and (in my weaker moments) even some Lloyd Webber.[2] Though I dabbled in opera while a student at Phillips Academy (even taking direction from a spiky-haired Peter Sellars for a production of Mozart's *Le Nozze di Figaro*), I arrived at Yale College as something of a *naïf* with regard to art music. Professor Janet Schmalfeldt, now at Tufts University, saw to it that I did not remain that way. It was through my study of cadential harmonic processes and nineteenth-century *lieder* with her that I developed an abiding interest in tonal drama and its relationship to the text in dramatic vocal works, and became a music theorist.[3]

The singer-theorist is an exceedingly rare breed in the music-theoretical community, where the piano, for both practical and historical reasons, reigns supreme: Professors Elizabeth West Marvin of the Eastman School of Music, Cynthia Gonzales of the Texas State University, and Matthew Shaftel of the Florida State University are among the few other singer-theorists active at the national level. Perhaps this is due to a perceived "knowledge gap" between singers and theorists, who are stereotypically placed at opposite ends of the intellectual spectrum in descriptions of the music conservatory environment. Although most singers begin the formal study of their craft later than instrumentalists, it would be a mistake to assume that they do not have equally valuable insights to offer with regard to music theory and analysis. They are often highly attuned to aspects of melodic structure, register, and timbre, and they deal with text/music relationships on a daily basis. Moreover, a significant portion of the core tonal repertoire is comprised of operatic works—including the operas of Händel, Mozart, Rossini, and Verdi, to name just a few—and such leading Romantic composers as Schubert, Schumann, and Brahms lamented their inability (usually blamed on a poor librettist) to produce a successful work in one of the most important genres of their time.[4] It is the singer who is uniquely qualified to bring an insider's perspective to these important works.

To the singers who are interested in this book: unless you are preparing one of the roles discussed in Chapters 4 through 7, you are probably most familiar with the music of *Porgy and Bess*. Read the sections on "Scoring a Role" and "Applying the System to the Analysis of Opera" in Chapter 2 to get a sense of Stanislavsky's system of dramatic objectives, and then skip to Chapter 5. You may want to read through Table 1 first, to evaluate my interpretation of Porgy's objectives, then read through the analyses of his individual numbers—compare Figure 5 ("I Got Plenty O' Nuttin'") to Figure 13 ("Bess, Oh Where's My Bess?") to see how closure and lack of closure are displayed differently in the graphs (beamed open-note descent vs. beamed open-note repetition). Try to sing these two popular song/arias to yourself while following the abstracted scores in the figures, and consider whether the closure or lack of closure shown in the graphs would impact the way you or your peers would perform these two songs.

To the broader theatrical community: the ongoing publication of new English translations of the complete works of Stanislavsky by Routledge Press is a testament to the enduring influence of his ideas on the current generation of actors, directors, and theatre educators. Overlooked amidst this flurry of activity is the fact that Stanislavsky ended his career as an opera director and devoted considerable time and energy to the genre throughout his lifetime. He saw opera as a new and greater challenge for the director, and despite his efforts, in many ways it remains so today; see the section on "Applying the System to the Analysis of Opera" in Chapter 2. Translations from the Russian of any production notes held in the Stanislavsky Archive for the operas directed by Stanislavsky (listed in Chapter 2, Figure 8) would be a valuable resource for further research into the dramatic analysis of opera.

To the Schenkerians who are interested in this book: aside from the occasional graphical oddities arising from the jazzy harmonic vocabulary of Gershwin and Weill (e.g., the multiple implied tones and substitutions in the background of Figure 11, "I Loves You Porgy"), the two primary innovations in the book are the permanent interruption and the multi-movement *Ursatz*. Both structures are discussed at length in the Introduction, and then incorporated into the subsequent analytical chapters. I have found similar structures in the nineteenth-century song cycles of Schubert and Schumann, as well as the operas of Verdi, Massenet and Puccini—the topics of my current research. What pieces do you know that end with an interrupted or broken line, or that might contain background structures spanning multiple movements, given their tonal plans?

There are several additional items of theoretical interest in the graphs: in Chapter 5, the chromatic *Aussensatz* in Figure 5 (I Got Plenty O' Nuttin'"), the augmented initial arpeggiation in Figure 9 ("Bess, You Is My Woman Now"), and the "gapped" 5-line in Figure 15 ("Oh Lawd, I'm On My

Way"); in Chapter 6, the interrupted 8-line in Figure 2 ("Lonely House"), and the imperfect authentic "interruption" at $\hat{3}$ in Figure 8 ("We'll Go Away Together"); in Chapter 7, the deceptive cadence from V^{11}_{7} to IV harmonizing $\hat{1}$ in Figure 1c ("Once I Thought").

To the broader music-theoretical community: while the four operas studied here are certainly not representative of early twentieth-century opera in general, they do speak to a broader trend in late nineteenth-century and early twentieth-century "transitional" music toward what I call the "strategic use of tonality." Ignoring for a moment the specter of intentionality raised by this turn of phrase, reconsider your favorite pieces from this period. Given that post-Wagnerian composers were no longer bound by the common-practice rules of harmonic progression and cadential resolution, don't those occasional authentic cadences, all the more prominent for their isolation and strangeness, take on more semantic significance? I have found numerous moments that are semantically significant in this way in the works of Debussy, Scriabin, Janáček, and Britten, among others. For other instances of unusual harmonies and modulation schemes that make great teaching examples, see the following figures: in Chapter 4, the ♭VI—V—♭III—IV modulation scheme in Figure 2c ("The Bag of Luck"); in Chapter 5, the use of i^{add6} in Figure 1 ("They Pass By Singin'"), the use of ♯IV in Figures 4 and 5, and the I—III♯—♭VI (♯V) modulation scheme in Figure 9 ("Bess, You Is My Woman Now").

ENDNOTES

1 I define "dramatic vocal music," as any vocal genre or individual piece that is built around one or more characters who attempt to overcome obstacles to achieve a specific objective, including most operas, operettas, musicals, and oratorios, as well as some cantatas, art songs, and song cycles. Other vocal genres include "narrative" and "poetic" vocal music.

2 Composer Maury Yeston, however, currently ranks first on my list, as the only Yale-educated music theorist that I know of that makes a living writing Broadway musicals. For his theoretical work, see Maury Yeston, *The Stratification of Musical Rhythm* (New Haven: Yale University Press, 1976), and Maury Yeston, ed., *Readings in Schenker Analysis and Other Approaches* (New Haven: Yale University Press, 1977).

3 See Janet Schmalfeldt, "Cadential Processes: The Evaded Cadence and the 'One More Time' Technique," *Journal of Musicological Research* 12/1-2 (1992): 1–52, and "Towards a Reconciliation of Schenkerian Concepts with Traditional and Recent Theories of Form," *Music Analysis* 10/3 (1991): 233–87.

4 Several important twentieth-century composers, including Debussy (*Pelléas et Mélisande*) and Schoenberg (*Moses und Aron*), in addition to the composers studied in this book, considered their lone operas to be their greatest masterpieces.

Acknowledgments

General thanks are due to the dozens of people who have read my work and encouraged me along this arduous journey. Special thanks first to my family—my wife Cara, my children Elizabeth, Marie, and John, and my parents for believing in me. Thanks also to my teachers, especially Peter Warsaw, Janet Schmalfeldt, Patrick McCreless and Allen Forte. Thanks to God, who needs no thanks from me.

CHAPTER 1

Tonality as Drama: An Introduction

Is tonality, as defined by harmonic and linear progression, inherently dramatic? It should be clear from its title where the present book and its author stand on that issue. Though Austrian music theorist Heinrich Schenker's declaration that "in music the drama of the fundamental structure [das Drama des Ursatzes] is the main event"[1] was later cited by would-be detractors as an example of his narrow-minded focus on "the music itself," it is actually an explicit acknowledgment of Schenkerian theory as a theory of musical drama, an idea that will be further explored in Chapter 3. Carl Schachter notes that "elements of the fundamental structure ... become charged with dramatic tension through their suppression or their transformation"[2] and analytical work by other scholars has developed this theme.[3] In fact, the unfolding of tonal musical structure—with all its detours, roadblocks, dead ends, and arrivals—is a roadmap for an inherently dramatic journey. This idea, implicit in some of the best writing on music (e.g., Edward T. Cone's article on Schubert's "promissory note"),[4] is one of the most valuable and invigorating insights of musical scholarship, and a vital aspect of Schenkerian theory. Despite its significance, the relationship between musical and dramatic structure, particularly in vocal music, has not yet been formalized in an explicitly interdisciplinary analytical methodology.

Perhaps, part of the problem is a lack of precedent. Though Schenker was an opera critic in the early stages of his professional life,[5] as an analyst he broke his customary silence on the subject of opera only to comment negatively on Wagner's music. Schenker, as Carolyn Abbate and Roger Parker point out, "did not otherwise venture into the brackish waters of opera, not even as far as the illusory purity of the Mozartean set-piece."[6] However, since Schenker's death in 1935, music theorists—particularly in the United States—have adapted his ideas for application to a wider repertoire. As will be indicated in Chapter 2, this "Americanization" of Schenker (to use William Rothstein's term) bears some resemblance to the dissemination of Russian director Konstantin Stanislavsky's ideas on acting, in that "disciples" of varying degrees of orthodoxy—including the present author—have appropriated Schenker's system for their own purposes and to serve their own agendas.[7] If combined with an equally nuanced and flexible mode of dramatic analysis, this expanded form of Schenkerian analysis might provide a model for the analysis of opera and other forms of "dramatic vocal music."[8]

Merging Tonal and Dramatic Analysis

What would be the methodological requirements for this new "linear-dramatic" hybrid?[9] When Abbate and Parker, in the preface to *Analyzing Opera*, boldly declared that "'analyzing opera' should mean not only 'analyzing music' but simultaneously engaging with equal sophistication, the poetry and the drama,"[10] they set a very high standard. Like the conundrum regarding the relative importance of text versus music in opera composition, captured by the famous seventeenth-century "words as the mistress of music" debate between the brothers Monteverdi and the critic Artusi, opera analysis has historically tended to migrate from one pole (music) to the other (poetry) and back again, while drama remained in a no man's land between the two, an uncharted territory that must be crossed in order to reach the true destination. A formalist enterprise at the outset, music analysis has been adapted, only with difficulty, to the demands of the operatic genre.

The results of this adaptation have largely tended to reinforce the notion of polarization.

One of the earliest examples of opera analysis, the fundamental-bass analysis by Jean d'Alembert of *"Enfin, il est en ma puissance,"* from Lully's *Armide*, places opera analysis firmly in the formalist camp, presenting a harmonic analysis devoid of any commentary on the accompanying text.[11] By the end of the nineteenth century, however, composer-critics such as Berlioz, Schumann, and Carl Maria von Weber, all of whom, like Wagner after them, had a vested interest in maintaining the air of mystery surrounding the act of musical composition, had steered opera analysis away from the music and toward the poetry.[12] In 1912, music criticism had devolved to such a state that Schoenberg could complain that the critics "prattle almost exclusively about the libretto, the theatrical effectiveness, and the performers."[13] Schoenberg does not exempt composer-critics. He asserts:

> This is even true in the case of a composer's writing criticisms. Even if he is a good composer. [*sic*] For in the moment when he writes criticisms he is not a composer, not *musically inspired*. If he were inspired he would not describe how the piece ought to be composed, but would compose it himself.[14]

Later in the twentieth century, several explorers made the trek back towards analysis focused on the music itself. Led by Edward J. Dent, in whose capable hands music criticism began to take on a more analytical aspect once again, opera analysts began to return their focus to the music.[15] Foremost among the resurgent formalists was Alfred O. Lorenz, whose studies of Wagnerian leitmotif were responsible for the creation of an entire cottage industry.[16] Armed with their newfound focus on the music and, specifically, the motive, opera analysts tackled works by Mozart, Verdi, and Berg, as well as Wagner.[17]

In the 1990s, the pendulum began to swing back toward the text, as opera analysis was swept up in a broader cross-disciplinary examination of the meaning of musical structure.[18] As a result, a more balanced approach—one that includes the examination of text and music in equal proportions—is apparent in several recent opera studies.[19] Amid all the attention paid to the music and the poetry, either individually or collectively, drama *per se* has nonetheless received short shrift, often relegated to a brief plot summary or outline.[20] While the method presented in Chapter 2—Stanislavsky's system of character objectives—is not intended to provide a comprehensive response to Abbate and Parker's challenge, it attempts to provide a more sophisticated and detailed means of analyzing what characters *want*, as opposed to what they say or sing. By seeking a method of dramatic analysis that focuses on the successes and failures of individual characters *vis à vis* their spoken and unspoken desires, the opera analyst can move beyond surface issues of plot to examine character motivations at a deeper level.

The Permanent Interruption and the Multi-Movement *Ursatz*

Linear-dramatic analysis—if it is committed to examining the dramatic goals or objectives of individual characters, both those that are successfully achieved and those that are undermined—must also define tonal success and failure in order to facilitate a comparison of the two. In Schenkerian analysis, ultimate tonal success in a given piece is defined by the completion of its *Ursatz*, or fundamental structure, comprised of the *Urlinie* (fundamental line) and the *Bassbrechung* (bass arpeggiation). An *Ursatz* is considered complete upon linear and harmonic arrival at its tonic pitch and triad, respectively, usually in a piece's final measures. This arrival at tonic is an example of musical closure in the broadest possible terms, often prefigured by the many smaller linear completions and cadences during the course of the piece.

Given Schenker's perceived emphasis on the fundamental structure in his analytical system (an emphasis that has drawn occasional criticism due to its drastic graphical simplification of the musical surface)[21] any compositional strategy that he allowed to impede the progress of the *Ursatz* ought to receive pride of place in a theory of tonal drama. That strategy—the most dramatic of all Schenkerian concepts—is the interruption. Typically a breaking of the line at $\hat{2}$ over the dominant followed by a return of the primary tone and a completed descent to $\hat{1}$ over the tonic, the interruption is typically discussed in relation to sonata form. Recent articles on form in music of the common-practice period include representative discussions of this concept.[22] Its role as a marker of formal or phrase-structural division notwithstanding, the interruption is by its very nature a dramatic event—even its symbol (two vertical lines breaking the horizontal beam of the background line: –‖) is visually striking.

Schenker's discussion of the interruption is primarily confined to two sections of *Der freie Satz*, the latter of which is devoted to sonata form. The first section occurs in the context of his presentation of structural aspects of the first middleground.[23] After demonstrating an interrupted 3-line, Schenker notes that "the initial succession $\hat{3}$–$\hat{2}$ gives the impression that it is the first attempt at the complete fundamental line," but that "$\hat{2}$/V appears as the limit of an initial forward motion of the fundamental line."[24] As Peter Smith has noted, this statement contradicts Schenker's later assertion that the interruption "has the effect of a delay, or retardation, on the way to the ultimate goal."[25] The apparent contradiction concerns the relative importance of the first half of the interruption. According to the first statement, the initial descent from $\hat{3}$–$\hat{2}$ is subordinate to the completed version that follows it, while the latter statement gives the interruption more weight, de-emphasizing the subsequent retracing of the $\hat{3}$–$\hat{2}$ as a mere "delay." In an editorial note on the two contrasting descriptions, Ernst Oster points out that although Schenker used two different notations for the interruption, both were intended to show the same thing: the relative importance of the first half of the interruption or what Allen Cadwallader and David Gagné call the "first branch."[26]

Schenker's emphasis on this "first branch" of the interruption makes phenomenological sense. He makes his emphasis explicit by stating that "with respect to the unity of the fundamental structure, the first occurrence of $\hat{2}/V$ is more significant than the second."[27] Because it receives priority of place in a musical work, the initial interrupted descent is of primary importance. In fact, it is possible to argue that the term "interruption" properly belongs only to the initial "broken" descent: the reinstatement of the primary tone and closure to $\hat{1}/I$, as noted by Smith, are more correctly identified as the "completion" or "continuation" of the fundamental line. As Cadwallader and Gagné put it, the actual "'point' of interruption" occurs at the end of the first branch.[28]

Given the teleological significance of the point of interruption, should the analyst not then admit the possibility of a "permanent" or "sustained" interruption, one in which the second "branch," the completion or continuation, is omitted? Schenker implicitly dismissed the possibility of such a broken structure in *Der freie Satz*, maintaining that "if recent musical products have almost no end or seem to find no end, it is because they do not derive from a fundamental structure and hence do not arrive at a genuine $\hat{1}$; without the $\hat{1}$ a work is bound to give the effect of incompleteness."[29] But what if "the effect of incompleteness," particularly as it pertains to a fundamental structure, is precisely the effect a composer seeks to create?

Two articles, in particular, have addressed this issue in various ways: David Loeb's essay on "dual-key movements" in *Schenker Studies*, and Schachter's article on "*Das Drama des Ursatzes*" in *Schenker Studies 2*.[30] While Loeb's essay includes some trenchant observations, most notably that "when pieces begin and end in different keys such that neither key is understood as subsidiary to the other, then we must abandon our usual approach and seek a different kind of overall structure,"[31] his focus is primarily on Baroque instrumental forms. Schachter, for his part, notes that in the absence of a normative background structure, "what the analyst must do is to arrive at the intuition of some higher level—middleground or background—and to test that intuition against the totality of impressions made by the piece."[32] He then goes on to graph Chopin's *Mazurka in A♭ major*, Op. 41/3 as a 5-line in which "the ghostly presence of the missing $\hat{2}$ and $\hat{1}$ is so clearly evident that the analysis should suggest something like the following: $\hat{5}$–$\hat{4}$–$\hat{3}$—but where are $\hat{2}$ and $\hat{1}$?"[33] His graph uses question marks and parentheses to indicate the absent, implied structural pitches.

Schachter maintains that "often, as here, Schenkerian theory is able to accommodate structural anomalies without the need for extending it by postulating, for example, new *Ursatz*-forms"; the mazurka would count as "a transformed 5-line piece, and not one that simply traverses a third from $\hat{5}$ to $\hat{3}$."[34] When the "totality of impressions" made by a piece includes a narrative in which a protagonist fails to reach a desired goal, however, it is tempting to disagree with Schachter. A ***permanent interruption***—a broken background line descending only as far as $\hat{5}$ (for an 8-line) or $\hat{2}$ (for a 5-line or a 3-line)—is an effective, and indeed compelling, compositional response to such a scenario.[35] Schenker pupil Adele Katz puts it best when she claims that Wagner's music, and by extension dramatic vocal music in general, must be studied

> from two different points of view: first, whether it demonstrates the principles of structural unity; second, whether any sacrifice of these principles is due to the demands of the text.... [One must] consider any deviations in the basic techniques in relation to the text or dramatic action they represent.[36]

Even with the permanent interruption representing musical failure, linear-dramatic analysis requires a second theoretical concession in order to compare the changing objectives of a character across an entire role to that character's music—namely, the ***multi-movement Ursatz***, a "meta-fundamental structure" in which each of the notes of the fundamental line is the primary tone of a separate aria, number, or movement, supported by the tonic of that number. Traditionally, Schenkerian analysts have restricted their analytical endeavors to the tonal structure within a single piece or movement. David Neumeyer and Patrick McCreless, however, have argued for a widening of analytical scope to include multi-movement works. McCreless, as part of a bid to reconcile Schenkerian analysis with Leo Treitler's work on key associations, claims that "linear analysis ... is by no means incompatible with a point of view that finds tonal meaning echoing from moment to moment in a single movement, or from movement to movement in a multipartite work."[37] In his writing, Neumeyer lays the groundwork for the future development of a model for multi-movement works, which is worth quoting in its entirety. He writes:

> when the closed analytic system—in our case, Schenker's method applied to single movements—is confronted with a situation outside its capacities—here, the problem of multi-movement forms—the way to proceed is to add other pertinent structural criteria and develop an expanded, but again closed, methodology. Thus, for the song cycle and other expanded vocal works (including opera?), we need to add to Schenker's harmonic-tonal and voice-leading model, as expressed in the *Ursatz*, the narrative or dramatic criteria, and from this develop a broader analytic system which can treat these two as co-equal structural determinants.[38]

Strategic Tonality in Four Post-Wagnerian Operas

Permanent interruption and the multi-movement *Ursatz* will form the theoretical basis for much of the discussion in Chapters 4 through 7, and early twentieth-century American opera serves as the analytical focus of the book for two reasons. First, as a sub-genre, early twentieth-century American opera provides perhaps the best collective example of ***strategic tonality***, the use of linear and harmonic tonal processes to bolster or undercut moments of dramatic success or failure.[39] Second, although the operas of Joplin,

Gershwin, Weill, and Copland vary greatly in style and conception, they each contain characters who fail to attain their ***superobjectives***—their goals for the entire opera—which in turn suggests the possibility of permanent interruption.[40] Naturally, this particularly dramatic situation is prevalent in operatic tragedies—especially, it seems, in love stories. Among the main *dramatis personae* of the operas studied in the analytical chapters, only Treemonisha and Sporting Life (the career-minded characters) achieve dramatic success, proving Lysander's assertion in the opening scene of Shakespeare's *A Midsummer Night's Dream* that "the course of true love never did run smooth."

The rubric "twentieth-century opera" typically evokes the dark, post-Expressionistic sound worlds of Strauss and Berg, the angular and sharp-edged twelve-tone masterpieces of Schoenberg and Dallapiccola or the eclectic, psychologically driven styles of Janáček and Britten. Yet for a handful of composers in the United States, it came to signify something quite different. Determined to develop a uniquely American operatic style and laboring to various degrees under the strong influence of the European grand opera tradition, composers from Joplin to Sondheim opted to continue the development of a strategic approach to tonality begun by late Romantic composers such as Verdi, Massenet, and Puccini, among others.[41] Their incorporation of elements from the folk, popular and jazz idioms necessitated a compositional approach that included a substantive role for tonality, broadened to include extended chords (ninths, elevenths and thirteenths) and non-dominant cadential progressions, an approach made all the more striking by virtue of the fact that, following Wagner's operatic "emancipation of the cadence" with his opera *Tristan und Isolde* (1859), tonality as defined by standard linear and harmonic progression was no longer considered to be a requirement for a successful composition.

Scott Joplin's *Treemonisha* (1911) was considered by some to be "the first truly American opera, not imitative of the European form."[42] Although the subject of its libretto—the plight of slaves working on plantations in the South—is distinctively American and many of its melodies are inspired by African-American spirituals and folk songs, *Treemonisha* shares much in common with the European grand opera tradition in its strategic use of tonality. The "King of Ragtime" himself certainly thought of the work as grand opera, noting that

> I am a composer of ragtime music but I want it thoroughly understood that my opera *Treemonisha* is not ragtime. In most of the strains I have used syncopations (rhythm) peculiar to my race, but the music is not ragtime and the score complete is grand opera.[43]

The most significant difference between *Treemonisha* and the other operas considered in this volume is that it does not focus on the romantic relationship between a man and a woman. Instead it depicts two political adversaries, Treemonisha and Zodzetrick, vying for control of the plantation's slave community. Because the two main characters are not dependent on one another to achieve their dramatic superobjective—quite the opposite, in fact—Joplin is free to have one succeed at the expense of the other, and this he does in a most convincing fashion. Treemonisha is the only character studied in Chapters 4 through 7 that completes a background descent to the tonic, though Joplin appends a coda in the final scene that moves the tonal center back to the key of the dominant in order to suggest the work that lies ahead for Treemonisha as the new leader of the community.[44] Zodzetrick's music, by contrast, concludes without a return to his tonic key, though it does not comprise a permanent interruption like those analyzed in *Porgy and Bess*, *Street Scene*, and *The Tender Land*, since it does not end in the key of the dominant.

Schenkerian analyses frequently depict the coda as a passage of music that occurs after the descent of the fundamental line has reached its conclusion, acting as a prolongation of the final structural tonic in both the melody and the bass line. What makes Joplin's tonal structure for Treemonisha's role unusual is that the coda does not remain in the tonic key, reinforcing the earlier structural arrival on the tonic. Rather, it modulates to the dominant, harmonically suggesting the possibility of a permanent interruption. In the absence of a narrative or dramatic context, the notion of a modulatory coda would be far less convincing, given the overwhelming amount of rhetorical emphasis that would have to be accorded to the structural cadence in order to overcome the phenomenological priority generally given to openings and conclusions. The motion to the dominant in the final two scenes of *Treemonisha*, however, can be considered peripheral to the main structure of the eponymous character's role only because, unlike the ill-fated couples in the other three operas, she successfully achieves her superobjective before the opera's conclusion. Thus, *Treemonisha* presents an example of an **open-ended coda**, a passage following closure at the background level that modulates away from the tonic key.

In contrast to *Treemonisha*, the dramatic event in George Gershwin's *Porgy and Bess* (1935) that initiates the main character's quest to achieve his superobjective does not occur at the beginning of the opera. It is not until after Crown murders Robbins in the middle of Act 1, forcing Bess to abandon him for Porgy, that Porgy is able to begin building a happier life together with her. In order to convey the gradual crystallization of this new superobjective, Gershwin gives Porgy's first number ("They Pass By Singin'") an ambiguous tonal center, suggesting but ultimately withholding linear and harmonic closure in his home key (A minor). In Act 2, after Bess has come to stay with Porgy and has been living with him for a while, Gershwin reintroduces A minor with a strong primary tone and closes a local *Ursatz* in that key in "Buzzard Song." "Oh Little Stars" and "I Got Plenty O' Nuttin'," the previous two numbers set in E major and G major respectively, are incorporated as part of a large-scale *Anstieg* (initial ascent) that spans Porgy's first four numbers, leading to the initiation of his background primary tone and his quest to build a new life with Bess. Thus, the first half of Porgy's role in *Porgy and Bess* comprises a **multi-movement initial ascent**—a series of at least three separate numbers, the primary tones of which form a stepwise ascent from the tonic to the primary tone of a multi-movement fundamental structure.

A second distinguishing feature of Gershwin's opera is the almost total absence of solo material for its leading female character. In contrast to Porgy, who has four solo numbers and solo sections in two more, Bess has only one solo ("What You Want Wid Bess?"), which becomes a duet with Crown. The other time she sings alone on stage (III/i), she borrows the first half of Clara's lullaby ("Summertime") to sing Jake and Clara's newly orphaned baby to sleep. She and Porgy do, however, share two important duets together ("Bess, You Is My Woman Now" and "I Loves You Porgy"), and it is primarily through these that she conveys her main objectives.

Kurt Weill immigrated to the United States in 1935, arriving in time to accept an invitation from Gershwin to attend the dress rehearsal for *Porgy and Bess*.[45] According to his wife, Lotte Lenya, "he listened very closely and he said 'you know, it is possible to write an opera for Broadway.'" From that point onward, Weill was "always consciously working towards an opera."[46] Though Gershwin called *Porgy and Bess* a "folk opera" and Weill referred to his *Street Scene* (1946) as an "American opera," they both premiered on Broadway and later made their way into the repertories of either the Metropolitan Opera or the New York City Opera and thus can also be referred to as "Broadway operas."[47]

Like Porgy and Bess, whose intertwined superobjectives are not firmly established until Act 2, Sam Kaplan and Rose Maurrant are not a couple at the beginning of *Street Scene*. Instead of using a multi-movement *Anstieg*, however, by setting each of their opening numbers in the same key (E♭ major) Weill creates an initial arpeggiation that tonally links the two characters but denies them a common primary tone: Sam's aria "Lonely House" contains an 8-line, while Rose's aria "What Good Would the Moon Be?" contains a 5-line. When the common primary tone (G) does arrive in their first duet, "A Sprig With Its Flower We Break," it is supported not by an E♭ major tonic but by C major, the major submediant. This large-scale harmonic substitution emphasizes the fact that Sam and Rose have not yet decided to join together to achieve their respective superobjectives; that task is preserved for their next duet, "We'll Go Away Together," where E♭ is reintroduced as the tonic key and G is presented as a viable multi-movement primary tone. *Street Scene* therefore contains a ***multi-movement initial arpeggiation,*** a series of at least three separate numbers that prolong the tonic key, the primary tones of which form an arpeggiation concluding with the primary tone of a multi-movement fundamental structure.

Copland's *The Tender Land* (1954) represents another aspect of the evolution of American opera. Although, like Gershwin, he labeled his work a "folk opera," Copland interpreted the phrase differently, incorporating hymn tunes and other folk songs rather than elements of popular music, Broadway or jazz.[48] A second feature that separates Copland's opera from the other three operas is its asymmetrical dramatic trajectory. Whereas *Porgy and Bess* and *Street Scene* take several scenes to establish the superobjectives of their respective characters and initiate a background primary tone, *The Tender Land* establishes both the background key and the primary tone in the opening scene, in Laurie's aria "Once I thought I'd never grow." Though all three operas contain permanent interruptions, the arrival at $\hat{2}$ over the dominant occurs much earlier in Copland's opera: at the end of Act 2, rather than in the final scene of Act 3. Laurie's grandfather calls a precipitous halt to Martin and Laurie's budding romance and orders Martin off his farm. This pivotal moment that concludes Act 2 prompts Copland to create a ***prolonged permanent interruption***—a series of two or more separate numbers concluding a multi-movement work, the primary tones of which prolong background arrival at $\hat{2}$ over the dominant.

All four examples of post-Wagnerian strategic tonality demonstrate remarkable sensitivity to the dramatic trajectories of their main characters. Perhaps because they were all forged in the fiery crucible of New York City, where they were judged (often harshly, especially by the *New York Times*) by the standards of both opera and musical theater, these four works display an affinity for character and drama that is more a hallmark of musical theater than opera, even while they display all the musical characteristics of opera. In the next six chapters, a method for examining how they go about creating this affinity will be put forth and then applied to each one in turn.

ENDNOTES

[1] Heinrich Schenker, *Free Composition: Volume III of "New Musical Theories and Fantasies,"* 2 vols., ed. and trans. Ernst Oster (New York: Longman, 1979), 137 n14.

[2] Carl Schachter, "Structure as Foreground: 'Das Drama des Ursatzes'," in *Schenker Studies 2,* eds. Carl Schachter and Hedi Siegel (Cambridge: Cambridge University Press, 1999), 309. The title of the recent *Festschrift* for Schachter testifies to his belief in the meaning inherent in tonal structure. See L. Poundie Burstein and David Gagné, eds., *Structure and Meaning in Tonal Music: Festschrift in Honor of Carl Schachter* (Hillsdale, NY: Pendragon, 2006).

[3] See Rudy Marcozzi, "The Interaction of Large-Scale Harmonic and Dramatic Structure in the Verdi Operas Adapted from Shakespeare" (PhD diss., Indiana University, 1992); Wayne Petty, "Imagining Drama as an Aid to Musical Performance" (paper presented at the annual meeting for the New England Conference of Music Theorists, Wellesley College, Wellesley, MA, April 1995); Arthur Maisel, "Voice Leading as Drama in Wozzeck," in *Schenker Studies 2,* ed. Schachter and Siegel, 160–91; and Walter Everett, "Singing About the Fundamental Line: Vocal Portrayals of Directed and Misdirected Motions" (paper read at the annual meeting for the Society of Music Theory, Phoenix, AZ, October 1997), and "Deep-Level Portrayals of Directed and Misdirected Motions in Nineteenth-Century Lyric Song," *Journal of Music Theory* 48/1 (2004): 25–68. For a related combination of Schenkerian theory and "energetics," see Frank Samarotto, "Sublimating Sharp $\hat{4}$: An Exercise in Schenkerian Energetics," *Music Theory Online* 10/3 (2004), http://mto.societymusictheory.org/issues/mto.04.10.3/mto.04.10.3.samarotto.html.

[4] Edward T. Cone, "Schubert's Promissory Note: An Exercise in Musical Hermeneutics," *Nineteenth-Century Music* 5/3 (1982): 233.

[5] Giorgio Sanguinetti, "L'opera italiana nella critica musicale di Heinrich Schenker [Italian Opera in Heinrich Schenker's Music Criticism]," *Nuova rivista musicale italiana* 29/3 (1995): 431–67.

[6] Carolyn Abbate and Roger Parker, "On Analyzing Opera," in *Analyzing Opera: Verdi and Wagner,* ed. Carolyn Abbate and Roger Parker (Berkeley: University of California Press, 1989), 4. For a recent and thorough list of Schenker's most important publications as well as secondary sources on Schenkerian theory, see David Carson Berry, *A Topical Guide to Schenkerian Literature: An Annotated Bibliography with Indices* (Hillsdale, NY: Pendragon, 2004). See also David Damschroder, *Music Theory From Zarlino to Schenker: A Bibliography and Guide* (Stuyvesant, NY: Pendragon Press, 1990), 304–17; Nicholas Rast, "A Checklist of Essays and Reviews by Heinrich Schenker," *Music Analysis* 7/2 (July 1988): 121–32; and Larry Laskowski. *Heinrich Schenker: An Annotated Index to His Analyses of Musical Works* (Hillsdale, NY: Pendragon, 1978).

[7] See William Rothstein, "The Americanization of Heinrich Schenker," *In Theory Only* 9/1 (1986): 5–17. Reprinted in *Schenker Studies,* ed. Hedi Siegel (Cambridge: Cambridge University Press, 1990), 193–203.

[8] See Preface, note 1.

[9] The adjective "linear-dramatic" is taken from the title of the author's dissertation, and references Allen Forte's use of the term "linear-motivic" to describe post-Schenkerian analyses of linear structure. See Edward D. Latham, "Linear-Dramatic Analysis: An Analytical Approach to Twentieth-Century Opera" (PhD diss., Yale University, 2000), and Allen Forte,

"New Approaches to Linear Analysis," *Journal of the American Musicological Society* 41/2 (1988): 315–48.

[10] Abbate and Parker, "On Analyzing Opera," 4.

[11] Jean Le Rond d'Alembert, *Élémens de musique, suivant les principes de M. Rameau* (Lyon: Bruyset, Père et Fils, 1779), appendix.

[12] Two of the few exceptions where nineteenth-century opera critics did address the music directly may be found in Ian Bent, ed., *Music Analysis in the Nineteenth Century* (Cambridge: Cambridge University Press, 1994). See Hector Berlioz, "*Les Huguenots*: The Score," 39–57, and Hans von Wolzogen, "Prelude, Act I [*Parsifal*]," 88–105.

[13] Arnold Schoenberg, "The Relationship to the Text," in Arnold Schoenberg, *Style and Idea: Selected Writings of Arnold Schoenberg*, rev. ed., ed. Leo Stein and trans. Leo Black (Berkeley: University of California Press, 1984), 143.

[14] Ibid.

[15] Edward J. Dent, *Mozart's Operas: A Critical Study* (London: Chatto and Windus, 1913).

[16] Alfred O. Lorenz, *Das Geheimnis der Form bei Richard Wagner*, 4 vols. (Berlin: M. Hesse, 1924–33).

[17] See, for example, Siegmund Levarie, *Mozart's "Le Nozze di Figaro": A Critical Analysis* (Chicago: University of Chicago Press, 1952); Frits Noske, *The Signifier and the Signified: Studies in the Operas of Mozart and Verdi* (The Hague: Nijhoff, 1977); George Perle, *The Operas of Alban Berg*, 2 vols. (Berkeley: University of California Press, 1980); and Janet Schmalfeldt, *Berg's "Wozzeck": Harmonic Language and Dramatic Design* (New Haven: Yale University Press, 1983).

[18] In his own writing, and as the editor of Indiana University Press's *Musical Meaning and Interpretation* series, Robert Hatten has been particularly influential in effecting this broader disciplinary shift in music theory. See Robert S. Hatten, *Musical Meaning in Beethoven: Markedness, Correlation, and Interpretation* (Bloomington: Indiana University Press, 1994), and *Interpreting Musical Gestures, Topics, and Tropes: Mozart, Beethoven, Schubert* (Bloomington: Indiana University Press, 2004). In the *Musical Meaning* series, see especially Byron Almén and Edward R. Pearsall, eds., *Approaches to Meaning in Music* (Bloomington: Indiana University Press, 2006); Peter H. Smith, *Expressive Forms in Brahms's Instrumental Music: Structure and Meaning in His Werther Quartet* (Bloomington: Indiana University Press, 2005); and Michael L. Klein, *Intertextuality in Western Art Music* (Bloomington: Indiana University Press, 2004). For other recent studies of musical meaning, see Daniel K. L. Chua, *Absolute Music and the Construction of Meaning* (Cambridge: Cambridge University Press, 1999), and Peter Hadreas, "Deconstruction and the Meaning of Music," *Perspectives of New Music* 37/2 (1999): 5–28.

[19] See Peter Kaminsky, "How to do Things with Words and Music: Towards an Analysis of Selected Ensembles in Mozart's *Don Giovanni*," *Theory and Practice* 21 (1996): 55–78; Ted Conner, "Cherubino Rediscovered: Text, Music, and Narrative in Mozart's Trio," *Theory and Practice* 25 (2000): 27–64; and Janet Schmalfeldt, "In Search of Dido," *The Journal of Musicology* 18/4 (2001): 584–615.

[20] The end of the millennium, viewed by many at the time as the *ne plus ultra of* dramatic events, must have inspired some notable exceptions. See Joachim Herz, "*Wozzeck*: Musikalische Struktur und Dramaturgie [*Wozzeck*: Musical Structure and Dramaturgy]," in *Alban Bergs Wozzeck und die Zwanziger Jahre*, ed. Jürgen Kühnel et. al. (Anif-Salzburg: Mueller-Speiser,

1999), 199–217; Carl S. Leafstedt, *Inside Bluebeard's Castle: Music and Drama in Béla Bartók's Opera* (Oxford: Oxford University Press, 1999); and Giorgio Sanguinetti, "La funzione drammatica del campo tonale: Il duetto tra Carlo ed Elisabetta nel secondo atto del Don Carlo [The Dramatic Function of the Tonal Field: The Duet between Carlo and Elisabetta in the Second Act of *Don Carlo*]," in Giorgio Sanguinetti, *Intersezioni: Quattro studi di teoria e analisi musicale* (Cosenza: Università della Calabria, 1999), 109–36.

[21] The misperception that Schenker privileged the fundamental structure at the expense of the musical surface is perpetuated largely by the current practice of teaching Schenkerian analysis in a large university seminar format, instead of in individual instructional sessions, as Schenker taught the system to his first students. The lack of individual instruction leads inevitably to a greater focus on the *Ursatz* as a consensus builder in classroom discussion. In actuality, as a performer and conductor, Schenker considered the musical surface (the foreground) of equal importance for its integral and aurally salient interrelationship with the background. On the importance of the foreground, see John Rothgeb, "Design as a Key to Structure in Tonal Music," *Journal of Music Theory* 15/1–2 (1971): 230–53. For Schenker's views on performance, see Heinrich Schenker, *The Art of Performance*, ed. Heribert Esser and trans. Irene Scott Schreier (Oxford: Oxford University Press, 2000), and William Rothstein, "Analysis and the Act of Performance," in *The Practice of Performance: Studies in Musical Interpretation*, ed. John S. Rink (Cambridge: Cambridge University Press, 1995), 217–40.

[22] See David Smyth, "'Balanced Interruption' and the Formal Repeat," *Music Theory Spectrum* 15/1 (1993): 76, and Peter H. Smith, "Brahms and Schenker: A Mutual Response to Sonata Form," *Music Theory Spectrum* 16/1 (1994): 77. For a more recent discussion of the interruption, see Irna Priore, "The Case for a Continuous $\hat{5}$: Expanding the Schenkerian Interruption Concept—With Analytical Interpretations of Beethoven opp. 101, 109, and 111" (PhD diss., University of Iowa, 2004), and "Further Considerations of the Continuous $\hat{5}$ with an Introduction and Explanation of Schenker's Five Interruption Models," *Indiana Theory Review* 25 (2004): 115–38.

[23] Schenker, *Free Composition*, 36–40. Carl Schachter, however, includes interruption as an element of background structure. See Schachter, "Structure as Foreground," 299.

[24] Schenker, *Free Composition*, 36.

[25] Ibid., 37.

[26] Allen Cadwallader and David Gagné, *Analysis of Tonal Music: A Schenkerian Approach*, 2nd ed. (Oxford: Oxford University Press, 2007), 113.

[27] Ibid.

[28] Ibid., 168.

[29] Schenker, *Free Composition*, 126 n6.

[30] See David Loeb, "Dual-Key Movements," in *Schenker Studies*, ed. Siegel, and Schachter, "Structure as Foreground."

[31] Loeb, "Dual-Key Movements," 76.

[32] Schachter, "Structure as Foreground," 302.

[33] Ibid., 304.

[34] Ibid.

[35] The interruption at $\hat{3}$ is another less widely accepted but nonetheless intuitively attractive option for a permanent interruption, reflecting an imperfect authentic cadence at the piece's conclusion.

[36] Adele T. Katz, *Challenge to Musical Tradition: A New Concept of Tonality* (New York: Alfred A. Knopf, 1945), 195.

[37] Patrick McCreless, "Schenker and Chromatic Tonicization: A Reappraisal," in *Schenker Studies*, ed. Siegel, 144.

[38] David Neumeyer, "Organic Structure and the Song Cycle: Another Look at Schumann's *Dichterliebe*," *Music Theory Spectrum* 4 (1982), 97.

[39] I have intentionally avoided the use of the word "intentionally" in the definition of strategic tonality. Whether Joplin and his peers were aware of the large-scale structural implications of the key schemes and melodic structures they created in their operas is an impossible question to answer, and largely irrelevant per the "intentional fallacy." The relationships between dramatic and musical structure are there to be considered, and possibly aurally perceived by those blessed with perfect pitch, excellent relative pitch, and/or the gift of "structural hearing" (Salzer, 1952). For two different perspectives on the "intentional fallacy," see Ethan Haimo, "Atonality, Analysis, and the Intentional Fallacy," *Music Theory Spectrum* 18/2 (1996): 167–99, and Edward D. Latham, "Review of Ethan Haimo's 'Atonality, Analysis and the Intentional Fallacy' *Music Theory Spectrum* 18/2 (Fall, 1996)," *Music Theory Online* 3.2 (1997), http://mto.societymusictheory.org/issues/mto.97.3.2/mto.97.3.2.latham.html.

[40] Stanislavsky's concept of superobjectives is discussed at length in Chapter 2.

[41] Britten and Janáček explored similar techniques in their early works, especially Peter Grimes and Jenufa, respectively. See Edward D. Latham, "Britten's Strategic Use of Tonality: A Review-Essay on Philip Rupprecht's Britten's Musical Language (2001)." Theory and Practice 28 (2003): 137–46, and Matthew M. Werley, "From Alienation to Abnegation: Jenufa and the Metaphysics of Dramatic and Musical Discourse at the Turn of Century" (paper presented at the annual meeting for the Music Theory Society of the Mid-Atlantic, Baltimore, MD, April 4–5, 2003).

[42] James Haskins, *Scott Joplin: The Man Who Made Ragtime* (New York: Scarborough, 1980), 177.

[43] Edward A. Berlin, *King of Ragtime: Scott Joplin and His Era* (Oxford: Oxford University Press, 1994), 226.

[44] Sporting Life, a character in Gershwin's *Porgy and Bess*, is also successful in achieving his superobjective and reaching tonal closure at the background level. See Edward D. Latham, "It Ain't Necessarily So: Sporting Life's Triumph in Gershwin's *Porgy and Bess*," *Indiana Theory Review* 25 (Fall 2005): 29–45.

[45] David Farneth, *Kurt Weill: A Life in Pictures and Documents* (Woodstock, New York: Overlook Press, 2000), 272.

[46] Lotte Lenya to Joseph Horowitz, October 26, 1979 interview in the *New York Times*. Quoted in Douglas Jarman, *Kurt Weill: An Illustrated Biography* (Bloomington: Indiana University Press, 1982), 136.

[47] Later examples in this genre that also use strategic tonality include Leonard Bernstein's *West Side Story* (1957) and *Candide* (1976), and Stephen Sondheim's *Sweeney Todd* (1979).

[48] Copland's librettist, the dancer Erik Johns, labeled *The Tender Land* an "operatic tone poem." See Erik Johns to Aaron Copland, not dated, Aaron Copland Collection, Music Division, Library of Congress, Washington, D. C. Cited in Christopher W. Patton, "Discovering 'The Tender Land': A New Look at Aaron Copland's Opera," *American Music* 20/3 (2002): 317–40.

CHAPTER 2

Dramatic Closure: The Stanislavsky System and the Attainment of Character Objectives

"Constantin Stanislavski (1863–1938) is the most important single figure in the history of acting."[1]

A system of dramatic analysis that is both multi-leveled and richly detailed can be found in the work of the Russian actor, director and teacher Konstantin Stanislavsky (1863–1938).[2] Stanislavsky was born to wealthy parents on January 5, 1863.[3] Baptized as Konstantin Sergeievich Alekseiev, he adopted the stage surname Stanislavsky in 1884 in order to conceal from his parents his performance in amateur regional productions of vaudeville, which they considered to be beneath him.[4] The majority of Stanislavsky's early acting experiences, however, came as a part of the Alekseiev Circle (founded in September 1877), a family theatrical troupe that staged plays and operettas at the Alekseiev estate.[5] From the beginning, in his acting work as a member of the Circle, Stanislavsky was interested in systematizing the craft of acting: in his notebook for 1885, he listed thirteen "aspects" which one should consider when preparing a role.[6] This list is reproduced below as Figure 1.

1. What is the temperament of the role?
2. To what nationality or period it belongs.
3. The physiological aspect of the role.
4. The psychic aspect of the role.
5. Relationship to other roles.
6. Age.
7. Maturity.
8. What type (*emploi*) of role.
9. The most recent presentation of the character.
10. The author's intention.
11. Opinions of other characters concerning this role.
12. The most outstanding passages in the roles.
13. The outward appearance of the role.

Figure 1   Stanislavsky on Preparing a Role (1885)
(J. Benedetti, *Stanislavski*)

When, in 1886, the Alekseiev Circle began to die out, as sisters and brothers grew up or moved away, Stanislavsky began searching for a new outlet for his creative ambition.[7] In 1887, pursuant to a discussion he had with Fyodor Kommisarzhevsky, his voice teacher at the Moscow Conservatory, he founded the Moscow Amateur Music-Drama Circle,[8] and then in 1888, he established the Society of Art and Literature along with Kommisarzhevsky and Aleksandr Fedotov, a successful actor, director, and the husband of Stanislavsky's friend Glikeria Fedotova.[9]

With the Society, Stanislavsky scored many successes as an actor, as well as his first as a director (of Pimeski's *Burning Letters*), but he remained dissatisfied with the progress of his acting technique.[10] Instead of relying upon his own instincts and developing an individual method, he relied largely on his ability to imitate methods developed by other famous actors, as well as the models presented to him by his director, Fedotov. As Benedetti notes:

the most he was able to achieve, as he ultimately recognized, was a passable imitation of the role [of Georges Dandin in Molière's play of the same name] which Fedotov step-by-step demonstrated for him. He did not act on the basis of his own experience or on the observation of real-life models but on the basis of a reality mediated by Fedotov's personality and skill.[11]

What Stanislavsky ultimately sought was a way to circumvent clichéd theatrical gestures and characterizations and to bring about naturalness on the stage. Directing him in *Georges Dandin*, Fedotov passed on to Stanislavsky the lessons he had learned from Mikhail Shchepkin, the most famous Russian actor of the previous generation and its foremost proponent of realism on the stage. For Shchepkin, the actor has two sources of inspiration: knowledge of his own nature and observation of life.[12] As Shchepkin noted in a letter to the actress Aleksandra Shubert:

> It is so much easier to play mechanically—for that you only need your reason. Reason will approximate to joy and sorrow just as an imitation approximates to nature. But an actor of feeling—that's quite different…. He just begins by wiping out his own self … and becomes the character the author intended him to be. He must walk, talk, think, feel, cry, laugh as the author wants him to. You see how the actor's task becomes more meaningful. In the first case you need only pretend to live—in the second you really have to live.[13]

Despite the enormous aesthetic assumptions underlying Shchepkin's statement, his meaning is clear: self-conscious acting is inferior to a realistic portrayal of the character. It was to be almost twenty years before Stanislavsky was able to solidify his thoughts on acting into a system capable of producing the desired results. In order to be able to internalize and ultimately to achieve the psychological realism desired by Shchepkin, he had first to create a working environment in which he could develop a "system" of acting in collaboration with an ensemble of dedicated and open-minded actors. Such an environment was eventually to be provided by the studios of the Moscow Art Theatre, which Stanislavsky founded with Vladimir Nemirovitch-Dantchenko after a sixteen-hour conversation begun at the Slavyansky Bazaar Restaurant in Moscow on June 22, 1897.[14]

At first, Stanislavsky, in his new role as director, poured his energy into manufacturing external "naturalism," in his productions, traveling great distances to procure authentic props and costumes for plays such as Shakespeare's *The Merchant of Venice*, which he directed for the Moscow Art Theatre's first season in October 1898.[15] Influenced by his observance in April 1890 of the working methods of the Duke of Saxe-Meiningen's theatrical troupe, which compensated for the mediocre talent of its actors with disciplined rehearsal and authentic settings, Stanislavsky devoted himself to reproducing real life on the stage.[16] By producing absolutely authentic settings for his productions, a practice for which he was later heavily criticized, he thought to bring about realistic characters.[17]

The Moscow Art Theatre's naturalistic productions were initially well received. Vsevolod Meyerhold, one of Stanislavsky's star pupils, praised the setting for Tolstoy's *Tsar Fyodor Ivanovitch*, which was also part of the theatre's opening season in 1898, declaring that "in terms of originality, beauty, and truth the décor for the settings can go no further. You can look at them for hours and never tire."[18] One St. Petersburg critic, G. Arseniy, nonetheless scorned the praise by the Moscow critics for the production:

> Having seen "real" headdresses, ancient kaftans with swept-
> back collars and slits in the sleeves, not badly done, although
> with rather lacklustre sets, and a more or less strictly
> disciplined crowd, they decide that they have witnessed the
> eighth wonder of the world.[19]

The success of the Moscow Art Theatre's naturalistic approach to the staging of plays continued through its first six seasons, from 1898 to 1903, culminating in the production of Maxim Gorky's *The Lower Depths* in 1902. The 1899 production of Chekhov's *Uncle Vanya* was applauded, and the famous "chirping crickets" introduced as a naturalistic sound effect by Stanislavsky were praised by the critic Aleksandr Kugel', becoming a trademark of the production.[20] With each successive season, however, the problems of the naturalistic approach became increasingly evident. Nemirovitch-Dantchenko's production of Ibsen's last play, *When We Dead Awaken*, in November 1900, "foundered beneath the weight of . . . naturalistic detail," including a genuine mountain stream, croquet mallets, and hunting dogs.[21] Finally, with the production of Tolstoy's *The Power of Darkness* in 1902, even Nikolay Efros, the Moscow Art Theatre's most sympathetic critic, began to protest, noting that "external detail took away the play's 'spirit and reason,' which not even the presence of no less than three different horses at three different times, 'munching oats, snorting quietly and moving their ears,' could compensate for."[22]

It was only after 1905 that Stanislavsky was able to procure the freedom to experiment, test boundaries, and develop his system. In this year he created a new, experimental Theatre-Studio with Meyerhold who had left the Moscow Art Theatre in 1902 to pursue his own ideas on directing. Stanislavsky had begun to realize that the kind of external "facsimile" realism that he had been using in his direction of Chekhov and Ibsen (i.e., buying authentic props, visiting actual locales, etc.) was insufficient without an internal "psychological" realism in the actors' portrayal of the characters.[23]

Stanislavsky wanted to demonstrate that his ideas on acting could be applied to all types of theatre, Symbolic and Realistic, farcical and tragic. As Maeterlinck, the preeminent Symbolist dramatist, expressed it, the task of the Symbolist theater was to produce "an *inner* drama, which has its own logic and its own development, which never coincide with the logic and development of the events in the material outer world."[24] Stanislavsky had been aware that his conception of realism had been missing this "inner drama" as early as 1902, when he commented on his production of Tolstoy's *The Power of Darkness*:

> Realism only becomes naturalism when it is not justified
> by the artist from within ... the external realism of the
> production of *The Power of Darkness* revealed the absence
> of inner justification in those of us who were acting in it.
> The stage was taken over by things, objects, banal outward
> *events* ... which crushed the inner meaning of the play and
> its characters.[25]

In 1908, during the rehearsals for his production of Maeterlinck's *The Blue Bird*, Stanislavsky began to implement techniques that he had begun developing in 1906 and 1907. In his rehearsal notes to the cast, Stanislavsky explained:

> The blocking is not understood. Everyone moves because the
> director has said "move" and because the move corresponds
> to the director's ideas. Nobody is digging around and so
> there is no search for inner motive. All the moves are false
> because they are unthinking. It's not enough to understand,
> you must take your positions and moves to your heart.[26]

For the next thirty years, he would continue to change, adapt, and discard different features of what came to be called the Stanislavsky "system," but the essential goal of truthfulness in acting always remained the same.

Beginning with the 1911 production of Tolstoy's *The Living Corpse,* the Stanislavsky system was adopted as the official pedagogical system of the Moscow Art Theatre.[27] Though it was constantly evolving and changing up until Stanislavsky's death in 1938, the system was given its most complete representation in his book *Building a Character*, drafted in the 1930s after serious illness forced him to cut back on his production schedule.[28] A diagram of the complete system, distilled from the discussion in the book, is presented in Figure 2. In his discussion, Stanislavsky adopts a dialogical format, in which, as the fictional teacher Tortsov, he explains the system to a group of students by hanging a series of banners on the wall. Each of the lines in Figure 2 represents one of Stanislavsky's banners. At the base of his diagram, Stanislavsky places the motto "an actor prepares," the title of his first major treatise on acting, in order to remind his students that good acting requires hard work and dedication at its foundation.[29] Above this, he places three other fundamental principles: 1) that acting is primarily about *action*; 2) that emotion on the stage must always be sincere; and 3) that the actor accesses the subconscious through the conscious use of theatrical techniques.

Overall, the system is divided into two parts, "psycho-technique" and "external technique," indicated by the headings on each side of Figure 2.[30] External technique encompasses all the various disciplines that the actor is required to master in order to effectively produce a physical embodiment of a character on the stage. Several of the terms require brief definition: "expressive body training" is a general rubric for the study of "gymnastics, dance, acrobatics, fencing (foils, rapiers, daggers), wrestling, boxing, carriage, all aspects of physical training,"[31] "external tempo-rhythm" has to do with pacing and timing of action on stage, and "external characterization" covers all of the idiosyncratic physical gestures that an actor might use to define a character.

The left side of Figure 2 enumerates the techniques available to the actor for internal preparation, meaning the internalization of the character. "The magic 'If'" helps actors to imagine realistic, personal responses to situations in the play by having them ask "*If* I were in this situation, what would I do?"[32] "Given circumstances" are essentially bits of background information that actors create for their characters, information not provided by the script, particularly their history immediately prior to the opening of the play.[33] "Emotion memory," also called affective memory or emotional recall, is the ability of actors to remember events from their own past that can be applied to analogous situations in their roles, creating a truthfulness of emotion based on personal experience.[34]

It is the left side of the diagram, the side dealing with psycho-technique that was subjected to the most frequent revisions during Stanislavsky's development of the system. In earlier formulations, particularly in *An Actor*

INTERNAL PREPARATION	EXTERNAL PREPARATION
(preparation of the part)	(preparation of the actor)
(inner qualities)	(physical attributes)
"living a part"	"clothing a part"

OVERALL CREATIVE STATE

Internal Creative State   External Creative State

Imagination and its inventions	Relaxation of muscles
The Magic "If"	Expressive Body Training
Given Circumstances	Plasticity (movement)
Units / Objectives	Voice (vocal production)
Attention / Object	Speech (diction)
Sense of Truth / Faith	Discipline
(Desire-->) Action	Ethics
Communion (-->Goal)	Ensemble Sense
Adaptation	Coherence
Inner Tempo-Rhythm	External Tempo-Rhythm
Emotion Memory	External Characterization
Repeated Feelings	External Stage Charm
Sincerity of Emotions	Restraint and Finish
Logic / Continuity	Logic/Coherence of Action
Internal Habit	External Habit
Internal Training	External Training

Mind Will Feelings

Psycho-Technique   External Technique

"Action" "Sincerity of Emotions" "The Subconscious
      (Pushkin)   via the Conscious"

AN ACTOR PREPARES

Figure 2 The Stanislavsky System (adapted from Stanislavsky,
    Building a Character)

Prepares, Stanislavsky stressed the importance of emotion memory, and it was this version of the system that was eventually adopted and promulgated by many of Stanislavsky's American disciples.[35] Near the end of his life, however, Stanislavsky developed a new method of working on a play, which he dubbed the "method of physical actions," and it was this method that was to become what he felt was his most important contribution to acting theory.[36]

Scoring a Role

In its entirety, the Stanislavsky system represents an attempt to address every aspect of the actor's craft. Much of the system, which is presented in three volumes (*An Actor Prepares*, *Building a Character*, and *Creating a Role*), focuses on practical matters of stage acting such as movement, relaxation, and vocal projection. The portion of the complete system that is relevant to the present undertaking, however (i.e., the portion that relates to the analysis of a dramatic text), is the subsection of Figure 2 listed under "Internal Preparation" as "Units/Objectives." This portion of the system is unique in that it was conceived during a stage of Stanislavsky's development of the system (1924–28) in which he concentrated on analysis of the play itself, on the roles contained within the drama rather than on the performance of those roles. From 1909 to 1916, Stanislavsky developed the essentials of his system, constantly shifting emphasis from one element to another and refining the whole. Subsequently, from 1916 to 1924, he focused on affective memory, including the concepts of sense memory and emotional recall. During these first two periods of the system's development, Stanislavsky approached the system from the actor's perspective; he himself was still acting and considered the problems of the actor to be of the utmost importance. From 1924 to 1928, however, Stanislavsky's perspective changed to that of the director. It was during this period that he emphasized the "table sessions" where he (as director) would gather his actors around a large table for days, and even weeks, at a time before rehearsals began and analyze the play.[37]

Stanislavsky described a dramatic text as being comprised of a series of "units" of varying length: acts, scenes, subsections, and individual lines. During the table sessions, Stanislavsky and his actors would divide the play into its "main organic episodes," breaking the text down into smaller and smaller units until arriving at the individual lines themselves.[38] Stanislavsky would then help each of his actors prepare a "score" for their role, which he defined as an "outline of the character's objectives," each corresponding to a specific unit of the text.[39] An "objective" is the goal of a character for a given unit of the drama, while "the overarching goal of a character" for the play is that character's "superobjective."[40] The superobjective has been variously defined by Stanislavskians as the "seed," the "overall action," the "ruling idea," the "overlaying problem," and the "spine" of a role.[41]

> In *An Actor Prepares*, the only book published during his lifetime, Stanislavsky offers the following guidelines on the process of breaking down the role into its constituent units: The largest pieces you reduce to medium size, then to small, and then to fine, only to reverse the process eventually and reassemble the whole.... Do not break up a play more than is necessary, do not use details to guide you. Create a channel outlined by large divisions, which have been thoroughly worked out and filled down to the last detail.[42]

He then goes on to offer advice on the selection of objectives for each unit, noting, "every objective must carry in itself the germ of action" and urging the actor to "introduce something more definitely active, state a question so that it requires an answer."[43]

In *A Challenge to the Actor*, an updated adaptation of the Stanislavsky system that focuses on the concept of objectives, Uta Hagen follows Stanislavsky's advice and outlines a six-step process that poses the sort of direct questions he had in mind (see Figure 3).[44] Steps 4 through 6, in particular, address the character's objectives, while the first three steps deal with what Stanislavsky called "given circumstances," a sort of background sketch that the actor creates to help fill in the details of the character's life and situation prior to the opening of the play.[45]

1. Who Am I?
2. What Are the Circumstances?
3. What Are My Relationships?
4. What Do I Want?
5. What Is My Obstacle?
6. What Do I Do To Get What I Want?

Figure 3 Hagen's Six Steps (Hagen, *A Challenge for the Actor*)

Though Stanislavsky's original formulation of the system of objectives provided for an almost infinite number of different levels, he himself discussed only three: the superobjective (the character's goal for the play), the main objective (the character's goal for each scene), and the objective (the character's goal for each line).[46] He described the relationship between the three levels with a number of insightful metaphors, including the following passage from *Building a Character*:

> As if you had a threaded needle in your fingers now pass it through the elements already set up inside you, the objectives you have prepared in the detailed score of your part, and string them on the unbroken line leading to the supreme goal of the play being produced.[47]

Later, Stanislavsky's disciples expanded his tripartite system to include several other types of objectives. Uta Hagen, for example, adds the notion of an "immediate objective," for each "beat" of a scene, which she defines as an objective that "stays in effect from the moment of its inception until the wish has been fulfilled or has failed, at which point it will be replaced by another one."[48] Thus, a scene may have more than one "beat objective," if the character's goal shifts during the progression of the scene.

Hagen also discusses "hidden" and "subconscious" objectives, opening up the possibility of multiple layers of objectives coexisting during the same temporal span, but at different levels of the character's consciousness.[49] In addition, Irina and Igor Levin, two later proponents of the Stanislavsky system, describe an "interrupted event," which they define as a "string of events with the same conflict, leading character, and main objective."[50] An interrupted event could span a series of beat objectives, or even main objectives, until it was either resolved or discarded.[51]

Finally, Georgi A. Tovstonogov introduced the concept of meta-objectives when he discussed the "super-superobjective." Tovstonogov differentiates the superobjective and the super-superobjective in noting that "the superobjective, or idea of the performance, is inherent in the play…. The super-superobjective is the bridge that connects the performance with life…. It requires an awareness of life, of the people for whom we are working."[52] In broaching the subject of objectives that extend beyond the domain of the play itself (i.e., the performer's objectives, in addition to the character's objectives), Tovstonogov calls to mind Edward T. Cone's work on the different "voices" present in a performance of a musical work: those of the composer and the performer can be heard in addition to the character being portrayed by the performer.[53] Stanislavsky describes the distinction between the performer and the character in these terms:

> One half of an actor is absorbed by his super-objective, by the through line of action, the subtext, his inner images, the elements which go to make up his inner creative state. But the other half of it continues to operate on a psycho-technique more or less in the way that I demonstrated it to you. An Actor is split into two parts when he is acting. You recall how Tommaso Salvini put it "An actor lives, weeps, laughs on the stage, but as he weeps and laughs he observes his own tears and mirth. It is this double existence, this balance between life and acting that makes for art."[54]

The hierarchical system of objectives, with its additions by various Stanislavskians, may be summarized, from the top down, as follows: 1) the super-superobjective (SSO); 2) the superobjective (SO); 3) the interrupted objective (IO); 4) the main objective (MO); 3) the beat objective (BO); and 4) the line objective (LO). Other types of objectives that may be included at each level are the hidden objective (HO) and the subconscious objective (SbO).

Sample Analyses: Griboyedov and Shakespeare

In order to clarify further how one actually goes about scoring a role, I will now provide two examples drawn from Stanislavsky's own scores, the first from his analysis of Griboyedov's comic masterpiece, *Woe from Wit*, and the second from his analysis of *Othello*. Because he planned to use it as a pedagogical tool in his book *Creating a Role*, Stanislavsky went through several additional analytical stages before arriving at the actual score for the role of Chatski in *Woe from Wit*. One of these preliminary stages is represented by the list of "external circumstances," the "facts" of the play, created by Stanislavsky for the first act (see Figure 4).[55] The list resembles a traditional plot summary, and it is indicative of the degree to which Stanislavsky changed the face of dramatic analysis that he considered it only a rudimentary first step.

The short list given in Figure 5 represents a second preliminary stage in the analytical process. Here, Stanislavsky uses the facts of the play as the springboard for a deeper investigation of the circumstances of the play "on the social level." As he notes in *Creating a Role*:

> Often the facts of a play derive from a way and kind of life,
> a *social* situation; therefore it is not difficult to push down
> from them into a deeper level of existence. At the same
> time the circumstances which make up a way of life must
> be studied not only in the actual text but also in a variety
> of commentaries, pieces of literature, historical writings
> concerning the period, and so forth.[56]

1. A meeting between Sophia and Molchalin has continued all night.
2. It is dawn. They are playing a duet of flute and piano in the next room.
3. Liza, the maid, is asleep. She is supposed to be keeping watch.
4. Liza wakes up, sees that day is breaking, begs the lovers to separate quickly.
5. Liza sets the clock ahead to frighten the lovers and turn their attention to danger.
6. As the clock strikes, Sophia's father, Famusov, enters.
7. He sees Liza, flirts with her.
8. Liza cleverly evades his attention and persuades him to go away.
9. At the noise Sophia enters. She sees the dawn and is astonished at how quickly her night of love has passed.
10. The lovers have not had time to separate before Famusov confronts them.
11. Astonishment, questions, angry uproar.
12. Sophia cleverly extricates herself from embarrassment and danger.
13. Her father releases her, while he goes off with Molchalin to sign some papers.
14. Liza upbraids Sophia and Sophia is depressed by the prose of daytime after the poetry of her nighttime meeting.
15. Liza tries to remind Sophia of her childhood friend Chatski, who apparently is in love with Sophia.
16. This angers Sophia and causes her to think all the more of Molchalin.
17. The unexpected arrival of Chatski, his enthusiasm, their meeting. Sophia's embarrassment, a kiss. Chatski's bewilderment, he accuses her of coldness. They speak of old times. Chatski is witty in his friendly chatter. He makes a declaration of love to Sophia. Sophia is caustic.
18. Famusov returns. He is astonished. His meeting with Chatski.
19. Exit Sophia. She makes a sly remark about being out of her father's sight.
20. Famusov cross-examines Chatski. His suspicions about Chatski's intentions with regard to Sophia.
21. Chatski is lyrical in praise of Sophia. He leaves abruptly.
22. The father's bewilderment and suspicions.

Figure 4 External Circumstances (Griboyedov, *Woe from Wit*, Act I)
(Stanislavsky, *Creating a Role*)

1. The rendezvous between Sophia and Molchalin. What does it show? How did it come about?
   Is it due to the influence of French education and books?
   Sentimentality, languor, tenderness, and purity on the part of a young girl; yet at the same time, her laxity of morals.
2. Liza watches over Sophia. You must understand the danger which threatens Liza: she could be sent to Siberia or demoted to farm work. You must understand Liza's devotion.
3. Famusov flirts with Liza at the same time that he poses as being monk-like in behavior. This is an example of a Pharisee of those times.
4. Famusov is afraid of any misalliance; there is Princess Maria Alexeyevna to be considered.
   What is the position of Maria Alexeyevna? Her family are afraid of her criticism. One can lose one's good name, prestige, and even one's place.
5. Liza favors Chatski; she will be ridiculed if Sophia marries Molchalin.
6. Chatski arrives from abroad. What does it mean to come home in those days, traveling by coaches with relays of horses?

Figure 5 Social Circumstances (*Woe from Wit*, Act I) (Stanislavsky, *Creating a Role*)

After completing his preliminary investigation of the background and circumstances surrounding the character of Chatski, Stanislavsky scored Chatski's role for Act I, Scene 2: his encounter with Sophia.[57] Again because it is intended for pedagogical use, his outline of Chatski's objectives is considerably expanded, with explanations following each item in the outline. The score has been re-compressed in Figure 6 for the sake of expediency.

A. I desire to hasten the moment of my meeting with Sophia, something I have dreamed of for so long.
    a. I must speak to[the yardman], be agreeable, exchange greetings.
    b. I must quickly rouse the sleepy doorman.
    c. I desire to greet the dog, and pet this old friend of mine.
    d. I must say how do you do to [the doorman], be nice to him, exchange greetings.
    e. I must greet [the steward and the housekeeper] too, I must ask about Sophia. Where is she? Is she well? Is she up?
    f. I want to get to main goal quickly, see Sophia, the dear friend of my childhood, almost my sister.

B. I wish to greet the dear friend of my childhood, one who is almost a sister to me; I want to embrace her and exchange pent-up feelings with her.
    a. First of all I want to look at Sophia carefully, to see her familiar and dear features, to appraise the changes that have taken place in my absence.
    b. I want to convey my feelings in a brotherly kiss.
    c. I must caress Sophia by look and by word.

C. I must understand the reason for this cold reception.
    a. I must get Sophia to confess what is the matter.
    b. I must shake her up with interrogation, reproaches, cleverly put questions.
    c. I must draw her attention to me.

D. To cross examine Sophia about herself, her relatives, acquaintances, and all the life of this house and of Moscow.

Figure 6 The Score of Chatski's Role (*Woe from Wit*, I/ii) (Stanislavsky, *Creating a Role*)

Because this is the score of a single scene, the upper-case letters of the outline refer to beat objectives, rather than main objectives; each letter represents a fundamental shift in the scene, prompted by a turn of events. Chatski's first beat objective, for example (to hasten the moment of his meeting with Sophia) is abandoned once she arrives in the room. It is replaced by a second beat objective (marked "B" in the figure): to exchange pent-up feelings with Sophia. When Chatski is coldly received, another beat change occurs in the scene; his new beat objective is to determine the reason for Sophia's disinterest. Each of the line objectives represented by lower-case letters is designed to promote the attainment of its attendant beat objective.

The analysis of *Othello*, Act III, Scene 3, dates from 1929–30, when Stanislavsky took a rare vacation to Nice to recover from illness and was forced to write out his comments on the production and mail them back to his actors at the Moscow Art Theatre.[58] A comparison of the production notes for *Othello* with Stanislavsky's only other published production notebook, on Chekhov's *The Seagull*, reveals a host of differences.[59] Though his notes for *The Seagull*, written in 1898, were quite detailed, including complete blocking cues, suggested emotional cues, and insights into the nature of the play, Stanislavsky did not mention objectives at all, because he had not yet developed his system.[60] A typical example from the notebook reads as follows:

> I can't help thinking that all through this scene [I/i] Konstantin is very excited. The performance of his play is to him an event that is of decisive importance to his future career.... The more jumpy and agitated he is now, the stronger will his mood of despair be after the failure of his play.[61]

The sort of generic emotional cues given by Stanislavsky in the above-quoted passage ("excited ... jumpy and agitated ...") became anathema to him by the time he wrote the production notes for *Othello* in 1929–30. During the last years of his life (1924 to 1938), Stanislavsky developed what he called "The Method of Physical Actions," a way of working that emphasized physical objectives and physical improvisation on the stage early in the rehearsal process.[62] As Grigori V. Kristi notes:

> The method of physical actions developed by Stanislavski during the last years of his life differs fundamentally from everything previously elaborated by him in the field of dramatic creativity. It was not only a new technique, but

a new conception of creativity, firmly based in science. It was no accident that Stanislavski considered this method the summary of his whole career, his legacy to the artistic generations of the future.[63]

Stanislavsky's score for Act III, Scene 3 of Othello's role, shown in Figure 7, is a good example of a score influenced by the need to find "means which the actor can control."[64] Like the analysis of Chatski discussed above, it focuses on concrete and performable actions.

A: "...[to] *decide why Desdemona deceives me.*"

B: "...'to get away from Iago, not to see or hear him.'"
"...[to] escape to-day your doctor's tortures."

C: "...[to] understand, feel for yourself—this is what you have done to me!"
"... [to] *force* Iago the cold-hearted to perceive with his inner sight and experience everything he has done, all the tortures Othello is undergoing."

D: "...'to make it clear to Iago—look out, you cannot joke like this with impunity.'"

E: "...[to] hide, to get away from oneself and from others."

F: "...[to] soften Iago and gain his help."
"...to move him to pity and physically show him what a hell he is in."

G: "...[to] find my bearings and understand. Othello does everything to make Iago talk."

H: "...[to show] *the change which has taken place within him, a change irrevocable and final.*"

 I: "...to cut all roads of retreat (to secure your decision as firmly as possible and to deprive yourself of any possibility of escape)."

J: "...to share a terrible secret of a kind that is difficult to confess even to your own self."

Figure 7 Stanislavsky's Score for Othello (*Othello*, III/iii) (Stanislavsky, *Stanislavsky Produces "Othello"*)

Stanislavsky and Schenker in the United States

Although the system of units and objectives may well prove to be Stanislavsky's most enduring legacy, his reputation in the United States was founded primarily on the concept of affective memory, particularly in its incarnation as Lee Strasberg's "Method."[65] Strasberg, who, along with Stella Adler, Robert Lewis, and Harold Clurman, founded the Group Theater (1931–1941) to apply Stanislavsky's ideas to American productions, emphasized affective memory above all the other aspects of the system, despite Adler's assertion that the study of the text was of paramount importance.[66] As Sonia Moore explains, this is because the majority of Stanislavsky's admirers in the United States became acquainted with his ideas only through *An Actor Prepares*.[67] Since Stanislavsky was constantly adapting and refining his system (*An Actor Prepares* was planned as the first book in a three-volume series) and his final ideas were not systematically written down, his American disciples ended up distorting his teachings. Moreover, as Elizabeth Reynolds Hapgood, a close friend of Stanislavsky's and the primary translator of his written works, points out (with obvious reference to Strasberg):

> Some actors tended to choose what appealed to them the most
> and did not make the effort to become what ideally might be
> called the "compleat" actor in a part, just as some teachers
> who claim to expound Stanislavski's method actually use
> only a fraction of his all-embracing technique.[68]

The problem created by the absence of a definitive written form of Stanislavsky's complete system was compounded from the outset by the proliferation of acting teachers, all former students of his in Moscow, desiring to differentiate themselves from Stanislavsky and stake out their own territory by creating personalized adaptations of his system. Three of Stanislavsky's star pupils, Michael Chekhov, Vsevolod Meyerhold, and Eugene Vakhtangov, set out on their own to create competing dramatic theories. Chekhov, whom

Stanislavsky called "his most brilliant student," left the Moscow Art Theatre and established a studio in England, where he combined Stanislavsky's ideas with aspects of Eurhythmy drawn from the work of Rudolf Steiner, attracting students such as Marilyn Monroe and Yul Brynner.[69] Meyerhold, for his part, rejected the Naturalist tendencies of the system, embracing Symbolism and creating what many came to see as a diametrically opposed method of creating surreal, fantastical productions.[70] The defense of Stanislavsky's original system was left to Vakhtangov. Though he "understood Stanislavski's teachings thoroughly and passed them on to his students as a true follower of his great teacher,"[71] he was also determined to improve upon Stanislavsky's system. He assumed the task reluctantly, attempting to forge a compromise between the ideas of Stanislavsky on the one hand and Meyerhold on the other. As Michael Benedetti notes:

> Eugene Vakhtangov (1883-1922) worked with Stanislavski and Meyerhold and admired them both. Although he won Stanislavski's admiration as the best teacher of the Stanislavski system, Vakhtangov remained aware of the shortcomings of naturalism. He attempted a compromise between the Stanislavski and Meyerhold systems in his own approach to acting, which he called "Fantastic Realism." This was fundamentally a realistic form, but one in which the selected details of performance were abstracted and exaggerated in order to stimulate the audience's imagination. Vakhtangov was, in a sense, attempting to use Stanislavski's means for Meyerhold's ends.[72]

In 1923, following their participation in the highly successful American tour of the Moscow Art Theatre, a second wave of disciples brought Stanislavsky's ideas to the United States. When the rest of the company returned to Moscow, these three students, Leo Bulgakov, Richard Boleslavsky, and Maria Ouspenskaya, remained behind and established the Laboratory Theatre and School in New York City.[73] In the 1930s, the Group Theatre, led by Strasberg, began to distance itself from the teachings of the Lab School. A confrontation between its members was forced when Stella Adler, returning from a series of private lessons with Stanislavsky in Paris in 1933, presented Strasberg with a more complete interpretation of the system:

> [Adler] returned with a conflicting idea of the Russian system, one which put much less stress on personal experience and more on imagination and study of the text. Strasberg in particular rejected this new interpretation, and the long-awaited publication of *An Actor Prepares* in 1936 seemed to confirm Strasberg's position, particularly since Stanislavski's projected subsequent volumes were left incomplete at his death.[74]

The Group Theatre was disbanded, and Adler and Strasberg each founded their own studios. Strasberg's Actors' Studio, of which Elia Kazan was a part, attracted the interest of Marilyn Monroe in the 1950s, and the future of his Method was assured.[75] Actors from Marlon Brando to Jack Nicholson, including Warren Beatty, Paul Newman, Frank Sinatra, Liz Taylor, Jason Robards, Anthony Perkins, and James Dean, have since adopted Strasberg's Method.[76] Today, the studios of both Adler and Strasberg are part of the Tisch School of the Arts at New York University.

Although they were certainly operating independently, disciples of the Austrian music theorist Heinrich Schenker (1868–1935) and Stanislavsky took remarkably similar routes to disseminate their respective theories. Both Schenker and Stanislavsky published their definitive masterworks in the mid-1930s.[77] Both masters also had "official" representatives who emigrated to the United Sates from Europe in the 1930s and 40s; for Schenkerians, these authentic disciples were Hans Weisse, Ernst Oster, Oswald Jonas, and Felix Salzer, while for Stanislavskians they were Richard Boleslavsky and Maria Ouspenskaya.[78] Both schools set up shop in New York, the Schenkerians at the Mannes School of Music and the Stanislavskians at the American Laboratory Theatre and School.[79]

Eventually, these original disciples attracted American followers: Carl Schachter and Allen Forte, for the Schenkerians and Lee Strasberg and Stella Adler for the Stanislavskians. These new disciples, in turn, began teaching the systems to students of their own, Forte at Yale University and Schachter at the City University of New York, Strasberg at the Actors' Studio and Adler at the Stella Adler Theatre Studio.[80]

In addition to the similarities in the dissemination of their respective theories in the United States, there are also a number of conceptual parallels between Schenker's theory of structural levels and Stanislavsky's system of objectives.[81] To begin with, both systems are hierarchical, though not in the strict sense suggested by Cohn and Dempster in their critical evaluation of Schenkerian theory, and both are comprised of three primary structural levels.[82] Each system emphasizes the connection between its levels, the dependence of the foreground on the background and vice versa. Stanislavsky even uses the terms foreground and background to denote different structural levels, though, as the following passage from *Building a Character* makes clear, their meaning for him is opposite to their meaning for Schenker:

> The lines of perspective which are used to convey complex feelings move on the subtextual, inner plane of a role. These are the lines of inner objectives, desires, ambitions, efforts, actions which are grouped, inserted, separated, combined, accented, toned down. Some represent important fundamental objectives and appear in the foreground. Others of medium or minimum value are grouped on a secondary plane, or sink quite into the background, according to the peculiar factors causing the development of the emotions throughout the play.[83]

Like the system of objectives, Schenker's theory of structural levels is a powerful tool for explaining a temporal art form, where different events, occurring later in time, can be seen as fulfilling processes begun much earlier. Moreover, both Schenker and Stanislavsky consciously strove to justify their theories as organic and rooted in nature.[84] As Stanislavsky notes in one of his last comments on the system, "there is really no question of my method or your method. There is only one method, which is that of organic, creative nature."[85]

Stanislavsky clearly regarded his system as a musical one, at least in a metaphorical sense. He draws the analogy himself when he says that "objectives are like the notes in music, they form the measures, which in turn produce the melody . . . the melody goes on to form an opera or a symphony, that is to say the life of a human spirit in a role, and that is what the soul of the actor sings."[86] He was inclined to think in musical terms, given that he was trained as a singer before he became a director and he turned to opera for inspiration in the last stage of his career, first as the director of the Opera Studio in 1918, then as the director of the Opera-Theatre Studio in 1935.[87]

Perhaps the strongest link between the two systems, however, lies in their mutual emphasis on the relevance of theory to performance. Although Schenkerian analysis has since been used almost exclusively in the service of musical analyses that reduce the music to its essence simply to demonstrate the intricacy of musical structure for its own sake, Schenker clearly intended his ideas to be used in the service of musical performance. Music theorists have begun to reclaim Schenker's emphasis on the link between analysis and performance, to such a degree that analysis and performance studies has become a recognized subdiscipline in the field.[88]

Stanislavsky's attitude toward the relationship between theory and performance is well documented in the writings of his students. It is certain that he intended for the complete system to be practical, a tool to be used by working actors and directors in their training and for the preparation of specific productions. As Harold Clurman notes, "the system *is* a technique, it is not an end in itself. Nor is it a *theory*. It exists and has value only in practice, in the work of the actor, the director, the company."[89] Moreover, as Uta Hagen observes, it is in the performer's best interest to carry out an analysis of the role:

Let me stress that an intellectual approach to the play, *a thorough analysis of it*, is and always has been the director's responsibility, *not* the actor's. However, if we want to claim the right to be creative participants in bringing it to life, we must be armed with more than our technical skills. We should be able to make an *intelligent* evaluation of the play's purpose: first, in order to be able to follow the director's analysis when he shares his intentions with us, and, perhaps more importantly, so that we don't go interpretively astray in the initial stages of our homework on the role.[90]

Consequently, in the analyses that are included in the subsequent chapters, the scoring of individual roles will always be undertaken with an eye toward how the analyses may be applied in a performance context. As Stanislavsky puts it, an objective "must have the power to attract and excite the actor"; units and objectives are "merely a technical method of arousing inner, living desires and aspirations."[91]

Applying the System to the Analysis of Opera

Though he is certainly most famous as a director of the naturalistic dramas of Tolstoy, Ibsen, and Chekhov, Stanislavsky devoted increasing amounts of time in his later years to the direction of opera, which he regarded as the greatest challenge to the director. In fact, Stanislavsky directed opera precisely because it offered "an opportunity to refute the accusation that the System only had validity for 'naturalistic' plays. If it could be made to work in opera … it could prove its universality and its claim to be rooted in the real world of nature."[92] A list of the operas directed by Stanislavsky is given in Figure 8.[93]

8/2/21:	Werther (Massenet)
6/15/22:	Eugene Onegin (Tchaikovsky)
4/5/25:	Il Matrimonio Segreto (Cimarosa)
11/28/26:	The Tsar's Bride (Rimsky-Korsakov)
4/12/27:	La Bohème (Puccini)
1/19/28:	May Night (Rimsky-Korsakov)
3/5/28:	Boris Godunov (Moussorgsky)
2/26/29:	Queen of Spades (Tchaikovsky)
5/4/32:	The Golden Cockerel (Rimsky-Korsakov)
10/26/33:	The Barber of Seville (Rossini)
4/4/35:	Carmen (Bizet)
5/22/36:	Don Pasquale (Donizetti)
3/10/39:	Rigoletto (Verdi) - completed by Meyerhold

Figure 8 Operas Directed by Stanislavsky (adapted from J. Benedetti, *Stanislavski*)

In his work at the Opera Studio, founded in 1918, and later at the Opera-Theatre Studio, founded in 1935, Stanislavsky emphasized that the singer-actor had to create a perfect blend of "vocal, musical, and stage arts."[94] He insisted, as Jean Benedetti notes, "Actions, motivations ... were to be found in the score not in the stage directions which were often added later, without reference to the composer and in blatant contradiction to the music. A bar by bar examination of the structure of the music ... would supply the information needed for a truthful performance."[95]

Stanislavsky describes the bond between music and action in the following passage on operatic preludes, excerpted from *Stanislavsky's Legacy*:

> In opera I take my point of departure from the music. I try to discover what it was that prompted the composer to write his work. Then I try to reproduce this in the action of the singers. If the orchestra plays a prelude, introducing a scene before the action begins we are not content to have the orchestra simply play this, we put it in scenic terms, in the sense of actions, words, phrases. Thus we often use

action to illustrate other instruments which lend color to the orchestra. If an instrument gives the theme of death, the singer will feel the corresponding emotions. He must not disregard these preludes and use the time to clear his throat or prepare his entrance, he must already be part of the life of a human spirit in his part, in the play.[96]

He clarifies his methodology for analyzing the roles in an opera in a section entitled "Opera Rules," also from *Stanislavsky's Legacy*:

Concert music is pure music. By contrast opera music is subject to theatrical rules. These rules are to the effect that every scenic performance is action, hence the division into *acts*. In revivifying opera productions the point of departure should be the music. The objective of the director of an opera is to sift out the *action inherent in the musical picture* and restate this composition of sounds in terms of the dramatic, that is to say the *visual*. In other words: the action should be determined to a far greater degree by the musical score than merely by the text. The objective of the director is to explain exactly what it is that the composer wished to say when he wrote each phrase of his score, and what dramatic action he had in mind, even though this last may have been only subconsciously in his mind.[97]

Stanislavsky's model for the perfect singer-actor was Fyodor Chaliapin, the great Russian bass. He even went so far as to declare, "I have copied my system from Chaliapin. When I told him my views on the art of acting, Chaliapin yelled 'Help! I've been robbed!'"[98] Chaliapin's interpretations, especially his portrayal of the eponymous character in Moussorgsky's *Boris Godunov*, were universally admired. As Vincent Sheehan notes:

Chaliapin had an infallible sense for stage action in the representation of a character. For this he never had an equal, so far as we know, except Mary Garden. Neither could have created a character in this way—*lived* a character, *been* a character—in the ordinary theater with its totally different demands, but in the lyric theater, where everything up to and including the innermost soul of the personage is the function of the music, they were the first and so far the only examples of their kind…. Her Mélisande and his Boris … were spun from within like spider's web, and the beholder had nothing left to do but to marvel, and perhaps to weep.[99]

Because he believed that "*every* opera is a musical drama,"[100] Stanislavsky made no distinction between the epic tragedies of Tchaikovsky and the light comedies of Rossini in terms of analytical rigor, directing everything from *Eugene Onegin* to *The Barber of Seville*. He even commented on Wagner, noting, "you can bring Wagnerian heroes to life and make human beings out of them if you can wean them from everything 'operatic' and plan their actions in consonance with the *inner meaning* of the music and not the *external* effects."[101]

Keeping Stanislavsky's comments on the priority of music in mind, what is the best way to go about analyzing both the text and the score of an opera? As the aesthetician James Merriman notes, in order to compare features of music and drama, those features must be possible in both mediums. He lists repetition, contrast, reversal, juxtaposition, and heterogeneity as potentially analyzable features.[102] If one were to distill Stanislavsky's system of objectives down to a single feature, however, that feature would be closure. A character's dramatic success is defined by the attainment of local objectives, main objectives, and a superobjective, and the attainment of each objective represents a kind of dramatic closure, a closing of a chapter in the character's history. Obviously, closure is also a prominent feature of music, and therefore it meets Merriman's basic requirement for analysis.

What follows is a general methodology for undertaking a "linear-dramatic" analysis of an operatic role: 1) complete a linear analysis of the music relating to the character selected (i.e., the musical passages during which the character is onstage, as well as other passages containing the character's motive, if applicable), making note of points of musical closure; 2) read the libretto all the way through and identify the character's superobjective (SO), noting whether or not it is attained;[103] 3) go though the scenes involving the character, identifying a main objective (MO) for each scene, taking note of the character's success or failure, and making sure that all main objectives support the attainment of the SO;[104] 4) go through each scene in detail, identifying the beats of the scene, if any, and listing a beat objective (BO) for each new beat that supports the MO; 5) identify any interrupted objectives (IOs) and note whether they are ultimately resolved and, if so, where the resolution occurs; 6) go back through the objectives chosen in Steps 2 through 5, searching for any hidden, or subconscious, objectives (HOs) and adding them beneath or beside the relevant conscious objectives; 7) identify the most salient lines of each scene and identify line objectives (LOs) for these, making sure they support the relevant BO or MO; 8) compare the musical and dramatic analyses, from Steps 1 and 2 through 7 respectively, identifying points of correlation and disjunction and drawing conclusions accordingly; 9) place the composite analysis in a performance context, identifying ways in which the performer might highlight points of musical and dramatic closure, or lack of closure.

The musical analysis described in the first step of the methodology outlined above is dependent upon the presence of moments of tonal closure (in both the linear and harmonic sense) in the scores of the operas selected for analysis. While the majority of the operas examined in Chapters 4 through 7 are comprised almost entirely of such moments (Copland's opera being an exception that, like the operas of Britten and Debussy, limits tonality to certain characters or passages), it is the fact that all of them were written in a post-Wagnerian world in which the use of tonal closure was a choice, not a requirement, that invites further inquiry. After defining multi-movement tonal closure in Chapter 3, the following chapters will undertake that inquiry.

ENDNOTES

[1] Robert L. Benedetti, *Seeming, Being and Becoming: Acting in Our Century* (New York: Drama Book Specialists, 1976), 41.

[2] The Anglicized version of Konstantin Stanislavsky's last name will be used throughout the book, unless quoting or citing a source in which the name is spelled differently (e.g., Constantin Stanislavski, Konstantin Stanislavski).

[3] Jean Benedetti, *Stanislavski: A Life* (New York: Routledge, 1988), 3.

[4] Ibid., 24. Stanislavsky borrowed his stage name from Stanislavskaia, his favorite Bolshoi ballerina. See J. Benedetti, *Stanislavski*, 10 and 23.

[5] Ibid., 13–14.

[6] Ibid., 23.

[7] Ibid.

[8] Ibid., 24.

[9] Ibid., 27–8.

[10] For a complete listing of the productions that Stanislavsky acted in or directed for the Society of Art and Letters, see J. Benedetti, *Stanislavski*, 331–2.

[11] J. Benedetti, *Stanislavski*, 23.

[12] Ibid., 16.

[13] Mikhail Shchepkin to Aleksandra Shubert, 27 March 1848, in Mikhail Shchepkin, *Zhizn I Tvorchestvo* (Moscow: Iskusstvo, 1984), vol. I, 199–200. Translated and quoted in J. Benedetti, *Stanislavski*, 16.

[14] This meeting is discussed at length in the autobiographies of the two participants. See Konstantin Stanislavsky, *My Life in Art*, translated by J. J. Robbins (Boston: Little, Brown, and Company, 1924), 292–9, and Vladimir Nemirovitch–Dantchenko, *My Life in the Russian Theatre*, translated by John Cournos (New York: Theatre Arts Books, 1968), 79–108. Originally published by Little, Brown, and Company, 1936.

[15] For a complete list of the Moscow Art Theatre productions in which Stanislavsky served as actor or director, see J. Benedetti, *Stanislavski*, 332–5. For more information on the Moscow Art Theatre, see Nick Worrall, *The Moscow Art Theatre* (London: Routledge, 1996); Jean Benedetti, ed. and trans., *The Moscow Art Theatre Letters* (London: Methuen Drama, 1991); and Oliver M. Sayler, *Inside the Moscow Art Theatre* (New York: Brentano's, 1925).

[16] J. Benedetti, *Stanislavski*, 40–2.

[17] For criticism of the Moscow Art Theatre's dedication to Naturalism, see, in particular, Vsevolod Meyerhold, "The Isolation of Stanislavsky," in Vsevolod Meyerhold, *Meyerhold on Theatre*, ed. and trans. Edward Braun (New York: Hill and Wang, 1969), 175–80. See also Theodore Kommisarzhevsky, *Myself and the Theatre* (London: William Heinemann Ltd., 1929), 140.

[18] Vsevolod Meyerhold, *Perepiska 1896–1939* (Moscow: Iskusstvo, 1976), 19. Translated and quoted in Worrall, *The Moscow Art Theatre*, 90. Stanislasvky's extensive preparations for the production, including trips abroad to procure props and costumes, are described in Worrall, 85–6.

[19] G. Arseniy, *Teatr i iskusstvo* 22 (1899), 230. Translated and quoted in Worrall, 102.

[20] Aleksandr Kugel', *Teatr i iskusstvo* 8 (1899), 169–70. Translated and quoted in Worrall, 117.

[21] Worrall, 126.

[22] Translated and quoted in Worrall, 133. Original source unspecified.

[23] For a discussion of this shift in Stanislavsky's thinking, see Helen Krich Chinoy, "The Emergence of the Director," in *Directors on Directing: A Source Book of the Modern Theatre*, ed. Toby Cole and Helen Krich Chinoy (New York: Bobbs-Merrill, 1963), 31–6.

[24] Translated and quoted in Kommisarzhevsky, *Myself and the Theatre*, 68. Original source unspecified.

[25] Konstantin Stanislavsky, *Sobranie Sochineii*, 8 vols. (Moscow: Iskusstvo, 1988–94), vol. I, 26. Translated and quoted in Benedetti, 118.

[26] Konstantin Stanislavsky, Notes to *The Blue Bird* cast, January/February 1908, taken down by Sulerzhitsky, Konstantin Stanislavsky Archive, No. 1392. Translated and quoted in Benedetti, 173.

[27] Christine Edwards, *The Stanislavsky Heritage: Its Contribution to the Russian and American Theatre* (New York: New York University Press, 1965), 91.

[28] Konstantin Stanislavsky, *Building A Character*, trans. Elizabeth Reynolds Hapgood (New York: Theatre Arts Books, 1949), 260–76. In her introduction (vii–viii), Ms. Hapgood cites 1930 and 1937 as years in which she discussed the preparation of the book with Stanislavsky.

[29] Konstantin Stanislavsky, *An Actor Prepares*, trans. Elizabeth Reynolds Hapgood (New York: Theatre Arts Books, 1936).

[30] It is tempting to make a "left-brain vs. right-brain" analogy, based on the "mind—will—feelings" lines of the diagram, as Robert L. Benedetti does in *The Actor at Work*, 4th ed. (Englewood Cliffs, NJ: Prentice Hall, 1986), 134–5, when he notes that "the left hemisphere is the side which is mainly involved in analysis and other *rational* activity. The right side is more *intuitive*." Stanislavsky often intermingled the two, however, placing imagination and emotions on the left, and logic and discipline on the right.

[31] Stanislavsky, *Building a Character*, 264.

[32] See Stanislavsky, *An Actor Prepares*, 43–9.

[33] For an extensive and imaginative use of given circumstances, see Stanislavsky's analysis of the character of Roderigo from Shakespeare's *Othello* in Konstantin Stanislavsky,

Stanislavsky Produces "Othello," trans. Helen Nowak (New York: Theatre Arts Books, 1963), 13–22.

[34] See Stanislavsky, *An Actor Prepares*, 154–81.

[35] This is because *An Actor Prepares* was published in the United States in 1936, following the Moscow Art Theatre's successful 1923 American tour, and was the only pedagogical work of Stanislavsky's available in English. Because his later teachings were not systematically recorded until long after his death, Stanislavsky's American "disciples" were free to distort his teachings to suit their own purposes. See the following section entitled "Stanislavsky and Schenker in the United States."

[36] See Grigori V. Kristi, *The Training of an Actor in the Stanislavski School of Acting*, excerpted in *Stanislavski Today: Commentaries on K.S. Stanislavski*, ed. and trans. Sonia Moore (New York: American Center for Stanislavski Theatre Art, 1973), 22–33, and Leslie Irene Cooper, "Stanislavsky Changes His Mind," *Tulane Drama Review* 9/1 (Fall 1964): 63–8.

[37] Mel Gordon, *The Stanislavsky Technique: Russia: A Workbook for Actors* (New York: Applause Theatre Book Publishers, 1988), 194.

[38] Stanislavsky, *An Actor Prepares*, 110.

[39] Konstantin Stanislavsky, *Creating a Role*, trans. Elizabeth Reynolds Hapgood (New York: Theatre Arts Books, 1961), 56. See also Konstantin Stanislavsky, *Stanislavsky's Legacy: A Collection of Comments on a Variety of Aspects of an Actor's Life and Art*, ed. and trans. Elizabeth Reynolds Hapgood (New York: Theatre Arts Books, 1958), 181.

[40] Stanislavsky, *Creating a Role*, 78.

[41] Vladimir Nemirovitch-Dantchenko defines "the deepest essence of a play or rôle" as the "seed" in *My Life in the Russian Theatre*, trans. John Cournos (New York: Theatre Arts Books, 1968), 159. Stella Adler uses the terms "overall action" and "ruling idea" in *The Technique of Acting* (Toronto: Bantam Books, 1988), 38. "Overlaying problem" is the translation given in Ottofritz Gaillard, *The German Stanislawski Book*, trans. Evelyn Hoffman (MFA diss., Yale School of Drama, 1957), 123. "Spine" is the term used by Robert Lewis in *Advice to the Players* (New York: Harper & Row, 1980), 106.

[42] Stanislavsky, *An Actor Prepares*, 108–9.

[43] Ibid., 116–7.

[44] Uta Hagen, *A Challenge for the Actor* (New York: Charles Scribner's Sons, 1991), 134. It is a testament to the pervasiveness of Stanislavsky's influence that, although his ideas form the foundation of Hagen's entire method, she does not mention him anywhere in the book, taking the knowledge of his theories as a given among the theatrical community. This is also true of the discussion of many of Stanislavsky's most important concepts in John Perry, *Encyclopedia of Acting Techniques* (Cincinnati: Betterway Books, 1997), 80–7.

[45] Cf. note 33.

[46] For a particularly lucid example of the scoring of a role using these three levels, see Stella Adler, *The Technique of Acting*, 46. Adler, the only American that studied in person with Stanislavsky, has written a book that is perhaps the most useful and practical guide to applying the system, complete with numbered exercises.

[47] Stanislavsky, *Building a Character*, 278.

[48] agen, *A Challenge for the Actor*, 279.

[49] Ibid., 281–3.

[50] Irina and Igor Levin, *Working on the Play and the Role: The Stanislavsky Method for Analyzing the Characters in a Drama* (Chicago: Ivan R. Doe, 1992), 34.

[51] On interrupted objectives, see also the section on "incomplete actions" in Adler, *The Technique of Acting*, 41–2.

[52] Georgi A. Tovstonogov, from *The Profession of a Director*. Excerpted in Moore, *Stanislavski Today*, 62. For more on the "super-superobjective," see Sonia Moore, *The Stanislavski System: The Professional Training of an Actor*, 2nd ed. (New York: Penguin, 1984), 75.

[53] Edward T. Cone, *The Composer's Voice* (Berkeley: University of California Press, 1974).

[54] Stanislavsky, *Building a Character*, 167.

[55] Stanislavsky, *Creating a Role*, 14–16.

[56] Ibid., 16–17.

[57] Ibid., 56–61. See also Stanislavsky's revised version of the first half of the score in a different "key," that of the lover instead of the friend, 71–5.

[58] Stanislavsky, *Stanislavsky Produces "Othello,"* 183–91.

[59] Stanislavsky, *"The Seagull" Produced by Stanislavsky*, ed. S. D. Balukhaty and trans. David Magarshack (New York: Theatre Arts Books, 1984). Though only the two production notebooks have been published, numerous secondhand accounts of Stanislavsky's rehearsal of other works abound. For commentary on plays, see Nikolai M. Gorchakov, *Stanislavsky Directs*, trans. Miriam Goldina (New York: Funk & Wagnalls Company, 1954), 33–122. For commentary on operas, see Konstantin Stanislavsky, *Stanislavsky on the Art of the Stage*, trans. David Magarshack (New York: Hill and Wang, 1961), 255–78; Konstantin Stanislavsky and Pavel Rumyantsev, *Stanislavsky on Opera*, ed. and trans. Elizabeth Reynolds Hapgood (New York: Theatre Arts Books, 1975), 46–151; and Joshua Logan, "Rehearsal with Stanislavsky," *Vogue* (June 1949), 134–8.

[60] The Moscow Art Theatre opened in October 1898; Stanislavsky's production of *The Seagull* was a part of its inaugural season. See Elizabeth Reynolds Hapgood's preface to Stanislavsky, *Stanislavski's Legacy*, vii.

[61] Stanislavsky, *"The Seagull,"* 143.

[62] See the discussion by P.V. Simonov, from *The Method of Konstantin Stanislavski and the Physiology of Emotion* (Moscow: Iskusstvo, 1962), trans. and excerpted in Moore, *Stanislavski Today*, 34–43.

[63] Kristi, from *The Training of an Actor*, excerpted in Moore, *Stanislavski Today*, 32.

[64] Cooper, "Stanislavsky Changes His Mind," 67.

[65] Lee Strasberg, *A Dream of Passion: The Development of the Method*, ed. Evangeline Morphos (Boston: Little, Brown, and Company, 1987). See also S. Loraine Hull, *Strasberg's Method as Taught by Lorrie Hull: A Practical Guide for Actors, Teachers, and Directors* (Woodbridge, CT: Ox Bow Publishing, 1985).

[66] See Marvin Carlson, *Theories of the Theatre: A Historical and Critical Survey, from the Greeks to the Present*, expanded edition (Ithaca: Cornell University Press, 1993), 379.

[67] Moore, *Stanislavski Today*, foreword.

[68] Elizabeth Reynolds Hapgood, preface to Stanislavsky, *Stanislavsky's Legacy*, v–vi.

[69] See Mel Gordon's preface to Michael Chekhov, *On the Technique of Acting*, ed. Mel Gordon (New York: HarperCollins Publishers, 1991), x–xvi.

[70] Stanislavsky and Meyerhold are contrasted in Benedetti, *Seeming, Being and Becoming*, 48–9. See also Meyerhold's scathing critique of the Moscow Art Theatre in Meyerhold, "The Isolation of Stanislavsky." For a complete exposition of Meyerhold's theories, see Marjorie L. Hoover, *Meyerhold: The Art of Conscious Theater* (Amherst: University of Massachusetts Press, 1974).

[71] Ruben Simonov, *Stanislavsky's Protégé: Eugene Vakhtangov*, trans. and adapted Miriam Goldina (New York: DBS Publications, 1969), 13.

[72] Benedetti, *Seeming, Being and Becoming*, 53. Meyerhold later reconciled with Stanislavsky, who recommended that Meyerhold succeed him as director of the Opera-Theatre Studio in 1938.

[73] Harold Clurman, "In the USA," *World Theatre* 8/1 (Spring 1959), 31. For more on the teachings of Boleslavsky, former director of the Moscow Art Theatre First Studio, see Richard Boleslavsky, *Acting: The First Six Lessons* (New York: Theatre Arts Books, 1933).

[74] Carlson, *Theories of the Theatre*, 379.

[75] Clurman, "In the USA," 32–3.

[76] Steve Vineberg, *Method Actors: Three Generations of an American Acting Style* (New York: Schirmer, 1991), passim.

[77] Stanislavsky, *An Actor Prepares*, was published in 1936. See also Schenker, *Free Composition*.

[78] Clurman, "In the USA," 31. On the dissemination of Schenker's theories in the United States, see Rothstein, "The Americanization of Heinrich Schenker."

[79] Clurman, "In the USA," 31.

[80] Ibid.

[81] There is no documentary evidence that the two men ever met or exchanged ideas. Though the existence of Gaillard's *Das Deutsche Stanislawski Buch* is intriguing, its date of publication (1946) guarantees that Schenker never read it.

[82] Richard Cohn and Douglas Dempster, "Hierarchical Unity, Plural Unities: Toward a Reconciliation," in *Disciplining Music: Musicology and its Canons*, ed. Katherine Bergeron and Philip V. Bohlman (Chicago: University of Chicago Press, 1992), 156–81.

[83] Stanislavsky, *Building a Character*, 170.

[84] For two recent studies devoted to Schenker and organicism, see Nadine Hubbs, "Schenker's Organicism," *Theory and Practice* 16 (1991): 143–62, and Kevin Korsyn, "Schenker's Organicism Reexamined," *Intégral* 7 (1993): 82–118.

[85] Stanislavsky, *Stanislavsky's Legacy*, 158.

[86] Stanislavsky, *Creating a Role*, 51.

[87] James William Flannery, *Nemirovitch-Danchenko, Stanislavsky and the Singer-Actor* (MFA thesis, Yale University, 1961), 14 and 31–2.

[88] See Edward D. Latham, "Analysis and Performance Studies: A Summary of Current Research," *Zeitschrift der Gesellschaft für Musiktheorie* 2/2 (2005), http://www.gmth.de/www/zeitschrift.php?option=show&ausgabe=7&archiv=1. Significant articles and books on the subject include: Janet Schmalfeldt, "On Performance, Analysis, and Schubert," *Per musi: Revista de performance musical* 5–6 (2002): 38–54; Heinrich Schenker, *The Art of Performance*, ed. Heribert Esser and trans. Irene Scott Schreier (Oxford: Oxford University Press, 2000); John S., Rink, ed., *The Practice of Performance: Studies in Musical Interpretation* (Cambridge: Cambridge University Press, 1995); David Epstein, *Shaping Time: Music, the Brain, and Performance* (New York: Schirmer, 1995); Jonathan Dunsby, *Performing Music: Shared Concerns* (Oxford: Clarendon Press, 1995); Wallace Berry, *Musical Structure and Performance* (New Haven: Yale University Press, 1989); Janet Schmalfeldt, "On the Relation of Analysis to Performance: Beethoven's Bagatelles Op. 126, Nos. 2 and 6," *Journal of Music Theory* 29/1 (1985): 1–32; Edward T. Cone, *Musical Form and Musical Performance* (New York: W. W. Norton, 1968), and "Musical Form and Musical Performance Reconsidered," *Music Theory Spectrum* 7 (1985): 149–58; George Fisher and Judy Lochhead, "Analysis, Hearing, and Performance," *Indiana Theory Review* 14/1, (1993): 1–36, and "The Performer as Theorist: Preparing a Performance of Daria Semegen's *Three Pieces For Clarinet and Piano* (1968)," *In Theory Only* 6/7 (1982): 23–39.

[89] Harold Clurman, *On Directing* (New York: Macmillan, 1972), 147.

[90] Hagen, *A Challenge for the Actor*, 236.

[91] Stanislavsky, *An Actor Prepares*, 119, 232.

[92] Benedetti, *Stanislavski*, 234.

[93] This list is extracted from the complete list of Stanislavsky productions given in Benedetti, 331–5.

[94] Stanislavsky, *My Life in Art*, 433. Quoted in Flannery, 5. For the best practical guide to applying the system of objectives as a singer-actor, see Lewis, *Advice to the Players*, 167–72.

[95] Benedetti, 234.

[96] Stanislavsky, *Stanislavsky's Legacy*, 43.

[97] Ibid., 40.

[98] David Magarshack, *Stanislavski: A Life* (New York: Chanticleer Press, 1951), 351. Quoted in Flannery, 6.

[99] Vincent Sheean, *First and Last Love* (New York: Random House, 1956), 60. Quoted in Flannery, 3. For a discussion of Nemirovitch-Dantchenko's views on good opera acting, see Flannery, 18–25.

[100] Stanislavsky, *Stanislavsky's Legacy*, 40.

[101] Ibid., 41.

[102] James D. Merriman, "The Parallel of the Arts: Some Misgivings and a Faint Affirmation," *The Journal of Aesthetics and Art Criticism* 31 (1972–3): 160–1.

[103] If a stage director were undertaking the analysis with the intent of mounting a new production, he or she might also want to identify the "super-superobjective" (SSO) of the production at this point, as well.

[104] As with Schenkerian analysis, opinions vary on whether to pursue a "top-down" or "bottom-up" approach to the analysis. In her explanation of the system, Sonia Moore advises that "the superobjective controls each character's logic of actions, which makes the theme concrete. While an actor is preparing his role the superobjective must be clear in his mind from the beginning through its very end" (Moore, *The Stanislavski System*, 75).

CHAPTER 3

Tonal Closure:
A Schenkerian Approach to Tonal Drama

Two forms of expansion—"vertical" and "horizontal"—exemplify the adaptation of Schenkerian theory. Many theorists inspired by Schenker have sought to expand the influence of his theory of structural levels by applying it to musical works that lie outside the boundaries of the chronological canon he established (Bach to Brahms, or roughly 1700–1900): a horizontal form of expansion. Others have focused on applying the theory to genres or composers that, though they lie within the chronological boundaries of the canon, were not analyzed by Schenker himself: a vertical expansion.[1]

In analyzing the operas of Wagner, Patrick McCreless has been among those active in the vertical expansion of the Schenkerian canon.[2] In his essay included in *Schenker Studies*, one of several essay collections exploring aspects of Schenkerian theory, McCreless tackles a problem facing the Schenkerian opera analyst: the lack of precedent for applying "extra-systemic" insights (i.e., information gleaned from other movements) to the analysis of a single movement from a larger work.[3] Though neither Wagner nor opera analysis in general is his intended subject, McCreless addresses many issues with regard to multi-movement works such as symphonies and overtures that are equally relevant to the analysis of operas.

To frame his discussion of this perceived gap in Schenkerian theory, McCreless opposes Schenker's notion of a single, all-encompassing triad that "subsumes all keys and modulations ... into an ultimate diatonic structure" to the analytical approach of Leo Treitler, who is willing to consider foreign keys as "viable analytical entities that are crucial to an ongoing musical discourse."[4] McCreless formulates a dichotomy between the two approaches, yet argues the merits of both sides, noting that "Schenker can make a more self-motivating, self-contained whole of individual movements, while Treitler can account better for inter-movement relationships, for why different keys are tonicized over the course of the work."[5]

What McCreless is after is a "third way," an alternative point of view that combines the advantageous aspects of both methods without overly diluting either one. The compromise that he proposes is based on the idea of harmony as motive, a concept he traces through Schenker's early writings and into *Der Freie Satz*.[6] Though he tends to give more weight to Schenker's role in the proposed partnership, sacrificing, for example, Treitler's historically based emphasis on affective connotations for foreign keys, McCreless accords greater status to harmonic events as motivic entities. He writes:

> Our alternative point of view, however, while by no means denying that such events are ultimately subsumable into a diatonic voice-leading structure, nevertheless claims for them a purely harmonic status; such events are unfolded through voice leading, but they are harmonic in character, and they do not necessarily originate in voice leading.[7]

Perhaps, as an opera analyst and a Schenkerian, McCreless had a subconscious agenda in combining Schenkerian analysis with a harmonic-motivic approach. Indeed, his choice of "Pause," Song 12 from Schubert's song cycle *Die Schöne Müllerin*, as the focal analysis of his article confirms his belief in the applicability of such a combined approach to vocal music that is decidedly dramatic in nature. Certainly, studies of the associative properties of key areas abound in the opera-analytic literature,[8] and recently Schenkerians have begun to build on such associations by creating graphs of the bass motion in large sections of operatic works that not only identify moments of tonal recurrence but also illustrate the means by which these moments are prolonged or reintroduced.[9]

Despite the abundance of bass-line graphs, however, complete Schenkerian reductions of operatic material are relatively rare. David Lawton, who helped to pioneer the use of bass graphs for opera analysis in his dissertation,[10] provides only one combined graph of both the fundamental line and the bass arpeggiation (i.e., a complete *Ursatz*[11]) in his subsequent article on the "Bacio" theme from Verdi's *Otello*: a middleground reading restricted to the theme itself that reveals a gapped fundamental line ($\hat{5}$–$\hat{3}$–$\hat{2}$–$\hat{1}$).[12] Roger Parker and Matthew Brown, who use Lawton's article as a springboard, offer a more detailed pair of graphs that compare the opening statements of Otello and Desdemona in their Act I "love duet," but their analyses also remain restricted to the thematic level.[13] Moreover, it is unclear, at least in their second analysis (of Desdemona's opening statement), whether the top voice of the orchestra and Desdemona's vocal line have been compressed: the graph comprises only two staves, the treble staff contains dyads as well as individual pitches, and a text underlay is not provided.

If Parker and Brown fail to provide adequate signposts in their analysis, they would nonetheless be justified in claiming ample precedent for the format they adopted. In his own analyses of the lieder of Schubert, Schumann, and Brahms, Schenker did not provide any textual markers, and though he privileged the vocal line throughout most of his analyses, he occasionally compressed the vocal line and the top line of the accompaniment into a single line when circumstances warranted such a maneuver.[14] The songs Schenker selected for analysis typically contained homophonic accompaniment or doubling of the vocal line in the top voice of the piano, obviating the need for a separate analysis of the accompanimental melody. In some cases, however, his neglect of the piano's melodic line causes him to omit important analytical details. In his analysis of Schubert's "Auf dem Flusse" (Song 7 from the song cycle *Winterreise*), for example, he shows a long middleground arpeggiation of the tonic triad (mm. 1–53) that leads to the initiation of the primary tone (G, $\hat{3}$ in E minor) only twenty-one measures before the end of the song, but neglects to show the series of interrupted descents ($\hat{3}$–$\hat{2}$) in the accompaniment that ultimately find their fulfillment in the final $\hat{3}$–$\hat{2}$–$\hat{1}$ descent.[15] This omission is particularly striking considering the fact that *Winterreise's* protagonist is male, and thus the vocal line would be sung by a tenor an octave lower than written, making the top voice of the piano literally the top voice of the song as well.

Two of Schenker's most detailed lieder analyses are of Songs 2 and 4 from Schumann's *Dichterliebe*.[16] In both instances, the vocal line and the top voice of the accompaniment have been compressed into a single fundamental line. In the case of Song 4, where Schenker's analysis is brief and uncomplicated, the compression has little effect on his interpretation: in m. 8, he adds the G from the piano's melody as a lower neighbor to A in order to highlight the motivic dyad G-A, while in m. 15 he adds G and F♯ from an inner voice of the piano in order to show the prolongation of $\hat{2}$ (A) over the dominant. In his analysis of Song 2, however, the privileging of the vocal line leads to a distortion of the fundamental line. Instead of following the paradigm established by his reading of mm. 1-4, where he correctly interprets the A in the top voice of the piano (m. 4) as completing a middleground replica of the fundamental line begun in the vocal line,[17] Schenker designates the arrival on $\hat{1}$ in the vocal line at m. 15 as the completion of the fundamental line. This interpretation distorts the relationship between the protagonist—whose longing for his beloved remains unfulfilled (he sings "*und wenn du mich lieb hast Kindchen...*")—and the piano, which has been literally "leading him on" since the opening bars of Song 1. The protagonist does not complete the fundamental line on his own; rather, he ends his line on $\hat{2}$ over the structural dominant (m. 16), and it is left to the piano to provide both melodic and harmonic closure to the tonic in the final measure of the song.[18]

In addition to Schenker's song analyses, two subsequent contributions to the analytical literature have begun to develop a more thorough approach to the linear analysis of dramatic vocal music. Perhaps because they and their particular specialty have been around longer than most, analysts of Wagner's music seem to feel they have to be more ambitious in the scope of their endeavors. Whatever the case, recent articles on Wagner by Patrick McCreless and Matthew Brown contain some of the most detailed and extensive opera analyses to date.[19] McCreless, in his analysis of the opening scene of *Götterdämmerung*, graphs 327 bars of music and provides both a foreground and a middleground graph of the linear-harmonic structure of the scene.[20] Brown, for his part, analyzes a complete episode from *Tristan und Isolde* (Isolde's Narrative, from Act I, Scene 3), providing detailed voice-leading models for all five sections of the episode.[21] Though the same superficial flaws that are present in the work of the Verdi analysis and in Schenker's lieder analyses (the lack of text and the compression of the vocal line and the top voice of the accompaniment) are present in these essays as well, they are significantly more sophisticated both in analytical detail and in the rigor with which the Schenkerian analytical technique is applied.

Incorporating Dramatic Analysis

The twin pillars of opera analysis—Verdi and Wagner studies—discussed above have each produced analysts who have tried, with varying degrees of success, to incorporate dramatic analysis into their work. Ironically, the earliest example of a detailed analysis of Wagner from a Schenkerian perspective may be found in the work of Adele Katz, whose *Challenge to Musical Tradition*, at first glance, seems to cultivate an orthodox Schenkerian image. Having just completed analytical discussions of the music of Bach, Haydn, and Beethoven in which she identifies prototypical examples of tonal structure, including large-scale neighbor notes, register transfers, and linear descents from $\hat{5}$ and $\hat{3}$, Katz argues that Wagner's music (and, by extension, opera in general) must be studied

> from two different points of view: first, whether, it
> demonstrates the principles of structural unity; second,

whether any sacrifice of these principles is due to the
demands of the text.... [One must] consider any deviations
in the basic techniques in relation to the text or the dramatic
action they represent.[22]

This insightful comment provides a useful point of departure for the
analysis of opera. Moreover, although Katz is usually considered to be an
orthodox Schenkerian attempting to explain modern works by demonstrating
how they do not conform to the tonal model, the statement quoted above is
one of several that reveal her more flexible approach to analysis.[23] Schenker's
own comments on Wagner, in contrast, do not account for the dramatic
action, but hold Wagner to the standard of instrumental music, chastising
him for his inability to compose from the background.[24]

Katz goes on to examine passages in two Wagner operas, *Parsifal* and
Siegfried, according to the premise outlined above. In her Example 53, she
identifies a middleground ascending the span of a third. She justifies the line,
which is harmonized by a chromatic mediant, by offering an explanation
based on *leitmotif* and dramatic character:

the doubtful element in the motion is the B♭ major chord
that originates in the repetition of the characteristic figure
of the motive, the ascending third, B♭–D♭.... Since there is
nothing in the voice leadings to necessitate the exchange
of the minor for the major mediant, we can only assume
that the FM chord was substituted because it gave a more
realistic picture of the strength and security of which the
Valhalla motive is the symbol.[25]

Katz's inclusive analytical attitude is further demonstrated by Example
64, in which she provides two alternative interpretations of the same passage,
without giving preference to one or the other as the "better" solution. Instead,
she notes that "the choice depends entirely on whether we hear the first
four measures as two groups of two-measure phrases or four phrases of a

measure each" and leaves it at that.[26] She again resorts to a motivic/dramatic explanation when discussing problematic elements in this passage:

> the presence of F in the top voice is due primarily to the nature of the motivic figure…. Had Wagner used a typical horizontalized motion in which he introduced the F♯ major instead of the F major chord, he would have created a tonal stability that would have been at variance with the instability and unrest of which the Wanderer is a symbol.[27]

Unfortunately, Katz does not investigate the "dramatic action" in Wagner's operas any further than the level of *leitmotivic* associations. It is the limitations of studies such as hers that Rudy Marcozzi criticizes in his dissertation on musical and dramatic structure in Verdi.[28] Citing studies by Verdi scholars such as Noske, Chusid, and Petrobelli, Marcozzi argues that opera analyses that deal with "tonal association" on the surface level have several problems, including "the failure to move beyond the musical and dramatic surface to test the validity of the associations at more structural levels," and "the corollary failure to demonstrate a unifying syntax within which these tonal associations operate."[29]

Marcozzi's study is, to my knowledge, the most ambitious and thoroughgoing attempt to combine analyses of musical and dramatic structure into a form of composite opera analysis that attempts to live up to Abbate and Parker's expectations. In his introduction, he poses three fundamental questions:

1. If tonal progression is a powerful means of achieving musical articulation, does Verdi utilize it in order to communicate the dramatic dimension of a text?

2. Is there a relationship between the overall dramatic structure of the text and the tonal structure of its musical setting?

3. If such relationships exist, what is their precise nature?[30]

To answer these questions, he undertakes the analysis of the three Verdi operas adapted from Shakespeare: *Otello*, *Macbeth*, and *Falstaff*. For his analysis of dramatic structure, Marcozzi borrows from Bernard Beckerman, who outlines a method of "horizontal analysis," which focuses exclusively on plot.[31] Beckerman's work contains traces of Stanislavskian influence, though the latter is not cited anywhere in Marcozzi.[32] For Beckerman, a dramatic analysis consists of four elements: identifying a "project," which occurs when "intent or motivation … is manifested in concrete physical activity," determining the "resistance" to the project, which is "that which inhibits completion of a particular project," locating the "crux," which is "the point at which the viewer knows whether resistance or project will dominate," and following the "decrescent," which is "the adjustment that follows as the result of crux."[33]

Marcozzi creates a system of graphical representation for Beckerman's four elements (consisting of arrows and circles) and proceeds to analyze the three libretti. He takes great pains to establish a degree of methodological "objectivity" by declaring that he has undertaken the dramatic and musical analyses separately, "in order to avoid biases which might be part of simultaneous analyses."[34] As for the musical analyses, he provides Schenkerian bass-line reductions of each of the complete operas, along with "occasional glimpses" of melodic voice-leading, which are intended to rectify the problems he identified in previous Verdi analyses.

Marcozzi's work has five major flaws. First, he is overly concerned with establishing analytical objectivity. Even if it were possible to separate out the musical and dramatic elements of an opera and analyze them individually, every decision made by the analyst in either realm is an *a priori* act of interpretation. Rather than being considered a weakness, the subjective nature of analytical interpretation creates the possibility for multiple readings of the same passage or piece, each with the potential to enrich the reader/listener's experience of the musical work. The primary goal of the analyst should be to create a convincing, persuasive reading, rather than a single solution that eliminates other possibilities.[35]

Second, Marcozzi's desire for objectivity leads him to privilege plot in his dramatic analysis, to the exclusion of character. He attempts to separate passages of text that advance the plot from those that delineate character, availing himself of what he calls "the luxury of an historic convention which confines segments of text that are more purely devoted to character delineation to closed textual and musical constructs, typically arias or similarly related designs."[36] The distinction that Marcozzi creates between plot and character is an artificial one. In Stanislavsky's system, they are united: the plot progresses only as a result of changes in the character's objectives. Take the beat objective, for example: though the plot is not necessarily advanced by each change of a character's beat objective within a given scene, it will not progress in the following scene until the character has achieved or forfeited his main objective for the same scene.

Third, because he does not regard analysis as an act of interpretation, Marcozzi struggles to justify analytical decisions by resorting to the "intentionality" argument. Previous analyses, he argues, are flawed because they do not provide "objective verification" of compositional intent. This verification, he posits, may be found in sketches, letters, notes, and other documentary evidence.[37] Such evidence is, however, not always reliable (especially with respect to objectivity), since composers, like the rest of us, always have personal agendas to advance and legacies to consider. Stravinsky and Schoenberg, for example, took great pains to seem impervious to the meaning of the texts they set, while Wagner carefully crafted an image of himself as an effortless genius.[38]

Fourth, in terms of his musical analysis, Marcozzi focuses almost exclusively on harmony, an inadvisable decision in a genre where melody is such a crucial thread in the musical fabric (particularly in Verdi). In his eagerness to provide a syntax whereby the surface moments of associative tonality identified by previous authors might be connected and contextualized,

Marcozzi neglects the important information provided by the melodic line, not only in terms of progression and closure, but also in terms of tessitura, range, and register.

Finally, after spending a great deal of time trying to justify the analysis of opera in terms of intentionality and audibility, Marcozzi spends only two sentences on the most pertinent justification of all: the relationship of analysis to performance. He notes "data generated by such analyses may be of particular help in the production of opera, where crucial elements such as tempi and blocking must clearly delineate and propel the dramatic structure. The analysis of both dramatic and tonal designs might suggest clearly to directors and conductors the ways in which best to achieve such delineation and momentum."[39] Unfortunately, he does not follow up these two astute observations with any concrete recommendations for the operas he has selected for analysis.

So, the question remains, what general principles, if any, may be abstracted from the discussion above? Despite their significant differences in both repertoire and scope, all three groups of analyses share at least three common features. First, they all privilege the vocal line as the primary conduit of melodic coherence. This is a logical choice, not only because the vocal line has the unique ability (given a performer with adequate diction) to convey semantic content, but also because it is undoubtedly the most aurally salient musical line (given a sensitive conductor and a singer with adequate vocal training), regardless of registral priority. Second, when necessary, all three groups incorporate the top voice of the accompaniment into the fundamental line in order to provide a more complete picture of the *Ursatz*. That kind of flexibility, while it can (as discussed above) lead to distortions if not employed cautiously, is ultimately beneficial because it enables the analyst to explore the relationship between singer and orchestra as characters in their own right and in relation to one another. Finally, all three groups of analyses are ultimately able to relate chromatic elements, even those present at the deep middleground level, back to the fundamental structure.

But what of McCreless's worthy goal of uniting rigorous analysis of the closed musical structure represented by the *Ursatz* with extra-systemic factors such as associative tonality? While I agree with both McCreless and Treitler that harmonic motives do indeed play an important role in multi-movement works, I wish to suggest an extension of the associative properties that such recurring tonal moments possess, one that, ironically, places them back under the influence of a linear fundamental structure.

As McCreless suggests in his discussion of the A♭ major passage in the opening of Beethoven's *Leonore Overture* No. 3, op. 72, such tonal recurrences are often highlighted by a variety of aurally salient features, including timbre, dynamics, tempo, rhythm, and register.[40] In an opera, the last of these features, register, especially as it relates to *tessitura*, plays a particularly important role in the construction of aurally salient connections between harmonic motives in opera. Male singers generally have five "registers" within their complete vocal range, distinguished by the amount of "head" voice versus "chest" voice in each register. In his book, *Training Tenor Voices*, Richard Miller identifies these five registers as the lower voice, the lower middle voice, the upper middle voice, the upper voice, and the falsetto.[41] Each register corresponds to a section of the complete vocal range: for a lyric tenor, these sections would be C–G, G–D1, D1–G1, G1–C2, and C2–G2.[42] Like any of the orchestral instruments, the timbral quality of the voice shifts depending on the register. Again, using the lyric tenor as an example, the lower voice has a darker quality, the lower middle voice is warmer, the upper middle voice is more powerful, the upper voice is strident and brilliant, and the falsetto is ethereal.[43]

When the *tessitura* of a particular musical passage lies primarily within one of these registers, it is marked, both for the performer and the listener, as a unique and salient event. Moreover, such demarcation may extend to the level of individual pitches, if they are registrally distinct from the surrounding context. If the composer used such an accentuated pitch in conjunction with the recurrence of a harmonic motive and the salient pitch is a member of the motivic triad, it may be seen as a structural pitch in relation to the local tonic represented by the harmonic motive. The salience of such a pitch is, of course, augmented exponentially when it also serves as the primary tone of a structural descent within a particular scene. When such coincidences may be identified, it becomes possible to combine a bass graph, such as those used by Verdi analysts to show recurring harmonic motives, with a reading of the aurally and structurally salient pitches of the melodic line to create a two-voice framework that spans multiple movements.

Were it based entirely on the notion of structural pitches accentuated through aurally salient musical features, such a two-voice framework would amount to little more than a whimsical exercise, however, since no two listeners hear an opera in exactly the same way. The model derives much of its power instead from the notion of "dramatic salience," a quality that is measurable with the use of the Stanislavsky system: the moment when a character achieves or forfeits an objective is marked as a dramatically salient event. What the bass graphs of Verdi are missing is an explicitly *linear* sense of the musical progression, in the sense of a stepwise descent that creates the expectation of closure to the tonic. As Walter Everett has persuasively argued, the fundamental line is inherently dramatic: the line's journey to closure on the tonic, with its many detours, obstacles, and delays, is a primary factor in maintaining the interest of the listener.[44]

ENDNOTES

[1] An extensive catalogue of the various expansions of Schenkerian theory may be found in David Beach's series of reviews of the literature. See David Beach, "Schenkerian Theory," *Music Theory Spectrum* 11/1 (1989): 3–14; "The Current State of Schenkerian Research," *Acta Musicologica* 57 (1985): 275–307; "A Schenker Bibliography: 1969–1979," *Journal of Music Theory* 23/2 (1979): 275–86; and "A Schenker Bibliography," *Journal of Music Theory* 13/1 (1969): 2–37. For more recent Schenkerian references, see D. Berry, *A Topical Guide*.

[2] See, for example, Patrick McCreless, "Schenker and the Norns," in Abbate and Parker, *Analyzing Opera*, 276–89.

[3] Patrick McCreless, "Schenker and Chromatic Tonicization." Other collections of Schenkerian essays include Burstein and Gagné, eds., *Structure and Meaning in Tonal Music*; Carl Schachter, *Unfoldings: Essays in Schenkerian Theory and Analysis*, ed. Joseph N. Straus (Oxford: Oxford University Press, 1999); Schachter and Siegel, eds., *Schenker Studies 2* (1999); Siegel, ed., *Schenker Studies* (1990); Allen Cadwallader, ed., *Trends in Schenkerian Research* (New York: Schirmer, 1990), David Beach, ed., *Aspects of Schenkerian Theory* (New Haven: Yale University Press, 1983), and Yeston, ed., *Readings in Schenker Analysis* (1977).

[4] McCreless, "Schenker and Chromatic Tonicization," 126. For a collection of Treitler's thoughts on music, see Leo Treitler, *Music and the Historical Imagination* (Cambridge: Harvard University Press, 1989).

[5] McCreless, "Schenker and Chromatic Tonicization," 128.

[6] Ibid., 130–5.

[7] Ibid., 131.

[8] Two examples are William Drabkin, "Characters, Key Relations and Tonal Structure in *Il Trovatore*," *Music Analysis* 1/2 (1982): 143–54, and Siegmund Levarie, "Tonal Relations in Verdi's *Un Ballo in Maschera*," *Nineteenth-Century Music* 2/2 (1978): 143–7.

[9] Schenkerian bass graphs have become particularly popular in the analytical literature on Verdi's works. See David Lawton, "Tonality and Drama in Verdi's Early Operas" (PhD diss., University of California, Berkeley, 1973), and "On the 'Bacio' Theme in *Othello*," *Nineteenth-Century Music* 1/3 (1978): 211–20; Roger Parker and Matthew Brown, "Motivic and Tonal Interaction in Verdi's *Un Ballo in Maschera*," *Journal of the American Musicological Society* 36/2 (1983): 243–65, and "*Ancora un bacio*: Three Scenes from Verdi's *Otello*," *Nineteenth-Century Music* 9/1 (1985): 50–61; and Marcozzi, "The Construction of Large-Scale Harmonic and Dramatic Structure in the Verdi Operas Adapted from Shakespeare" (Ph D diss., Indiana University, 1992).

[10] Lawton, "Tonality and Drama."

[11] A thorough explanation of basic Schenkerian concepts such as the *Ursatz*, fundamental line and bass arpeggiation is not practical within the context of the present undertaking. For a good introduction to Schenkerian analytical techique, see Allen Forte, "Schenker's Conception of Musical Structure," *Journal of Music Theory* 3/1 (1959): 1–30. Two textbook-length expositions are provided in Allen Forte and Steven E. Gilbert, *Introduction to Schenkerian Analysis* (New York, NY: Norton, 1982), and Cadwallader and Gagné, *Analysis of Tonal Music*.

[12] Lawton, "On the 'Bacio' Theme," 212. To be fair, Lawton does undertake a more extensive, three-level analysis of a complete fundamental structure in his recent article on Act III of *Aida*. See David Lawton, "Tonal Systems in *Aida*, Act III," in Abbate and Parker, *Analyzing Opera*, 272.

[13] Parker and Brown, "*Ancora un bacio*," 56.

[14] The majority of Schenker's published lieder analyses are included in Schenker, *Free Composition*. See Figures 22b, 37a, 39/1, 40/2, 152/1, 2, and 5. For a complete list of Schenker's published analyses, see Laskowski, *Heinrich Schenker: An Annotated Index*.

[15] Schenker, *Free Composition*, Fig. 40/2.

[16] Ibid., Figs. 22b and 152/1. These analyses are also included in the Norton Critical Score of the song cycle, along with Allen Forte's discussion of Fig. 22b, reprinted from Forte, "Schenker's Conception of Musical Structure." Schenker's previously unpublished analysis of Song 3 is also included. See Arthur Komar, ed., *Robert Schumann: Dichterliebe* (New York: Norton, 1971), 95–109.

[17] The middleground replica is displayed most clearly in the top level of Fig. 22b, where it is labeled with the scale-degrees 3–2–1.

[18] In Schenker's analysis, the protagonist's final pitch ($\hat{2}$), is left "hanging," an open notehead unconnected to the rest of the fundamental line, and is even subsumed under a slurred motion from C♯ to A, representing a sort of codetta.

[19] See McCreless, "Schenker and the Norns" and Matthew Brown, "Isolde's Narrative: From *Hauptmotiv* to Tonal Model," in Abbate and Parker, *Analyzing Opera*, 180–201.

[20] McCreless, "Schenker and the Norns," 282–5.

[21] Brown, "Isolde's Narrative," 190–2.

[22] Katz, *Challenge to Musical Tradition*, 195.

[23] On Katz as an orthodox analyst, see Beach, "The Current State of Schenkerian Research," 299.

[24] For a discussion of Schenker's comments on Wagner, see Allen Forte, "A Schenkerian Reading (of an Excerpt from *Tristan und Isolde*)," *Musicae Scientiae* (1998): 15–26.

[25] Katz, *Challenge to Musical Tradition*, 200–2.

[26] Ibid., 204.

[27] Ibid., 206.

[28] Marcozzi, "Harmonic and Dramatic Structure," passim.

[29] Ibid., 7. See also his criticism of David Lawton for not extending his keen analytical nsight to complete works, 24.

[30] Ibid., 2.

[31] Bernard Beckerman, *Dynamics of Drama* (New York: Knopf, 1970).

[32] In this regard, Marcozzi's RILM abstract (RILM no. 92–12447–dd), which makes reference to Stanislavsky, is misleading.

[33] Marcozzi, "Harmonic and Dramatic Structure," 21.

[34] Ibid., 58. This kind of supposed "objectivity" is reminiscent of Nattiez's attempts to create an objective "neutral" level in his tripartite analytical system (poietic-neutral-esthesic). See Jean-Jacques Nattiez, *Music and Discourse: Toward a Semiology of Music*, trans. Carolyn Abbate (Princeton: Princeton University Press, 1990), and "Varèse's 'Density 21.5': A Study in Semiological Analysis," *Music Analysis* 1/3 (1982): 243–340. Jonathan Bernard, among others, was quick to criticize the idea of a neutral level. See Jonathan Bernard, "On *Density 21.5:* A Response to Nattiez," *Music Analysis* 5/2–3 (1986): 207–32.

[35] On the value of analysis as interpretation, see Hatten, *Musical Meaning in Beethoven*, passim.

[36] Marcozzi, "Harmonic and Dramatic Structure," 18.

[37] Ibid., 6–7.

[38] For more on intentionality, see Haimo, "Atonality, Analysis, and the Intentional Fallacy," and Latham, "Review of Ethan Haimo's article."

[39] Marcozzi, 153. See also Marcozzi's arguments on the audibility of large-scale tonal connections, 25 and 28–29.

[40] McCreless mentions tempo and timbre (instrumentation). See McCreless, "Schenker and Chromatic Tonicization," 137.

[41] Richard Miller, *Training Tenor Voices* (New York: Schirmer, 1993), 4. For a comprehensive study of all voice types, see Richard Miller, *The Structure of Singing: System and Art in Vocal Technique* (New York: Schirmer, 1986).

[42] Miller, *Training Tenor Voices*, 7. The labels "D1" and "C1" refer to the Acoustical Society of America system for register classification, in which "middle C" is C4.

[43] For an excellent discussion of the different timbral qualities of instrumental registers, see Samuel Adler, *The Study of Orchestration*, second edition (New York: Norton, 1989), Chapters 3 and 7 passim.

[44] Everett, "Singing About the Fundamental Line" and "Deep-Level Portrayals of Directed and Misdirected Motions." On the dramatic tension created by conflicting tonal centers, see Petty, "Imagining Drama as an Aid to Musical Performance."

CHAPTER 4

The Completed Background Line
With Open-Ended Coda:
Scott Joplin's "Grand Opera" *Treemonisha* (1911)

"The music of Treemonisha is completely and distinctively American,
and it is the first truly American opera, not imitative
of the European form."[1]

From the turn of the century to World War I, most American composers were self-consciously trying to emulate (or rival) their European counterparts. Composers such as Walter Damrosch, desirous of acceptance by the European cultural elite, adopted many of the models established by eighteenth- and nineteenth-century European composers. This trend is exemplified in the world of instrumental music by Charles Ives' struggle to create a uniquely American style while adhering to the forms and technical elements of European art music. Operas written during this period, typified by Damrosch's *Cyrano de Bergerac* (1913), were often based on a European subject or a work by a European author. *Treemonisha*, Scott Joplin's "ragtime opera," then, stands out among this group of early operas as a singular attempt to combine the distinctly American sound of ragtime with the forms and idioms of European grand opera in the service of an American subject—namely, the plight of slaves working on plantations in the South.

Though he is primarily remembered as the composer of piano rags such as *The Maple Leaf Rag* and *The Entertainer*, Joplin aspired to write larger forms, part of his crusade to preserve the more serious style of "classic ragtime" in the face of competition from sideshow virtuosi and Tin Pan Alley hacks.[2] His first attempt at an opera, *A Guest of Honor*, was a one-act work comprised of twelve ragtime tunes, which he completed in 1903. According to James Marshall, a ragtime composer and Joplin's friend, *A Guest of Honor* was premiered in a large dance hall in St. Louis, but John Stark, Joplin's primary publisher, refused it based on the weakness of its libretto.[3] The Scott Joplin Ragtime Opera Company formed to perform the opera on tour throughout the Midwest, but was disbanded after only a few performances.[4] Although Joplin applied to copyright the opera, Library of Congress records indicate that a copy of the opera was never received.[5] Biographer James Haskins suggests that Joplin's possible dissatisfaction with the work may have led to its subsequent disappearance:

> Indeed, it is likely that in the face of his hopes for *Treemonisha* he became dissatisfied with the earlier opera, saw it as a merely adequate first attempt at an operatic form, and ceased to value it. This seems to be the only way to explain the fate he allowed to befall *A Guest of Honor*.[6]

Joplin completed a first draft of his second opera, *Treemonisha*, in 1907 while in St. Louis, but continued to revise it until 1910 when a second draft was submitted for publication.[7] Unable to come to an agreement with his former publisher John Stark, with whom he had a falling out over royalty payments, Joplin published the piano-vocal score himself in May 1911, under the imprint Scott Joplin Music Publishing Company.[8] Unlike *A Guest of Honor*, which Joplin had dubbed a "ragtime opera," *Treemonisha* was declared a "folk opera,"[9] though Joplin later amended this value-neutral generic designation, stating:

> I am a composer of ragtime music but I want it thoroughly understood that my opera "Treemonisha" is not ragtime.

> In most of the strains I have used syncopations (rhythm)
> peculiar to my race, but the music is not ragtime and the
> score complete is grand opera.[10]

Peter Gammond, one of Joplin's biographers, has suggested that his obsessive focus on getting *Treemonisha* published and performed accelerated his physical decline and ultimately hastened his death (from syphilis-related complications), remarking that "the death certificate ... didn't add that [Joplin's death] had been hastened by a violent addiction to *Treemonisha*."[11] Whether Gammond is correct or not, Joplin's single-minded devotion to *Treemonisha* in his last years did lead to neglect of his other sources of income, including a private studio that gradually dwindled to nothing. Indeed, his financial situation became so desperate that his wife Lottie ran their house as a brothel to support him.[12]

From 1908 to 1913, Joplin hawked *Treemonisha* to anyone who would lend him an ear, occasionally publishing announcements such as the following one in the *New York Age*:

> Music circles have been stirred recently by the announcement
> that Scott Joplin, known as the apostle of ragtime, is
> composing scores for grand opera.... Critics who have
> heard a part of his new opera are very optimistic as to its
> future success.[13]

He finally convinced Thomas Johnson, former president of the Crescent Theatre Company, to back a production in Atlantic City, but sadly, the production never materialized. Instead, Joplin used the last of his savings to rent the Lincoln Theatre, a music hall on 135th Street in Harlem, in July 1911 and mounted a single performance of the opera with an orchestra consisting of himself at the piano, devoid of sets and costumes, which, according to William Sullivan, one of his last remaining students, played to about seventeen people.[14]

The cancellation of two other scheduled productions is mentioned in biographies of Joplin, one in 1913 at the Lafayette Theatre under the auspices of manager Benjamin Nibur,[15] and the other in 1913 at the Washington Park Theatre in Bayonne, New Jersey.[16] These cancellations were a crushing blow to Joplin. Susan Curtis suggests a cultural disconnect as the primary reason for Joplin's failure to make inroads within the New York arts community, particularly the growing African-American community in Harlem. While white critics like Carl Van Vechten wrote approvingly of authenticity in African-American theatre, including the use of magic, voodoo, and folk dancing, in reality Harlem artistic circles consisted largely of college-educated intellectuals who could not relate to Joplin's tale of life on a Southern plantation.[17] Joplin died on April 1, 1917, unaware of the future acclaim that lay in store for the work that his lone treasured reviewer had hailed as "a thoroughly American opera."[18]

Knowing how much *Treemonisha* had meant to her husband, Joplin's widow tried unsuccessfully for years to get it staged on Broadway.[19] Lottie died on March 14, 1953, and it took another two decades before a full-scale production was premiered at the Atlanta Memorial Arts Center. The production was connected to an Afro-American music workshop sponsored by Morehouse College and featured a reconstruction of Joplin's score by T. J. Anderson, who wrote (rather ambitiously) of Joplin: "We see him now as one of the most important creators of his generation, certainly comparable to Schoenberg."[20]

The Atlanta production fueled an enthusiasm for *Treemonisha* that led to three more productions—at Wolf Trap Farm in Washington, D. C. in 1972, at the Houston Grand Opera in May 1975, and at The Uris Theatre on Broadway in September 1975—that established the opera's place in the canon of American opera and ultimately led to Joplin's posthumous reception of the Pulitzer Prize in 1976.[21] The Houston Grand Opera production was particularly noteworthy for its use of costumes, dance, and fantastical elements to overcome the inadequacies of Joplin's libretto. As composer

Gunther Schuller (who re-orchestrated the opera for the Houston production) noted, *Treemonisha* is "a very uneven piece and certainly not a great piece of drama but, on the other side of it, it has some of the most beautiful music Joplin ever wrote."[22]

The question of genre and appropriate venue, issues central to each of the works discussed in the subsequent chapters of this volume, has also colored the reception of *Treemonisha*. The 1911 review of the work in *The American Musician* placed it squarely between grand opera and light opera, labeling the work "character opera" or "racial opera," meaning that its characters sang in the style most particularly suited to them (i.e., the syncopated rhythms of African-American folk melodies).[23] As noted above, Joplin clearly considered the work grand opera, yet his wife Lottie persisted in calling it a "ragtime opera."[24] Biographer Peter Gammond claims that "with hindsight we might justifiably say that he aimed too high," and suggests "had he aimed at the sphere where ragtime more naturally belonged—the musical comedy stage—he might well have had a roaring success on his hands."[25]

Nonetheless, *Treemonisha* stands as a seminal achievement, a work that, written a quarter century before *Porgy and Bess*, "won popular national attention as a hybrid of African-American and European elements."[26] That an African-American composer wrote it makes it all the more important. As Haskins notes, "For Scott Joplin, a black man deeply committed to American Negro folk rhythms, to focus his energies on writing the folk opera *Treemonisha* was like W. E. B. Du Bois mounting a serious campaign for the presidency of the United States."[27] The influence of ragtime on the works of subsequent composers around the world, particularly the three studied in Chapters 3–5, is a testament to Joplin's belief in the flexibility and potential of the style.[28]

Synopsis

Treemonisha is set on a plantation deep in a forest somewhere in Arkansas, northeast of the town of Texarkana. Ned, a freed slave who manages the plantation for its white absentee landlords, and his wife Monisha are raising a daughter they found as an infant under a tree outside their cabin (hence her name, Tree-Monisha). Educated by a white woman in exchange for labor from Ned and Monisha, Treemonisha challenges the superstitious beliefs of the community in Act 1 by confronting Zodzetrick, one of the local "conjurors" ("The Bag of Luck"). He refuses to give up conjuring and, threatened by Treemonisha's pupil Remus, retreats into the forest, vowing vengeance on Treemonisha. After learning the truth from Monisha about her mysterious origin ("The Sacred Tree"), Treemonisha enters the forest with her friend Lucy to gather leaves for a wreath and is kidnapped by Zodzetrick and his accomplice, Luddud ("Confusion"). Remus and some of the other men run off in search of them.

Act 2 opens at the conjurors' forest hideout. Zodzetrick and Luddud present Treemonisha to the other conjurors, accusing her of trying to rob them of their livelihood ("Treemonisha in Peril"). Despite the objections of Cephus, the group condemns her and carries her off to a brush arbor to punish her. Simon suggests throwing her onto an enormous wasp nest, but before the punishment can be carried out Remus arrives dressed in a scarecrow costume (No. 14). Convinced that he is the Devil, the superstitious conjurors flee in panic and Remus rescues Treemonisha ("The Rescue").

Treemonisha and Remus return home in triumph at the opening of Act 3, and the other men arrive soon after with the captured Zodzetrick and Luddud in tow ("Treemonisha's Return"). The community wants to punish them with a severe beating, but Treemonisha urges their leader, Andy, to free the prisoners instead and pleads with the group to forgive them. When stern lectures from both Remus and Ned fail to sway the community ("Wrong is Never Right" and "When Villains Ramble Far and Near"), Treemonisha makes a personal appeal that finally persuades them to show forgiveness ("Conjuror's Forgiven"). She then calls for the appointment of a leader, and the community convinces her to accept the role herself ("We Will Trust You as Our Leader"). Finally, she "leads" everyone in a dance of celebration ("A Real Slow Drag").

Scoring and Analyzing the
Roles of Zodzetrick and Treemonisha

The plot synopsis above establishes Treemonisha and Zodzetrick as the central protagonist and antagonist of the opera. On one hand, scoring their roles provides a thorough catalogue of the local dramatic failures that ultimately lead to Zodzetrick's downfall, and on the other hand a detailed illustration of Treemonisha's emerging role as a successful leader of the community. Of the twenty-one beat objectives or main objectives shown in the score of Zodzetrick's role (Table 1), only seven are successfully achieved, five of them in Act 2. Zodzetrick's superobjective is to keep his business (selling "bags o' luck") thriving by preserving the plantation community's superstitious culture. In order to attain this goal, he has to strengthen his hold on the community and eliminate the opposition represented by Treemonisha and her friends and family, avoiding any appearance of weakness that might jeopardize his position as the leader of the conjurors. When his usual unctuous approach fails him in his first confrontation with Treemonisha ("The Bag of Luck"), he reverts to threats, intimidation, and kidnapping to frighten the community. Although in "Treemonisha in Peril," the accusation of Treemonisha at the hideout, he is successful in maintaining control of his band of conjurors by making her a scapegoat, Zodzetrick's bid to control the broader community through fear is thwarted by the rescue of Treemonisha and her election as leader.

	Y/N	KEY	CADENCE	LINE
SO: to keep his business thriving by preserving the community's superstitious culture	n	G	HC	3-2‖
MO_1 (I/2): to strengthen his hold on the community	n	G	---	---
BO_1: to con Monisha into buying a bag of luck	n	G	PAC/e: PHC	---
BO_2: to convince Ned of the bag's worth	n	e	IAC→EC	---
BO_3: to preserve his air of mystery	y	G	PAC	3-line
BO_4: to ingratiate himself with Treemonisha	n	d	---	8-5‖
BO_5: to intimidate Treemonisha	n*	e	PAC	---
BO_6: to spook Treemonisha	n*	C	PAC	---
BO_7: to intimidate the community	n	c	EC	---
[MO_2 (I/10): to weaken the community's resistance]	n	C?	---	---
BO_1: to conceal Treemonisha's disappearance	n	e	PHC	---
BO_2: to make Treemonisha vanish	n	C	DC/DC	3-line
BO_3: to sew anxiety and confusion	y*	a	PAC	---
MO_3 (II/12): to strengthen his power base	y	C	PAC	3-line
BO_1: to reassert his authority among the conjurors	y	a	PAC	3-line
BO_2: to shift blame onto Treemonisha	n	C	HC	---
BO_3: to make Treemonisha a scapegoat	y	C	PAC	3-line
[MO_4 (II/13): to quell doubts with a show of power]	y	e	PAC	(5-line)
MO_5 (II/14): to get rid of Treemonisha	n	C	---	---
BO_1: to persuade conjurors to kill Treemonisha	y?	C	IAC	---
BO_2: to maintain control of the conjurors	n	a	---	---
[MO_6 (III/20): to steal the community's spirit]	n	D	HC/IAC	5-(2‖)-3

Key

SO = Superobjective	PAC = Perfect Authentic Cadence
MO = Main Objective	IAC = Imperfect Authentic Cadence
BO = Beat Objective	PHC = Phrygian Half Cadence
y/n = Yes/No	EC = Evaded Cadence
I/2 = Act 1, No. 2	DC = Deceptive Cadence
HC = Half Cadence	IAC→EC = Imperfect-becoming-Evaded Cadence

Table 1 The Score of Zodzetrick's Role (Joplin, *Treemonisha*)

After their initial confrontation at the beginning of Act 1, each of the main characters is forced to make a decision: faced with resistance from a determined opponent, each must change their strategy or risk losing the battle of wills. In contrast to Zodzetrick, whose refusal to abandon his single-minded determination to remove her as an obstacle ultimately leads to dramatic failure, Treemonisha comes up with an alternate solution that represents a triumph of intellect over brute force, as shown in the score of her role in Table 2. Instead of running over Zodzetrick, she goes around him, asserting her leadership and strengthening her bond to the community with the help of Andy and Monisha. While Zodzetrick is absent for the remainder of Act 1, Treemonisha is constantly present, welcoming new laborers ("The Corn-Huskers"), planning entertainment ("We're Goin' Around"), participating in traditional activities ("The Wreath"), and showing respect to the elders of the community ("Treemonisha's Bringing Up"). Thus, when she is kidnapped, the entire community immediately decides to rescue her, and she then uses her near-martyrdom as leverage to persuade the people to abandon superstition and vengeance for faith and mercy, ending Zodzetrick's "reign of terror." It must also be noted that, although she initially demurs when asked by the people to be their leader, it is Treemonisha herself who proposed such an election, and the demurral is merely an adept public relations maneuver by an adroit politician.

	Y/N	KEY	CADENCE	LINE
SO: to free her community from fear	y	B♭	PAC	3-line
and lead them toward a brighter future	y*	B♭	HC	$\hat{3}$-$\hat{4}$-$\hat{5}$
[MO_1 (I/1): to establish the hope represented by her theme as the defining framework of the opera] with the help of the orchestra	y*	B♭	PAC	3-line
MO_2 (I/2): to convince Zodzetrick to change his ways	n	E♭	—	—
BO1: to stop Zodzetrick in his tracks	n	E♭	DC→HC	$\hat{3}$-$\hat{2}$‖
BO2: to shame Z. into giving up "conjury"	n	B♭	—	—
[MO_3 (I/4): to begin asserting her leadership] with the help of Andy	y*	G	PAC	5-line
[MO_4 (I/5): to strengthen her bond with the women] with the help of Monisha	y*	B♭	PAC	3-line
MO_5 (III/21): to capitalize on her near-martyrdom	y	B♭	PAC	3-line
MO_6 (III/25): to convince the community to be merciful and forgive Zodzetrick and Luddud	y	B♭	PAC	3-line
MO_7 (III/26): to persuade the community to elect a male leader (perhaps Remus)	n	C	—	—
MO_8 (III/27): to lead the community	y	F	PAC	5-line

Table 2 The Score of Treemonisha's Role (Joplin, *Treemonisha*)

The background structure of Zodzetrick's role, as defined by the connections between the tonal areas and primary tones of each of the numbers in which his influence is exerted, comprises a motion from G major (I) to C major (IV) and finally to A minor (ii), as shown in Figure 1. As a result of his confrontation with Treemonisha ("The Bag of Luck"), during which, with the help of her friends and family, she effects a shift to the subdominant key area (C major) and changes the prolonged tone from B to E, Zodzetrick is forced to spend Act 2 trying to establish a tonal center that will support a viable return to C as upper-neighbor to B, thereby enabling him to eventually return to his original key (G major) and primary tone (B) and successfully complete a closed tonal structure for the opera as a whole.[29] Though he accomplishes a shift to A minor ("Confusion"), he is unable to permanently install C as primary tone. Instead, E returns and is reinterpreted as $\hat{5}$ of A minor, and Zodzetrick ends the opera where he began: on the losing end of a (tonal) struggle with Treemonisha.

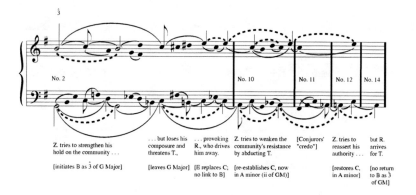

Figure 1 The Background Structure of Zodzetrick's Role (Joplin, *Treemonisha*)

As the source for all of the dramatic tension in the opera, "The Bag of Luck" deserves the most hermeneutically freighted modulations in *Treemonisha* (Figure 2). Zodzetrick makes his entrance in G major, initiating B as primary tone with his opening sales pitch to Monisha ("I want to sell to you"). Descent to $\hat{1}$ is interrupted over a half cadence at m. 8, as he gauges the effect of his words on Monisha, but is immediately followed by closure to a perfect authentic cadence at m. 12, completing a parallel period.[30] In his haste to make a sale, however, Zodzetrick omits $\hat{2}$ (A) over the cadential dominant, substituting an exuberant D instead. A hesitant Monisha restates the primary tone B and leads it again to an interruption at the half cadence in m. 14 as she questions the effectiveness of the "bag of luck." Zodzetrick abruptly changes his approach (he does not bother with a pivot chord), reinterpreting B as $\hat{5}$ of E minor, and adopting a more personal, conspiratorial tone (mm. 15–22).

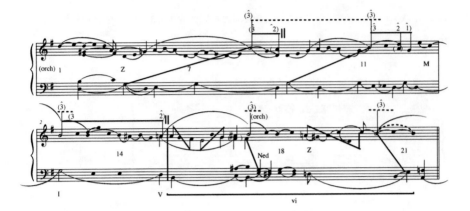

Figure 2a "The Bag of Luck," voice leading (Joplin, *Treemonisha*, No. 2)

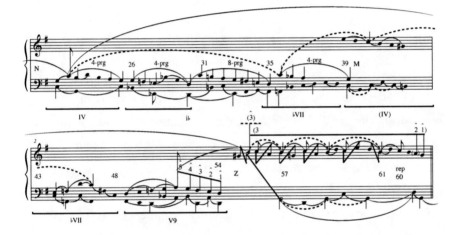

Figure 2b "The Bag of Luck," voice leading (cont.) (Joplin, *Treemonisha*, No. 2)

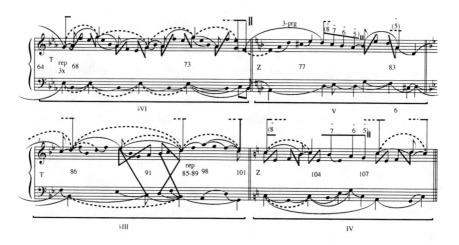

Figure 2c "The Bag of Luck," voice leading (cont.) (Joplin, *Treemonisha*, No. 2)

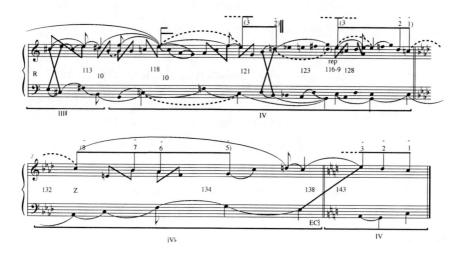

Figure 2d "The Bag of Luck," voice leading (cont.) (Joplin, *Treemonisha*, No. 2)

Ned objects to the tactics used by Zodzetrick, and he seizes control of the scene's tonality in mm. 22–49 and shifts it rapidly away from G major/E minor, cycling through C major, G minor, and F major in an attempt to discredit the conjuror and dissuade his wife. His failure to convince Monisha is demonstrated, however, by his inability to achieve full cadential closure— he reaches half cadences at mm. 30, 46 and 50, and abandons a cadential $^6_4$ at m. 37.[31] Finally, in mm. 49–54, Ned leaves Zodzetrick an opening when he asks Zodzetrick, in the key of D minor (the minor dominant of G major), to identify himself. Though he now realizes he will probably not get the sale, Zodzetrick seizes the opportunity to save face and reassert his authority, slyly reinstating G major with B as primary tone through sleight of hand (the use of a common-tone diminished seventh chord). However, though he again closes to the tonic over a strong perfect authentic cadence at m. 63, he avoids $\hat{2}$, this time substituting an added sixth above the dominant (B, $\hat{3}$). Though this sort of substitution is certainly idiomatic in ragtime and subsequent jazz styles, it nonetheless weakens the sense of linear closure inherent in Zodzetrick's melody.

At this point in the scene, Treemonisha picks up where Ned has left off. Once again moving the tonal area to the flat side of the circle of fifths by reinterpreting Zodzetrick's G major tonic as $\hat{3}$ of E♭ major (mm. 64–75), she challenges his moral integrity. In uncharted waters and uncertain how to proceed, the conjuror cautiously backpedals, returning to D minor (mm. 76–85) in order to reassert G major once more. Undeterred, Treemonisha transforms D minor into B♭ major (mm. 85–101) and chastises him for his many acts of deception. At this point, Zodzetrick begins to come unraveled, abandoning both his composure and his home key and threatening Treemonisha in C major: "An' it won't be long 'fore I'll make you from me run."

Unfortunately for the conjuror, his direct threat angers Remus, Treemonisha's friend and pupil, who joins the fray and puts further distance between Zodzetrick and his desired tonal goal by shifting the key to B major via another common-tone diminished-seventh chord (mm. 110) as he rebukes him. As he praises Treemonisha, Remus then appropriates Zodzetrick's C major and negates its potential to serve as support for an upper-neighbor to the original primary tone B by initiating E as local primary tone instead (mm. 115–31). Unlike Ned and Zodzetrick, Remus leaves no doubt as to his conviction and persuasiveness, reaching perfect authentic closure to $\hat{1}$ at mm. 131 via an explicitly stated $\hat{2}$ over the cadential dominant. Zodzetrick, off balance, is left to bluster ineffectually toward an evaded cadence in C minor (m. 138) before Treemonisha and Remus join forces and restore C major, banishing Zodzetrick from the stage with a strong perfect authentic cadence that concludes the number (m. 145).

In order to make his way back to G major, Zodzetrick has to rehabilitate C major/A minor as a "neighboring key" by reinstating C—not E—as primary tone. He is brought a step closer to this intermediate goal through the confusion caused by his abduction of Treemonisha at the end of Act 1. In the second half of "Confusion" (Figure 3), as Monisha describes the kidnapping to the community, the tonal area shifts to A minor, though still keeping E as primary tone (mm. 41–92). Each of the main characters reacts differently to the news. Monisha tries to remain brave by returning to C major, but her fear is telegraphed by the lack of closure in her music (half cadences at mm. 52 and 59 and a prominent deceptive cadence at m. 64). Ned, for his part, abandons reason and descends to Zodzetrick's level, using the conjuror's G major key and B primary tone to declare his murderous intentions ("I'll beat dat trifling Zodzetrick until he runs like a big cur dog, and I'll kill that scoundrel Luddud jus' lak I would kill a hog"). Like Zodzetrick, in letting his emotions get the better of him Ned omits $\hat{2}$ over the dominant, precluding linear closure to the tonic (m. 72). Even the staunch Remus is unnerved by Treemonisha's sudden disappearance: his confident C major promise ("I'll bring Treemonisha home") ends with a mode-mixed deceptive cadence to ♭VI (m. 80).[32] The number concludes in A minor, with the entire community urging Ned and Remus to hurry and save Treemonisha by closing a 5-line from E, albeit only with an implied $\hat{2}$ over the dominant (m. 87).

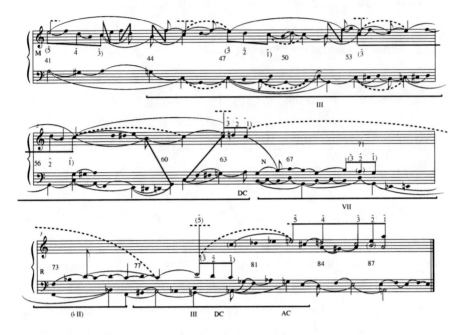

Figure 3 "Confusion," voice leading (Joplin, *Treemonisha*, No. 10)

As Act 2 opens, the scene shifts to the conjurors' forest hideout, Zodzetrick's stronghold. It is here that Zodzetrick has the best chance of regrouping and resuming progress toward the attainment of his superobjective. The "Superstition" number, a conjuror's credo of sorts, begins with an orchestral introduction in F major, establishing C as primary tone (Figure 4). After a transitional modulation to F minor, the band of conjurors enters in A♭ major (♭II in G major), reinterpreting C as the head note of a 3-line. As the litany of superstitions grows more bizarre and extreme ("If a neighbor comes to see you, an' squeezes yo' han' very tight, you had better speak loud 'Hee-Hoo,' that neighbor is not right"), the number modulates to F minor (mm. 73–100). A♭ major is restored for the final "amen" section, however, and a local 3-line is closed to the tonic.

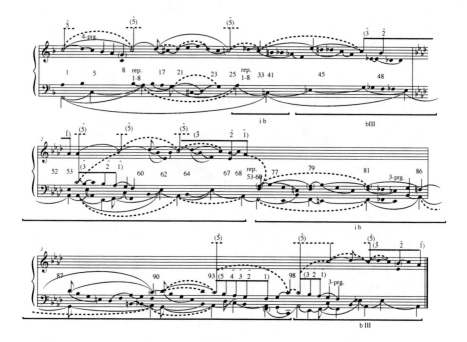

Figure 4 "Superstition," voice leading (Joplin, *Treemonisha*, No. 11)

"Treemonisha in Peril" brings Zodzetrick even closer to restoring C as a large-scale upper neighbor tone. As he and Luddud enter the camp with Treemonisha, the key shifts again to A minor (diatonic ii of G major, versus the mode-mixed ♭II of the previous number) and C is initiated as the primary tone of a 3-line (Figure 5). The conjurors' predisposition to harshly judge the captive stranger in their midst is demonstrated by the perfect authentic closure in their choral melody as Luddud calls for their attention (mm. 16–17). Luddud successfully demonizes Treemonisha in the eyes of the conjurors (via a perfect authentic cadence in mm. 25–26), but Cephus, a member of the group who is secretly in love with Treemonisha, tries to grant her a reprieve by effecting a modulation to C major (mm. 36–38). Simon, a lesser leader of the conjurors, implacably returns the key to A minor and Treemonisha is condemned. Because her punishment is temporarily deferred, however ("Come on ev'rybody to de brush arbor, dis gal mus' have de punishment dat's waitin' for her"), there is no closure in A minor. After a half cadence at

m. 42, the number modulates to C major and closes with a perfect authentic cadence (m. 46).

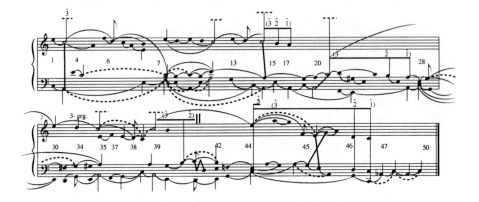

Figure 5 "Treemonisha in Peril," voice leading (Joplin, *Treemonisha*, No. 12)

Upon arriving at the brush arbor, Simon informs the other conjurors of his plan in "The Wasp-Nest": to throw Treemonisha onto an enormous wasp nest nearby. After an imperfect authentic cadence in C major indicating their assent (mm. 8–9), Simon begins a countdown, intoning the goal tone C and using it to pivot to A minor (mm. 9–12), as shown in Figure 6. Before he and the other conjurors can complete a descent to the tonic, however, Cephus again interrupts, distracting the group by calling attention to the arrival of a strange figure (Remus, dressed in a scarecrow costume) and restoring E as the primary tone. Mass confusion ensues as the conjurors, believing Remus to be the devil, flee in all directions, and the number closes in A minor, with an unresolved C as the final structural pitch in the melody.

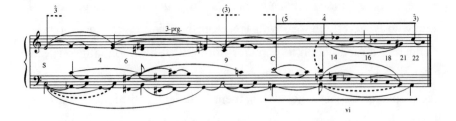

Figure 6 "The Wasp-Nest," voice leading (Joplin, *Treemonisha*, No. 14)

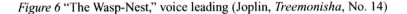

Although Zodzetrick does restore C as an upper-neighbor tone supported by A minor (ii), he is unable to use it to return to B over G major/E minor, and the background structure of his role remains incomplete and unresolved, even though it is not interrupted in the technical sense of the term.[33] His narrow-minded focus on getting rid of Treemonisha costs him his larger objective—to maintain control of the community. In contrast, Treemonisha is able to successfully bring about the return of her primary tone D ($\hat{3}$ of B♭ major), initiated in the overture, and achieve linear and harmonic closure to the tonic in No. 25 as she achieves her superobjective: to free her community from fear and lead them toward a brighter future (Figure 7).

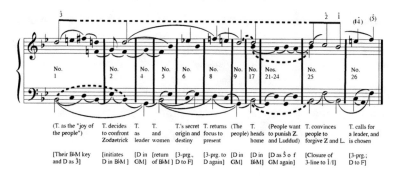

Figure 7 The Background Structure of Treemonisha's Role (Joplin, *Treemonisha*)

In a sense, Treemonisha's struggle to win the hearts and minds of the people can be represented as a struggle for control of the pitch D. Although D as primary tone ($\hat{3}$) is initially associated with the key of B♭ major (Treemonisha's key) in the overture, where it anchors the main theme of the opera representing "the happiness of the people when they feel free from the conjurors and their spells of superstition,"[34] it later becomes closely affiliated with the people's simplicity and ignorance, serving as $\hat{5}$ of G major (Zodzetrick's key) in the chorus numbers (Nos. 4, 9 and 21). Each time that D is introduced in a negative (G major) context, however, Treemonisha is able to redeem it in B♭ major: Zodzetrick's G major temptation of Monisha becomes a B♭ major reproach ("The Bag of Luck"), the raucous ring dance ("We're Goin' Around") becomes a meaningful springtime coronation ritual

("The Wreath"), the simplistic salvation offered by a traveling preacher ("Good Advice") becomes the actual salvation of Treemonisha herself from the conjurors ("Going Home"), and the condemnation of Zodzetrick and Luddud ("Treemonisha's Return") is transformed into an act of forgiveness ("Conjuror's Forgiven").

While it is tempting to simply read the struggle between Treemonisha and Zodzetrick as a conflict between flat keys and sharp keys, such a conflict does not entirely explain the tonal structure of the opera. Although the keys used by Joplin for Treemonisha (B♭ major), Ned (F major), Monisha (E♭ major) and Remus (C major) are primarily drawn from the flat side of the circle of fifths, the conjurors are represented both by sharp keys (G major and E minor for Zodzetrick) and flat keys (F major and A♭ major for the other conjurors). Moreover, Ned and Remus, in trying to convince the people to give up their desire for revenge at the end of the opera, speak to them in their own language, as it were, each adopting the key of D major for their moralistic exhortations ("Wrong is Never Right" and "When Villains Ramble Far and Near").

What does make Treemonisha's role especially compelling from the point of view of background structure, however, is its ability to simultaneously project large-scale closure and cyclic continuity. Joplin achieves this effect by bringing back Treemonisha's home key of B♭ major at the crux of the opera, where she convinces the people to forgive the conjurors (No. 25), but then prolonging it in the denouement through a motion to its dominant (F major) as the people look toward a brighter future by electing Treemonisha as the leader that will free them from ignorance and superstition (Nos. 26 and 27). This two-part structure is represented in Figure 7 by the background closure of a 3-line in B♭ major in No. 25 and the subsequent motion to the dominant in "A Real Slow Drag" that leaves open the question of whether or not Treemonisha becomes a successful leader and justifies the faith placed in her by the community, a question that remains unanswered as the curtain falls at the end of Act 3.

After brief appearances in "The Bag of Luck" (the confrontation with Zodzetrick) and "We're Goin' Around" (the ring dance) during which she is not the center of attention, Treemonisha comes into her own in No. 5, "The Wreath," reclaiming the key of B♭ major as she innocently but cleverly goes about preparing for her own "coronation" by steeping herself in the traditions of the community so as not to appear aloof or haughty. She establishes D as primary tone at m. 5, prolonging it through a third-progression involving raised $\hat{4}$ (mm. 5–12) that parallels the background structure of her role (Figure 8). After Monisha alludes metaphorically to Treemonisha's future success as a leader of the community ("an' very fine yo' wreath will be") by closing a middleground descent through $\hat{2}$ to the tonic (mm. 18–20), the key shifts to E♭ major. It is not yet time for Treemonisha to be crowned as leader, and the number concludes without closure in the home key.

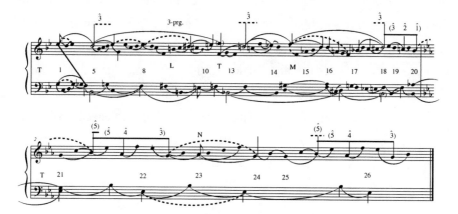

Figure 8 "The Wreath," voice leading (Joplin, *Treemonisha*, No. 5)

Treemonisha's triumphant return to the plantation in "Going Home" after her dramatic rescue in the forest brings with it the return of her home key, B♭ major. Remus initiates D as the local primary tone at m. 6, prolonging it through a fourth-progression before it is transferred up an octave to Treemonisha's vocal line at m. 8 (Figure 9). Because Treemonisha has not yet reached her destination (in both literal and dramatic terms), however, the primary tone is prolonged through the end of the number and does not resolve to the tonic. With its restatement of Treemonisha's key, yet absence of closure, this number provides perfect "traveling music" for her journey back to the community.

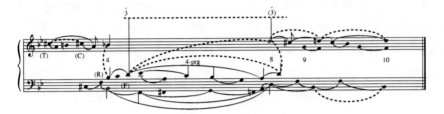

Figure 9 "Going Home," voice leading (Joplin, *Treemonisha*, No. 17)

With the joyous return of the opera's B♭ major main theme in the orchestra at m. 21 of "Treemonisha's Return," supporting a strong statement of the D primary tone in the choral soprano line, Treemonisha's iconic status within the community is confirmed with certainty (Figure 10). Treemonisha herself provides a strong linear descent to the tonic supported by a perfect authentic cadence that concludes the first section of the scene, in which she recounts the story of her rescue (mm. 23–32). She even showcases her charismatic flair as a storyteller and orator, keeping her audience in suspense by using an evaded cadence at m. 28 as she withholds just for a moment the crux of the story regarding the success of Remus's strategy.

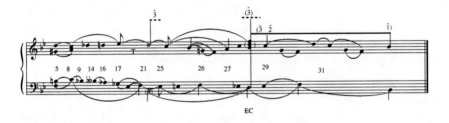

Figure 10 "Treemonisha's Return," voice leading (Joplin, *Treemonisha*, No. 21)

After an intriguing tonal struggle in No. 21, "Treemonisha's Return," in which Treemonisha's triumphant return (B♭ major, mm. 1–32) is jeopardized by the community's desire for revenge (G major, mm. 37–72), she again resorts to her inner circle of friends and family to help win over the rest of the people. First Remus (No. 22), then Ned (No. 24), appeal to the people in D major, the dominant of their old (superstitious) key of G major. When the people remain hesitant, Treemonisha finally takes matters into her own hands and there is a moment of extreme tension at the opening of No. 25 as she makes a personal appeal for forgiveness (mm. 1–15). It is far from certain, in fact, as the orchestra descends chromatically by step through an augmented octave from B to B♭ (mm. 11–15) that the community will give in to Treemonisha's demands (Figure 11). Only after she takes the initiative and becomes the first to shake hands with the conjurors (m. 16) do the others follow suit and permit the restatement of the primary tone D and background closure to the tonic (m. 37).[35]

Figure 11 "Conjurors Forgiven," voice leading (Joplin, *Treemonisha*, No. 25)

Summary

As a first example of multi-movement background structure in practice, *Treemonisha* provides an excellent introduction to the advantages and challenges of the model. Treemonisha's dramatic success at the conclusion of the opera is clearly evident in the libretto and in the surface features of her music (including mode, tempo, rhythm, and register), and is intuitively perceived by the audience. The interpretation of her music in the opera as a unified background structure in B♭ major, however, suggests that she consciously establishes her superobjective—to free her community from fear and lead them toward a brighter future—in her first scene, and that Joplin compositionally recalls that initial decision for the audience at significant moments in the plot ("Going Home" and "Conjuror's Forgiven") by returning to B♭ major and using D ($\hat{3}$) as the primary melodic tone. This makes her descent to her final perfect authentic cadence in "Conjuror's Forgiven" much more powerful, for the performer and thus also for the audience.

On the other hand, attempting to relate the considerable amount of music that intervenes between these B♭ major moments to the fundamental structure raises significant theoretical and phenomenological questions. How much latitude should be granted to a background structure that spans over two hours of music, particularly in terms of parallel voice leading and chromaticism? Traditionally, Schenkerians have frowned on both of these features, tending to exclude them from the background whenever possible. It is common, however, in the teaching of Schenkerian analysis to invoke the concept of structural levels to explain apparent middleground instances of parallel voice leading (i.e., parallel fifths or octaves revealed at the middleground level are ameliorated by the intervening intervals of the foreground). Since a multi-movement structure such as the one presented for Treemonisha's role is essentially a combined middleground-background structure for the opera as a whole, the same principle could be applied to the parallel fifths in No. 5 and Nos. 21–22. Instances of middleground chromaticism in individual pieces, on the other hand, are usually reduced out at the background level in a conventional Schenkerian graph, and the same principle could be applied to Treemonisha's background graph. The E and F♯ in No. 2 (refer again to Figure 7), prolong the primary tone D, while E in Nos. 8 and 26 serves as a dissonant passing tone filling in a consonant skip to F that represents Treemonisha's potential as a future leader of the community.

ENDNOTES

[1] Haskins, *Scott Joplin*, 177.

[2] Ibid., 170–1.

[3] Ibid., 130.

[4] Ibid., 137–8.

[5] Ibid., 162.

[6] Ibid.

[7] Ibid., 160, 172.

[8] Ibid., 166–7.

[9] Ibid., 161.

[10] Berlin, *King of Ragtime*, 226.

[11] Peter Gammond, *Scott Joplin and the Ragtime Era* (New York: St. Martin's Press, 1975), 100.

[12] Ibid., 98–100.

[13] *New York Age*, March 5, 1908. Quoted in Haskins, 161–2.

[14] Berlin, *King of Ragtime*, 214. Haskins has the date of the performance much later (in early 1915), but Berlin offers a convincing argument, based on secondary sources, for moving the date to 1911. See Haskins, *Scott Joplin*, 190.

[15] Susan Curtis, *Dancing to a Black Man's Tune: A Life of Scott Joplin* (Columbia: University of Missouri Press, 1994), 156.

[16] Berlin, *King of Ragtime*, 222.

[17] Curtis, *Dancing to a Black Man's Tune*, 157–9.

[18] *The American Musician*, June 24, 1911. Quoted in Haskins, *Scott Joplin*, 178.

[19] Kay C. Thompson, "Lottie Joplin," *The Record Changer* (October 1950), 18. Quoted in Haskins, *Scott Joplin*, 3.

[20] Dominique-Rene de Lerma, *Reflections on Afro-American Music*, 74 and 85. Quoted in Curtis, *Dancing to a Black Man's Tune*, 3.

[21] Haskins, *Scott Joplin*, 14–16.

[22] Ibid., 15.

[23] Ibid., 178.

[24] Ibid., 195.

[25] Gammond, *Scott Joplin and the Ragtime Era*, 146–7.

[26] Curtis, *Dancing to a Black Man's Tune*, 162.

[27] Haskins, *Scott Joplin*, 171.

[28] In an appendix, Peter Gammond gives a substantial list of compositions influenced by ragtime that includes works by Gershwin, Copland, Weill, and many other American and French composers. See Gammond, *Scott Joplin and the Ragtime Era*, 215–8.

[29] Though C major itself could provide adequate support for C as primary tone, this would create an 8-line, which is rare in the Schenkerian literature. The shift to A minor establishes C as the would-be primary tone of a local 3-line in No. 12, though a subsequent return to C major prevents local closure to the tonic.

[30] Measures are numbered from the beginning of each numbered scene in the 2001 Dover edition of the original piano-vocal score: Scott Joplin, *Treemonisha: Opera in Three Acts* (New York: Scott Joplin, 1911).

[31] The abandoned cadence is defined in William Caplin, *Phrase Structure in Classical Music* (Oxford: Oxford University Press, 1998).

[32] The Houston Grand Opera recording of *Treemonisha*, which includes many cuts throughout, also does not employ the $\flat$VI given in Joplin's score at m. 80, substituting a C major tonic instead. While the cuts do not substantially alter the structure of the opera, the harmonic substitution was an uninspired choice that weakens the sense of panic and desperation in the community at the end of No. 10.

[33] As noted in Chapter 1, Schenker defines interruption as a breaking of the line at $\hat{2}$ over V, followed by a return of the primary tone and a descent to $\hat{1}$ over I.

[34] Joplin, preface to *Treemonisha*, 3.

[35] The melodic substitution over the structural dominant here is the more conventional replacement of $\hat{2}$ with the leading tone (m. 36).

CHAPTER 5

The Multi-Movement *Anstieg* or Initial Ascent:
George Gershwin's "Folk Opera"
Porgy and Bess (1935)

During the period from the beginning of World War I to the end of World War II, a more characteristically American voice began to emerge in the operatic genre. The development of more innovative libretti (e.g., Gertrude Stein's text for Virgil Thomson's *Four Saints in Three Acts*, 1928), the addition of jazz elements to the harmonic lexicon (e.g., in George Antheil's *Transatlantic*, 1929), and the increasing use of American subjects (e.g., Douglas Moore's *The Devil and Daniel Webster*, 1939) promoted the search for a truly American opera. The apotheosis of these three trends was DuBose Heyward and George and Ira Gershwin's operatic masterpiece *Porgy and Bess*, which George dubbed a "folk opera," intended to be "the final meeting ground of the popular and the serious, both poised on the highest planes of artistic excellence."[1]

Gershwin, whom biographer Edward Jablonski compares to MacDowell, Griffes, Ives, and Copland, was instrumental in "energizing popular interest in the contemporary American composer and his music" and bringing native-born composers into the serious concert hall.[2] Though Gershwin called himself a "modern Romantic," he considered himself to be an American composer above all, claiming that music should reflect its age and "my people are American. My time is today."[3] Admired by composers as diverse as Ravel, Bartòk, Vaughan Williams, Schoenberg, and Berg,[4] Gershwin was regarded by supporters in the 1920s "as a kind of musical *naïf*, who had infused the American musical bloodstream with the illicit colorations of something called jazz," while his detractors regarded him "as an untutored Tin Pan Alley upstart who simply did not belong."[5]

Jablonski's comments on the early twentieth-century American composer's psyche are telling, particularly with regard to the previous chapter on Scott Joplin swimming against a tide of European operatic exports. Jablonski writes:

> Europeans take their musical heritage for granted because it seems to have always been there; American composers, musicians and critics are self-conscious about our early musical history and tended to reject our early music as inferior and not European enough. Generations of American composers were educated in Germany and later, when it became fashionable, France.[6]

Although there is no direct evidence that Gershwin knew Joplin's opera, the desire to further develop a uniquely American opera using popular or folk idioms was definitely in the air in the 1920s and '30s. The operetta composer Victor Herbert's *Natoma* was one of several unsuccessful attempts by self-consciously "American" composers to incorporate American Indian themes and subjects into an operatic framework.[7] As he remarked to his friend Isaac Goldberg in the late 1920s, Gershwin hoped to "write an opera of the melting pot, of New York City itself, with its blend of native and immigrant strains. This would allow for many kinds of music, black and white, Eastern and Western, and would call for a style that should achieve out of this diversity, an artistic unity."[8] He noted, "New York is a meeting-place, a rendezvous of the nations.... I'd especially like to blend the humor of it with the tragedy of it."[9]

In 1922, Gershwin had already attempted a one-act "jazz opera" about New York, collaborating with the lyricist Buddy DeSylva. Entitled *Blue Monday*, the opera was performed as part of George White's *Scandals of*

1922.[10] Though it lasted only one night in White's revue, it provided Gershwin with the impetus to write a full-scale opera. In a 1931 letter to Goldberg, Gershwin noted enthusiastically "I believe this work was the first ever to use recitative in the blues idiom."[11] His ambitions were further fueled by a trip to Europe in 1928, where he attended the April 28 performance of Ernst Krenek's *Jonny spielt auf*, in which the eponymous lead, a jazz violinist, was played in blackface. In the lobby afterward, pianist Lester Donahue protested, "if anyone should attempt a jazz opera, it should be George Gershwin."[12] Gershwin overheard him and responded "Oh, yeah!" Donahue noted with satisfaction the failure of *Jonny spielt auf* at the Metropolitan Opera in New York City the following year, after which several critics remarked, "they had never sufficiently appreciated Gershwin."[13]

On October 30, 1929, Gershwin received a contract from the Metropolitan Opera to compose an opera based on *The Dybbuk*, with a libretto by Henry Ahlsberg. Ahlsberg planned to use his translation of the 1926 Yiddish play by Solomon S. Rapoport, itself based on a popular Jewish folk tale, as the primary material for his libretto. When it was discovered that the rights to the play had already been granted to the Italian composer Lodovico Rocca, however, Gershwin abandoned the project.[14] Still in search of the proper subject for his American opera, Gershwin turned again to the idea of adapting DuBose Heyward's best-selling novel *Porgy*, a project he had discussed with the author on several occasions.

Gershwin first encountered *Porgy* in 1926, during rehearsals for his musical *Oh, Kay!* Inspired by the novel, which he had been reading for relaxation, Gershwin wrote to Heyward, inquiring about its availability for adaptation.[15] Heyward traveled to New York from his Hendersonville, North Carolina, home to discuss the matter with Gershwin, but upon his return his wife Dorothy confessed that she had already begun a stage adaptation of *Porgy*. Not wanting to disappoint her, Heyward informed Gershwin that any work on a musical treatment would have to be deferred until the completion of the play. Gershwin agreed, noting "he would want to postpone the project until he had made more serious study of music, for what he had in mind was to create an opera out of Heyward's story."[16]

In October 1926, Heyward and Gershwin met again in Atlantic City, New Jersey, while the Heywards were waiting for their play to be mounted by the Theatre Guild. They discussed the proposed opera in general terms, and came to a verbal agreement to begin work on the project once the Theatre Guild production was concluded.[17] Other projects demanded Gershwin's attention, however, and it was not until March 29, 1932, that he wrote to Heyward again, to make sure *Porgy* was still available. Heyward assured him that it was, but Gershwin wrote again on May 20 to say that he could not begin work on the opera until January 1933, following the premiere of his musical *Pardon My English*.[18] Heyward was in a difficult position: he was in dire financial straits, and he had been contacted by Al Jolson about doing *Porgy* in blackface as a musical, with the composer/lyricist team of Jerome Kern and Oscar Hammerstein. Perhaps because he did not know about Kern and Hammerstein's involvement in the project, Gershwin agreed to let Jolson have *Porgy* first, since his "play with a few songs" would not hurt a serious opera's chances. He wrote to Heyward:

> The sort of thing I had in mind for *Porgy* is a much more serious thing than Jolson could ever do.... I would not attempt to write music to your play until I had all the themes and musical devices worked out for such an undertaking. It would be more of a labor of love than anything else.... If you can see your way to making some ready money from Jolson's version I don't know that it would hurt a later version done by an all-colored cast.[19]

Luckily, the Kern/Hammerstein/Jolson *Porgy* never materialized. The three withdrew their claim, and on November 3, 1933, the Theatre Guild announced that it would be mounting a new production of *Porgy*, with music by Gershwin, despite the fact that Gershwin had not yet begun composing it.[20] On January 26, 1934, Gershwin began work on Act I, composing some of the songs and spirituals first.

The collaboration between Heyward and Gershwin was fruitful and relatively unimpeded by conflict. Though Heyward was deferential to Gershwin, he did suggest the opening sequence of *Porgy and Bess:* an orchestral overture that segues directly into Jasbo Brown's solo piano music.[21] A new conclusion for the opera was devised by Heyward's wife Dorothy: rather than having Bess go to Savannah, leaving a defeated Porgy behind, she would go to New York, pursued by a determined and faithful Porgy.[22] The only major disagreement between the collaborators concerned the use of recitative: Heyward favored spoken dialogue, underscored by the orchestra, but Gershwin remained committed to the use of sung recitative, and eventually convinced Heyward to go along with him.[23]

During *Porgy and Bess's* period of gestation, both Heyward and Gershwin became concerned about possible competition from other composers, particularly Virgil Thomson, whose *Four Saints in Three Acts* was done with an all-black cast. After attending a performance of *Four Saints*, a relieved Gershwin wrote to Heyward: "Musically, it sounded early 19th-century, which was a happy inspiration and made the libretto [by Gertrude Stein] bearable— in fact, quite entertaining."[24] Heyward, for his part, worried (needlessly, as it turned out) that the Metropolitan's production of Howard Hanson's *Merry Mount*, with its early American setting, might be more of a threat: "from the advance ballyhoo I thought something revolutionary was coming that might steal our thunder, but it seemed to me to be pretty much the conventional thing."[25]

Throughout the compositional process, Gershwin strove to combine elements of grand opera and musical theatre into a seamless tapestry. While in one notebook for *Porgy and Bess* he wrote, "Melodic, Nothing neutral, Utter simplicity, Directness,"[26] he also studied composition with Russian émigré Joseph Schillenger from 1932 to 1936 in preparation for writing some of the larger choruses and ensemble numbers in the opera.[27] Though Schillinger later claimed the opera was written under him, there is little evidence to suggest that the "Schillinger system," involving manipulation of the inverted and retrograde forms of the main theme, had more than a superficial effect on the opera's musical structure.[28]

The Theater Guild in Boston gave the first performance of *Porgy and Bess* on September 10, 1935. With the exception of John W. Bubbles (John William Sublett), of the vaudeville team Buck and Bubbles, who played Sporting Life, all the principals in the cast had operatic training, including Todd Duncan (Porgy) and Anne Brown (Bess). Although the tryout was a success, hailed by conductor Serge Koussevitsky among others as "a great advance in American opera,"[29] many cuts were made before the production opened at the Alvin Theatre in New York on October 10, 1935. These included Jasbo Brown's piano music, Maria's aria "I Hate's Yo' Struttin' Style," the trio section of Porgy's "Bess, Oh Where's My Bess," and the "Six Prayers" chorus in the storm scene, based on Gershwin's aural impression of a church service he had attended in North Carolina with Heyward.[30]

Despite the cuts, *Porgy and Bess* lasted only one hundred twenty-four performances at the Alvin Theatre. Many critics were uncertain of the work's genre: while Leonard Liebling called it "the first authentic American opera," Olin Downes of the *New York Times* charged that Gershwin failed to "utilize all the resources of the operatic composer," and found the mix of genres disturbing.[31] Writing in *Modern Music*, one of the most respected music journals of the day, Virgil Thomson claimed, "Gershwin does not even know what an opera is ... and yet *Porgy and Bess* is an opera."[32] Samuel Chotzinoff of the *New York Post* labeled *Porgy and Bess* a "hybrid," while Paul Rosenfeld regarded it as merely "an aggrandized musical show."[33]

Much of the criticism centered on Gershwin's use of recitative, rather than spoken dialogue. Brooks Atkinson, drama critic for the *New York Times*, complained that "turning *Porgy* into opera has resulted in a deluge of remarks that have to be thoughtfully intoned and that annoyingly impede the action,"[34] while Chotzinoff argued that Gershwin was trying to "impose the recitative on matter that did not require it."[35] In a particularly vitriolic review, Thomson declared that

> Gershwin's lack of understanding of all the major problems of form, of continuity, and of straightforward musical expression is not surprising in view of the impurity of his musical sources and his frank acceptance of them.... At best a piquant but highly unsavory stirring-up-together of Israel, Africa, and the Gaelic Isles.[36]

Perhaps most troubling was the reception that *Porgy and Bess* received among members of the African-American community. While John Mason Brown, drama critic for the *New York Post*, remarked that the work was "the most American opera that has yet been seen or heard: it is a Russian who has directed it, two Southerners who have written its book, two Jewish boys [*sic*] who have composed its lyrics and music, and a stageful of Negroes who sing and act it to perfection,"[37] James Hicks of the Baltimore *Afro-American* branded it "the most insulting, the most libelous, the most degrading act that could possibly be perpetrated against the Negro people."[38]

The controversy surrounding both *Porgy and Bess's* genre and its portrayal of the African-American community persisted in subsequent productions of the opera as well. In 1952, Robert Breen, director of the most famous and internationally renowned production of the opera, remarked, "I am a little weary of seeing all the type-space used up by the so-called music critics in discussing *Porgy and Bess* and whether it meets the specifications of being an 'opera.' We are not selling it as an opera but as a theatre piece."[39] For her 1961 production at New York City Opera, Jean Dalrymple reinstated the recitatives (cut in Cheryl Crawford's 1941 revival), causing Raymond Erickson of the *New York Times* to argue that the work's genre—musical show, play, light opera, folk opera, or opera—depended on the production.[40]

With Lorin Maazel's 1975 concert performance of the complete score with the Cleveland Symphony Orchestra and Sherwin M. Goldman's 1976 Houston Grand Opera production of the complete work, Peter G. Davis and Clive Barnes of the *New York Times* claimed that *Porgy and Bess* could truly be assessed as an opera.[41] Yet, if the issue of the opera's genre seemed resolved, its status in the African-American community remained uncertain. Goldman, in attempting to sell his idea for a production of the complete work with Houston Grand Opera, ran into black resentment of the work as "Uncle Tom," old-fashioned and demeaning in its portrayal of African-Americans. Prominent artistic figures such as choreographer Alvin Ailey and bandleader Duke Ellington both voiced their reservations to Goldman about the work, but by the time the opera opened in 1976 such concerns were far outweighed by the artistic success of the production.[42]

Synopsis

Porgy and Bess is set in "Catfish Row," an imaginary Charleston, South Carolina, riverfront community, peopled with African-Americans down on their luck. The curtain opens on an evening in late summer, in the early 1920s or '30s; the men of Catfish Row have gathered to play craps (I/i). Crown, a large man with a fearsome temper, enters, accompanied by Bess, and joins the game. He is drunk. During the course of the game, Crown gets into a fight with Robbins, Serena's husband, and kills him with a cotton hook. Crown goes into hiding and Sporting Life, a cunning drug dealer, "comforts" Bess by giving her "happy dus'" (cocaine) and offers to take her to New York with him. She accepts the first offer but refuses the second, and, when no one else will help her, she goes to stay with Porgy, a cripple who rides in a goat-drawn cart. The community gathers the following night to mourn Robbins and to take up a collection for his burial (I/ii).

A month goes by, and Porgy and Bess grow to love each other. Porgy obtains an "official" divorce from Frazier, the local mountebank, in order to be with Bess and "free" her from her supposed commitment to Crown (II/i). The community goes to Kittiwah Island for a picnic, including Bess, who, this time with the help of Porgy, refuses another offer from Sporting Life to go to New York, and declares that she has given up drugs (II/ii). As she is preparing to board the boat to return to the mainland, Bess, the last one to leave, encounters Crown, who has been hiding out on the island from the police. Crown forces Bess to stay and has his way with her, warning her that he will be coming to the mainland to reclaim her in two weeks. Bess returns to Catfish Row after two days, feverish and delirious, and is kept in bed for five days, while the community prays for her recovery (II/iii). On the day of Bess's recovery, Clara's husband Jake leads a fishing expedition to the Blackfish banks, despite Clara's warning that it is time for the September storms. Bess confesses to Porgy that she has slept with Crown and is still attracted to him, but she begs Porgy to let her stay with him. Porgy forgives her, and promises to protect her from Crown. The next morning a hurricane strikes and the community gathers in Serena's room to pray (II/iv). Crown bursts into the room, but before he can take Bess away from Porgy, Clara sees Jake's boat overturned in the river and runs out into the storm, giving her baby to Bess for safekeeping. To prove his manhood to Bess, Crown goes after Clara to protect her, but vows to return for Bess.

Jake and Clara both die in the storm. The following night, as the community mourns them, Crown reappears and sneaks over to Porgy's room (III/i). As he passes the window, Porgy stabs him in the back. They fight, and Porgy kills him. The next day, Porgy is hauled off to prison as a material witness to the murder, though not as a suspect, and Sporting Life succeeds in convincing Bess that he will surely be found out and imprisoned for life or hanged. In her despair, Bess accepts the cocaine that Sporting Life offers her, becomes hooked on the drug once again, and accompanies him to New York (III/ii). A week later, Porgy returns in triumph to Catfish Row, having avoided a conviction and won a handsome sum of money from the other inmates in the process (III/iii). He passes out gifts to his friends, but, when he discovers that Bess has gone to New York, he immediately sets out after her in his cart.

Scoring and Analyzing the Roles of Porgy and Bess

Scoring the roles of *Porgy and Bess* reveals a host of unfulfilled dreams and ambitions. Of the eight leading characters, four are killed (Robbins, Jake, Clara, and Crown), and three leave Catfish Row (Sporting Life, Bess, and Porgy). Only Serena, depicted as the pillar of the community, remains behind. The attainment of the final main objectives assigned to Porgy and Bess can therefore only be conjectured, since the opera ends in almost cinematic fashion (in such a way as to invite a sequel). Porgy goes off in search of Bess, but the audience never learns whether he finds her; Bess goes to New York, but the audience does not know whether she finds happiness there.

As will be demonstrated by the analyses, Porgy achieves many of his main objectives in scenes throughout the opera, reinforced by the closure of fundamental lines in the majority of his scenes. However, his failure to attain his superobjective (to build a new life together with Bess) is projected by the lack of closure in the background structure created by the tonal relationships between his musical numbers. Taken together, the musical and dramatic trajectory of Porgy and Bess's roles comprises a background interruption that spans the three acts of the opera, breaking off in Act III.[43]

Porgy's superobjective is not fully revealed until Act II, Scene 1, where the residents of Catfish Row declare that "Porgy change since dat woman come to live with he" in the ensemble section of Porgy's joyous "Banjo Song," "I Got Plenty O' Nuttin'" (R20). In his two previous numbers in Act I, "They Pass By Singin'" and "Oh Little Stars," Porgy must conceal his true intentions from the rest of the men, so as to protect himself from danger: if he is killed by Crown, then he will be unable to achieve his superobjective. Although he is successful in the majority of his scenes (see Table 1), the outcome of Porgy's primary task is still in doubt at the end of the opera.

	Y/N	KEY	CADENCE	LINE
SO: to put an end to his loneliness by sharing his life with a woman	?	a	HC	$\hat{3}$-$\hat{2}^{\|}$
MO₁ (I/i): to throw the other men off his trail ("They Pass By Singin'")	n	a	—	(1)
MO₂ (I/i): to impress Bess by winning money ("Oh Little Stars")	n	G	PAC	3-line
	E		EC	$\hat{5}$-$\hat{2}^{\|}$
MO₃ (II/i): to publicize his happiness and make Bess feel more like his woman ("I Got Plenty O' Nuttin'")	y	G	PAC	3-line
MO₄ (II/i): to defy and overcome a bad omen ("Buzzard Song")	y	a	PAC	3-line
MO₅ (II/i): to convince Bess to stay by showing her the depth of his devotion ("Bess, You Is My Woman")	n	B♭	HC	$\hat{3}$-$\hat{2}^{\|}$
	n	D	HC	$\hat{3}$-$\hat{2}^{\|}$
	y	F♯	PAC	3-line
MO₆ (II/iii): to reassure Bess and calm her fears ("I Loves You, Porgy")	y	F	PAC	(5-line)
MO₇ (III/iii): to force his friends to reveal Bess's whereabouts ("Oh, Bess, Where's My Bess")	n	E	—	(5)
MO₈ (III/iii): to rescue Bess ("Oh Lawd, I'm On My Way")	?	E	PAC	$\hat{5}$-$\hat{4}$/$\hat{2}$-$\hat{1}$

Table 1 The Score of Porgy's Role

Porgy's first song, "They Pass By Singin'," is a short, through-composed number. The lack of large-scale formal repetition, which is found in abundance in Porgy's other numbers, contributes to the casual atmosphere of the song. In addition, the uneven phrase structure of the song, 6: (4+2) + 11: [4: (2+2) + 4 + 3] + 10: (4 + 6), accentuated by the shifting meter in R79–80, creates a spontaneous, conversational tone.

The most striking thing about the harmonic structure of the song is the ambiguity that it creates with regard to the primary key. In the six-measure introduction beginning at R78, the lower voices of the orchestra outline a C major triad while the upper voices sound the pitches E, G, A, and C, which can be interpreted either as a C major triad with an added sixth or an A minor seventh chord. At R79, the ambiguity seems to be resolved in favor of C major when the orchestra plays a G dominant seventh chord, but the chord never resolves, and the accompaniment establishes A minor at R80 with a i^7–$V^{\sharp9}$–i^7 progression. Once again, when the music nears a cadence, arriving on a strong V^7 with a suspended sixth above the bass at R81–1, Gershwin avoids resolution, moving to a linear augmented-sixth chord that effects a transition back to V^7 of C major. C major then prevails for the final section of the song (R81–82), but the final cadence lacks tonal definition, both because of the absence of a V–I progression (vii^{o7} is substituted for the dominant), and because the added sixth is retained in the final tonic, leaving behind a hint of A minor. That Porgy also closes his vocal line on A only strengthens the sense of unresolved ambiguity inherent in the harmonic structure of the number.

The ambiguity created by the harmonic structure is echoed in the absence of a fundamental line in the melody (see Figure 1). The introduction arpeggiates the A minor seventh chord in the same order that it is stated in the opening measure: C, A, G, E, with the final pitch occurring at R79. E is then prolonged, though without tonic support, through R80, where it is re-emphasized as $\hat{5}$ over the new, but temporary, A minor tonic. Although Porgy's line moves to D at R81–3, creating the expectation of a 3-line in C major or a 5-line in A minor, an arpeggiation of the supertonic seventh chord (D, F, A, C) moves the vocal line away from D and towards an elaboration of the inner voice A. This inner voice dominates the rest of the aria, leaving Porgy to finish on a dissonant added sixth above the tonic triad.

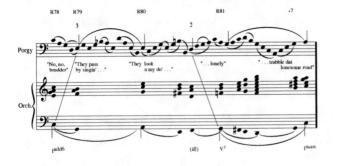

Figure 1 "They Pass By Singin'," voice leading

The lack of closure in "They Pass By Singin'" communicates Porgy's failure to convince the rest of the men that he is sincere in his scorn for women (at R78, he sings "No, no, brudder, Porgy ain' sof' on no woman"). The men share a laugh at R82, and are undoubtedly preparing to question Porgy further when Crown and Bess arrive on the scene, interrupting the conversation. Porgy's attempt to conceal his interest in Bess is necessitated by Jake's earlier accusation (R78–3) that he is "sof' on Crown's Bess," an accusation which, if proven, could bring a threat from Crown. Though he starts off with a firm denial, Porgy gets caught up in his own words, repeating the phrase "night time, day time he got to trabble dat lonesome road" with great sadness, as if the A minor element introduced at R80–81 ("They look in my do' an' they keep on movin'. When God made cripple, he mean him to be lonely") is too much to overcome and he cannot restore C major at the end of the number.

Porgy's second number, "Oh Little Stars," is also through-composed, though, like "They Pass By Singin'," it is divided into two broad sections. As in his first number, the phrase structure is uneven: 10: (3 + 2 + 5) + 12: (4 + 3 + 5). The only formal marker of any sort is the return to the G major tonic at R119+1, which makes the first section of the song a closed unit. The fluid formal structure accentuates the mysterious, almost prayerful atmosphere that Porgy is trying to create by invoking the power of his "little stars," the dice that he is rolling in the craps game.

Harmonically, "Oh Little Stars" is the simplest of Porgy's numbers. In a marked departure from his standard harmonic practice in the opera, Gershwin creates an almost entirely triadic accompaniment for the main body of the song (the applied dominant seventh chords at R118+3 and R119+2 are the only exceptions). The simplified chordal texture adds to the quasi-religious tone of the number, and also makes the arrival of the $F\sharp^{13}_9$ chord at R120 (F$\sharp$, A$\sharp$, C$\sharp$, E, G$\sharp$, D$\sharp$), where Crown grabs Porgy's arm, all the more striking.

The brief modulation to E major in the first section (R118+3 to R118+6) highlights the importance of chromatic third relations in the harmonic structure of the number. Another chromatic third relation is used in the retransition to G major at R118+6 (E: I–VI^t = G: ♯IV–V–I).[44] In the second half of the song, the modulation to E major is repeated (R119+2 to R119+8), but, instead of functioning merely as a parallel chromatic chord, VI^t is used as a pivot chord to F♯ major (E: I–VI^t = F♯: V–♭VI–I). When the new F♯ major tonic is transformed into a thirteenth chord (the most dissonant chord in the number), a descending-fifths progression is initiated (C♯–F♯^{13}–B^7) that should ultimately return the song to E major again ([V]→[V^{13}]→V^7–I). Gershwin obscures the arrival on the dominant at R121–2, however, by lowering the third of the chord, and the progression eventually moves deceptively to VI (C♯).[45] The evasion of an authentic cadence drives the music forward and foreshadows Porgy's eventual failure to win the game.[46]

Porgy initiates the primary tone (B) of a middleground 3-line in G major at R118+1 (see Figure 2). The primary tone is then prolonged by a third-progression in an inner voice of the melodic line, which descends from G to E.[47] The melody descends to $\hat{2}$ (A), harmonized by V, at R119–2, and then to $\hat{1}$ over the tonic at R119+1, ending the first section. When the harmony shifts away from G major in the following measures, B becomes reinterpreted as the primary tone of a 5-line in E major.

Figure 2 "Oh, Little Stars," voice leading

In retrospect, the inner-voice descent from G to E in the opening section can be seen as connecting the primary tone with its proper tonic (represented by the diagonal line in Figure 2). The fundamental line descends to an implied $\hat{4}$ (A) over IV at R119+4 and then moves to $\hat{3}$ over VI^t in the subsequent measure. After $\hat{3}$ (G♯) is prolonged through an arpeggiation of the C♯ major triad and a motion to A an upper-neighbor, the line moves to $\hat{2}$ (over [V]→V) and is interrupted.

The interrupted linear structure and evaded cadence both point to Porgy's failure to win the crap game (he eventually "craps out" at R123). Although he has some success early on (evidenced by the closure of the middleground 3-line in G major), his luck does not hold out and he is forced to pass the dice. As it turns out, though, fortune remains with Porgy, since Robbins, who takes up the "bones" next, is subsequently murdered by Crown in a fight after winning the money on his first roll. Having failed to achieve his second main objective, however, Porgy is still no closer to his primary goal.

Porgy's third song, "I Got Plenty O' Nuttin'," is constructed in rounded binary form on two separate levels. On the broader level, the entire A section (R13–R20), in which Porgy sings three statements of the main theme, is repeated after an eleven-bar contrasting B section in which the ensemble comments on Porgy's unusual behavior (R20–R22). A second rounded binary design is created by the repetitions of the main theme within the A section: after a two-bar introduction the main theme is presented and immediately repeated, closing the first half of the rounded binary design and following a ten-bar contrasting section ("I got no locks on my doors"), the main theme returns, rounding out the form (see Figure 3).

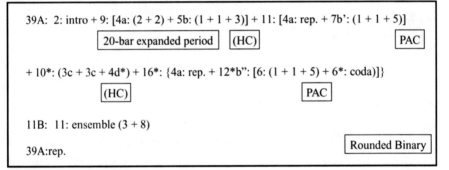

Figure 3 "I Got Plenty O' Nuttin'," form

In contrast to "They Pass By Singin'" and "Oh Little Stars," "I Got Plenty O' Nuttin'" projects confidence and triumphant joy, and much of this effect is achieved by formal repetition. In addition, Porgy's newfound stability and optimism are projected by the phrase structure of the A section, which comprises an expanded 16-bar parallel period (see Figure 4). The first nine bars form the antecedent, with a four-bar main idea followed by a five-bar contrasting idea. In the consequent phrase, Gershwin expands the contrasting idea to seven bars by adding a perfect authentic cadence at the end of the phrase (emphasizing Porgy's rhetorical question "what for?").

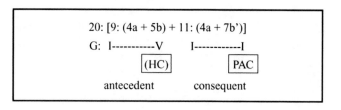

Figure 4 "I Got Plenty O' Nuttin'," main theme

Like that of "Oh Little Stars," the harmonic structure of "I Got Plenty O' Nuttin'" is straightforward. In addition to the opening section, which duplicates the brief modulation from G major to E major from "Oh Little Stars" before returning to G major once again, there is a brief contrasting section that tonicizes the mediant (B minor) with a series of tonic-subdominant chords, recalling the progression used in the E major section.

Porgy initiates the primary tone (B, $\hat{3}$ in G major) at R13+3, after arpeggiating the tonic triad in the opening two measures of his vocal line (see Figure 5). The primary tone and the tonic triad are then prolonged through an ascending middleground linear progression from D to G, which evolves in the following manner: 1) Porgy's vocal line skips up from the primary tone B to D; 2) D is coupled in the lower octave and then prolonged through continued arpeggiation of the tonic triad; 3) D moves up to E via a chromatic passing tone D♯, presented in the accompaniment (F♯ is substituted in the melody); 4) E is prolonged by a skip down to C♯ over an A major triad, the temporary subdominant (R14–2); 5) E moves to E♯ over a C♯ major triad, which then shifts directly up by half-step to the home dominant, D major, supporting F♯ in the melody; 6) F♯ moves to G over the tonic, completing the linear progression (R14+3), which is then repeated in its entirety.[48]

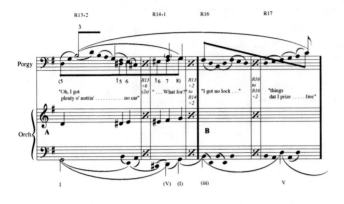

Figure 5 "I Got Plenty O' Nuttin'," voice leading

The B section begins by prolonging F♯ over a B minor triad, with the F♯ subsequently skipping down to D in the melody (R16). F♯ is then connected to C, functioning as an upper neighbor to the primary tone, via a large-scale unfolding of the diminished fifth F♯–C, which is perpetuated by the arpeggiation of the dominant at R17. The A section is then repeated, and the fundamental line closes to the tonic, though 2̂ is only implied in the vocal line: first F♯, then F (over a minor dominant), is substituted at R26+1ff., and the number finally closes with a plagal motion from IV to I.

This is Porgy's first truly successful musical number. Filled with jubilant repetitions and strong linear and harmonic closure, the song portrays a very different Porgy from the man the audience meets in Act I. It is clear that Porgy's situation has changed drastically for the better: Bess is living with him and they have grown to love each other. The only previous hint we get of their new relationship comes in Act I, Scene 2, when they enter together to give money to Serena to help with the burial of her husband, Robbins, who was killed by Crown. Serena refuses to accept money from Crown's woman, but Bess tells her: "Dis ain't Crown's money. Porgy give me my money now." Thus, the responsibility falls to "I Got Plenty O' Nuttin'" to convey the change in Porgy's situation.

The musical closure in the song also reflects Porgy's attainment of his main objective for Act II, Scene 1: to publicize his happiness (so that Bess feels more like his "woman"). In order to persuade Bess to stay with him, Porgy has to get the neighbors to accept and welcome Bess—and they begin to come around after seeing how Bess has transformed Porgy, noting "Porgy change since dat woman come to live with he. He ain' cross with chillen no more, an ain' you hear how he an' Bess all de time singin' in their room?"

In contrast to the brief, almost parenthetical ensemble section in "I Got Plenty O' Nuttin'," the B section of "Buzzard Song," Porgy's next number is longer than its main theme, making the song a more authentically ternary structure (see Figure 6). There are several aspects of the song that suggest a classical treatment in the style of a Schubertian art song, including the thirty-second-note sextuplet figuration in the accompaniment and the standard ternary form of the number.[49] Porgy's mastery of such an archetypal classical idiom demonstrates that he is on solid ground: he is confident enough to foray into a dissonant, atonal B section and return to complete a recapitulation of the main theme. In addition, the A section (R73–R75+2) may be interpreted as a 17-bar sentence, another marker of the aria's relationship to the art song. After an immediate repetition of the 4-bar main theme, the A section moves into a sequential continuation (R74) that leads to the perfect authentic cadence in A minor at R75+1.

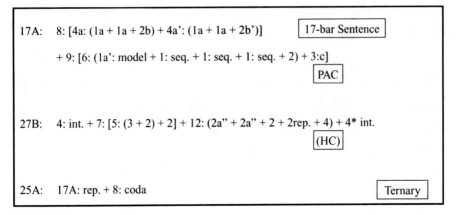

Figure 6 "Buzzard Song," form

Harmonically, "Buzzard Song" is one of the most striking numbers in *Porgy and Bess*. It begins, at R73, with a i–VI♭$^9_7$ progression that is embellished by upper-neighbor appoggiaturas on both chords.[50] At the half cadence that closes the antecedent phrase of the main theme (R73+3), Gershwin weakens the cadential dominant by adding the seventh and substituting an unresolved sixth above the bass for the fifth (V$^7_6$–). However, the use of the unresolved sixth (C♯ moves to C instead of B) permits Gershwin to maintain the motivic descending minor second that appears in each measure of the theme.

In the developmental interpolation within the consequent phrase (R74 to R75), Gershwin uses modal mixture to create a chromatic descending-step sequence, applying a secondary dominant seventh to each chord in the sequence: iv–[V^7]→ ♭iv♭^{5}– [V^7]→iii♭–[V^7]→ii♯^{5}–VI♭^{7}. The addition of the secondary dominants creates a sequence of tritone root movements in the bass (D–A♭, D♭–G, C–G♭, B–F) that add an enormous amount of dissonance and harmonic tension to the interpolation. In this context, the cadential $^6_4$ that arrives at R75–2 sounds particularly strong. Gershwin's subsequent evasion of the perfect authentic cadence implied by the cadential $^6_4$, which he accomplishes by substituting V$^4_2$ for V^7 and forcing the harmony to move to I^6 instead of I (R75–2), is therefore rendered all the more striking.

As for the B section (R76–4 to R78), it begins with an atonal passage that develops the tritones initially presented in the sequential interpolation. The five measures at the core of the section (R76 to R77–2) alternate octatonic tetrachords 4–z29 and 4–z15, built on the A–E♭ tritone. At R77, the atonal tetrachords are replaced by an ascending chromatic sequence of first-inversion chords that inverts the contour of the progression from the A section interpolation, leading the music to a strong half cadence on V that prepares the return of the A section.

Porgy initiates the primary tone (C, $\hat{3}$ in A minor) at R73, in the first measure of the number (see Figure 7). C is then prolonged through a descending arpeggiation of the tonic triad, and the antecedent phrase is repeated. In the interpolation, D ($\hat{4}$, harmonized by the subdominant) is prolonged as an upper neighbor to the primary tone via an 8–10 linear intervallic pattern in the outer voices that leads the melody down to A before returning it to D (over IV^t) again at R75–1.[51] $\hat{3}$ is then reinstated over III and a middleground replica of the fundamental line is closed over a perfect authentic cadence to end the A section (R75+1).

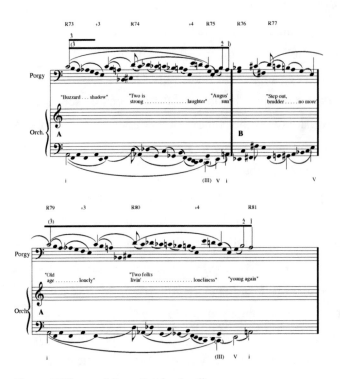

Figure 7 "Buzzard Song," voice leading

The B section prepares the return of D as a middleground upper neighbor with an arpeggiation of vii°7 of D major in the melody (G–B♭–C♯) at R76. A prolongation of the structural dominant ensues in R77 to R78: D is prolonged by arpeggiation to B over V^6, and B is then prolonged through a chromatic voice exchange (G♯→G, B→B♭) before moving down to E over V. C is reinstated at the beginning of the recapitulation and the 3-line closes to the tonic at the final cadence.

The form, harmony, and linear structure of "Buzzard Song" portray Porgy at his most confident. Porgy's main objective in this scene is to chase off doom (in the form of the buzzard); he hopes that by defying fate he will be able to convince Bess (and himself) that they have a chance at a future together. He is successful, though the chromaticism and atonal harmonies in the number indicate that the matter is far from settled. For the time being, however, Porgy has cleared himself some room to hope for a future with Bess.[52]

"Bess, You Is My Woman Now," the first duet between Porgy and Bess, is unlike the majority of the numbers discussed so far in that it does not have a large-scale contrasting middle section. Instead, Gershwin uses the main theme as a rondo refrain, creating a number that builds upon and strengthens the formal stability Porgy achieved in "I Got Plenty O' Nuttin'" and "Buzzard Song" (see Figure 8).[53] Having just given Sporting Life a warning never to come near Bess again, Porgy demonstrates his confidence by modulating from B♭ major to the distant key of F♯ major, using an intermediary modulation to D major as a transition from one key to the other. Because the contrasting B and C sections shown in Figure 8 also begin with variations of the four-bar A theme, the rondo form is also reflected in the four-bar phrases that form the subsections of the number, organized in an ABACABADAEA design (visible in Figure 8 by reading the lower-case letters from left to right).

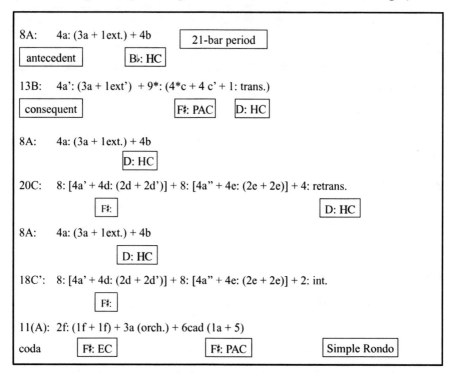

Figure 8 "Bess, You Is My Woman," form (Gershwin, *Porgy and Bess*, II/1)

The duet begins with an 8-bar theme in which Porgy establishes B♭ major. After a contrasting section, in which Porgy outlines the large-scale tonal plan of the number by modulating through D major to F♯ major, Bess follows Porgy's lead, singing the main theme in D major. Eager to prove her devotion to Porgy, she then jumps to a cadential $^6_4$ chord in F♯ major in the opening of the C section, hoping to convince him with both her determination and her passion (she sings her second highest pitch, A♯, in this section).[54] Porgy, who is more cautious, shifts the number back into D major at the end of the C section, showing he is not quite ready yet to declare victory. In the varied repetition of the C section, however, he is won over and declares "I knows you means it, I seen it in yo' eyes, Bess." He continues to lead the way for Bess, moving the music toward the final perfect authentic cadence in F♯ major.

As in "Buzzard Song" and "I Got Plenty O' Nuttin'," Porgy's newfound confidence and stability is reflected by the phrase structure of the duet. The opening two sections, for example, combine to form an expanded 20-bar parallel period: the A section forms the standard 8-bar antecedent phrase, stating the main idea and then leading the music to a half cadence at R96–1, while the B section serves as an expanded consequent, repeating the main idea and then sequencing the 4-bar contrasting idea to achieve the modulation to F♯ major.

The most striking harmonic feature of the number is the manner in which Gershwin modulates from B♭ major to F♯ major, both within the B section and in the duet as a whole. The first modulation takes place from R96 to R97, where Gershwin uses a combination of third-related shifts and parallel mode shifts to reach the new key. To begin with, he creates a common-chord modulation from B♭ major to D minor (the relative minor of the dominant) using a D minor triad as a pivot chord (R96+2). He then shifts to the parallel major (D major) by following a V$^4_3$ (common to both keys) with a B minor seventh chord (vi$^6_5$) instead of a B♭ major seventh chord and continuing on a G major ninth chord (IV$^9_7$). This entire process takes place within the span of only four measures, but because Gershwin's real goal is F♯ major, D minor and D major were only transitional keys. Thus, at R97–2, he creates another tonal shift, using the dominant/parallel combination once again. This time, a D major triad serves as the pivot chord (functioning as I in D major and VI in F♯ minor simultaneously), and the entire modulatory passage is transposed up a major third, exchanging F♯ minor for F♯ major and arriving at a perfect authentic cadence at R97+2.

Since the middle section of the duet is already in D major (thanks to a one-measure transition at the end of the B section), Gershwin accomplishes the large-scale modulation to F♯ major in the C section (at R99+2) by transposing the pivotal measure from the previous set of modulations (R96+2). Instead of moving from V⁴₃ to the submediant, however, the music moves directly to a cadential ⁶₄ chord in F♯ major, motivated by Bess's passionate declaration "I ain' goin'! You hear me sayin'," (R99+4). I⁶₄ is then prolonged through an octave descent in the bass, embellished by the addition of a French augmented-sixth chord preceding the return of I⁶₄ at R100. Despite the expectations created by the long prolongation of the cadential ⁶₄, cadential closure is ultimately evaded by motion to $\hat{4}$ in the bass, supporting a "blue note" chord (a V⁴₂ with a raised fifth) and the addition of a sixth to the subsequent tonic triad (R100+4).

Because it modulates twice and does not return to the key in which it began, "Bess, You Is My Woman Now" exhibits an unconventional fundamental structure (see Figure 9). The opening A section establishes D in the melody as the first note of what may be seen in retrospect as the initial note of an arpeggiation up to the primary tone A♯ ($\hat{3}$ in F♯ major). Supported by B♭ major harmony, D is prolonged by a descent to an inner-voice F in Porgy's melodic line, and then by a motion to C over F major ($\hat{2}$ and V, respectively, in the local key of B♭ major). The melodic motion D–C functions as an interruption in the local key of B♭ major, one that is never brought to completion, and a detail that will have important ramifications for the discussion of dramatic implications to follow. In the B section, D is reinstated in the melody, re-harmonized as $\hat{1}$ of D major, and prolonged by a middleground lower neighbor C♯, which is supported by the subsequent modulation to F♯ major. C♯ is then prolonged in the melody through an arpeggiation down to F♯, which also provides a middleground replica of the fundamental line (A♯–G♯–F♯).

In the repetition of the A section at R98, the opening material is transposed to D major, and F♯ becomes the prolonged pitch in the melody. Once again, there is an interrupted middleground descent from $\hat{3}$ to $\hat{2}$, supported by motion from the tonic to the dominant in the local key of D major. F♯ is re-harmonized as $\hat{1}$ in F♯ major and is prolonged by a downward arpeggiation of the tonic triad before the background arpeggiation up to the primary tone is completed at R100, where A♯ is established in Bess's vocal line over an F♯ major tonic triad in second inversion.

Although A♯ is prolonged by an arpeggiation down to $\hat{1}$ at R100+4, there is no intervening dominant to support a linear descent. A true structural dominant does not arrive to support a melodic descent to $\hat{2}$ until the coda, and when it does arrive, at R105+3, $\hat{2}$ is present in the melody only by implication. In fact, A♯ is substituted for G♯ in the top line of the orchestra and in Porgy's vocal line, further obscuring $\hat{2}$. The arrival of $\hat{1}$ in Bess's melody at R106 closes the fundamental line, but $\hat{1}$ does not receive solid tonic support until four measures later, further weakening the fundamental structure.

"Bess, You Is My Woman Now" sends mixed messages to the listener. On one hand, the rondo form and periodic phrase structure of the main theme project confidence and stability, akin to that of "I Got Plenty O' Nuttin'." On the other hand, the modulatory nature of the number, its many interrupted linear descents, and the evasion of both linear and harmonic closure in its final section betray an uncertainty that both Porgy and Bess are desperately trying to hide. Just before the duet begins, Sporting Life makes the first of two offers of cocaine to Bess. Though she musters the willpower to reject him three times, Sporting Life persists and the tension in the music (increased

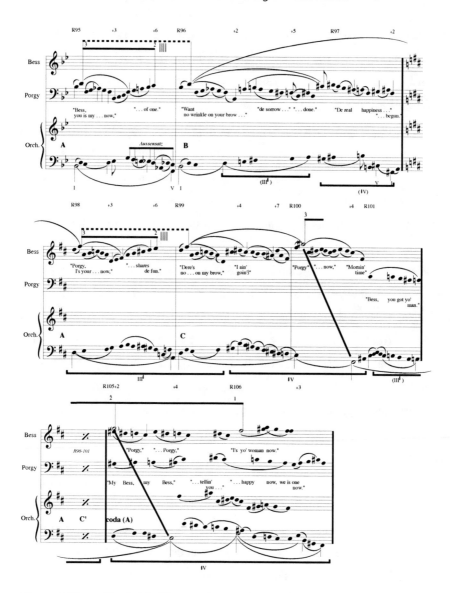

Figure 9 "Bess, You Is My Woman Now," voice leading

rhythmic activity, chromaticism, and a long trill, R88–89) indicates that he may prevail in the end. Porgy, who has been watching the exchange unobserved, grabs hold of Sporting Life and threatens to wring his neck if he comes near Bess again. Thus, both Porgy's main objective for this scene (to convince Bess to stay) and Bess's main objective (to prove her devotion to Porgy) take on a sense of urgency as the duet begins. Each time the duet modulates up a third, the sense of urgency increases, fueled primarily by the upward expansion of Bess's tessitura (which culminates with the arrival of the high A♯ at R100).

Within this larger context, Porgy's opening declarations may be seen in a different light. For example, the repetitions in his opening line "Bess, you is my woman now, you is, you is" show that he is trying hard to convince Bess of what he is saying, rather than simply making a statement. When he says, "de sorrow of de past is all done," there is no doubt that he is referring to Bess's addiction as well as to her relationship with Crown. Moreover, Bess's passionate declaration, "I ain' goin'! You hear me sayin', if you ain' goin', wid you I'm stayin'," (R99+4) comes after failed attempts by both Porgy and Bess to bring the main theme to closure on the tonic, and may thus be seen as a frantic bid to force closure upon the music. That it takes place over an unstable second-inversion triad and consists of nothing more than an expanded neighbor motion (C♯–D♯–C♯) reveals the frailty of Bess's resolve. Not coincidentally, the only moment in the duet where Porgy and Bess sing in unison, at the line "From dis minute I'm tellin' you, I keep dis vow," is a variation on this same neighbor note figure.

As he did in the case of the previous duet, Gershwin constructs "I Loves You Porgy" in simple rondo form, using the main theme as the refrain (see Figure 10). Because the subsections of the number do not contain repetitions, however, and because the contrasting sections depart substantially from the key, the effect of the recapitulation of the A section is markedly different in this number. It is as if Bess is clinging to the refrain for dear life, afraid that if she wanders too far from it, she will lose Porgy's love for good. Once again, it is Porgy who guides Bess back to the home key, re-establishing F major with a half cadence at the end of the B and C sections. The main theme, with its periodic structure, also echoes the previous duet, though in this case it is a much shorter and simpler 8-bar period that does not contain a modulation to a foreign key.

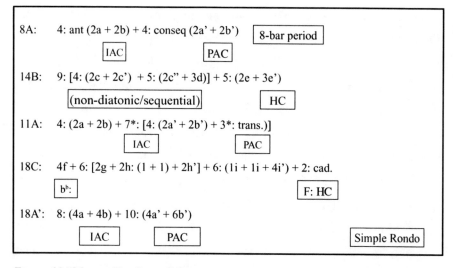

Figure 10 "I Loves You Porgy," form

The main harmonic points of interest occur in the "solo" departure sections of this concerto-rondo form, rather than in the refrain. In the B section, for example, as an anguished Bess describes what it will be like when Crown returns for her, Gershwin abandons F major entirely, in favor of a sequential passage filled with half-diminished seventh chords and augmented-sixth chords (R211 to 213–1). Anticipated by a chromatic wedge figure at R211–1, the first half of this dissonant passage consists of a three-measure passage that hints at A minor ($a^{add\#6}$, $E^{\flat 9}$, E^9), a sequential repetition of the passage in C minor, and a measure of linear augmented-sixth chords separating the two passages. At R212, the harmony becomes even more jarring—half-diminished seventh chords alternating with augmented triads—and the passage ends with an $F\#^{add\#6}$ chord leaping by tritone to a C^9, the dominant of the home key.

In the C section, the duet once again departs from F major, modulating into a B♭ minor/D♭ major hybrid (R214 to 217). This time it is Porgy's rising tide of emotion that prompts the key change: he tells her in this section that he will, in effect, take care of Crown. The section begins with motion from the tonic to the dominant in B♭ minor, but the diatonicism of both chords is complicated by chromatic pitches: the tonic includes a lowered seventh and the dominant contains both a major and a minor third, in addition to a lowered ninth. In the second half of the passage, Gershwin tips the balance toward D♭ major, creating a I^{9add6}–vi^9–IV^{13}–V^{11} progression in R215 to 216. The ending of the passage, however, like the ending of the B section, provides a final jolt of dissonance, with a descending chromatic sequence that winds up on an inconclusive second-inversion form of the D♭ major I^{9add6} before moving to V^{13} in F major for another half cadence in the home key (R216 to 217).

The primary tone, C ($\hat{5}$ in F major), is initiated by an arpeggiation at the opening of the duet (R210), and is subsequently prolonged by a middleground replica of the fundamental 5-line that spans the A section (see Figure 11). The analysis of this opening section from a linear perspective is complicated, however, by the fact that the melody consists almost entirely of five-note chordal arpeggiations (arpeggiated ninth chords). The arpeggiations create frequent displacements in the melody, as in the opening two bars of the number, where E arrives on the downbeat of R210 instead of the primary tone C. In addition, the use of sevenths and ninths in the arpeggiations leads to the substitutions of two pitches in the middleground replica of the fundamental line: C is substituted for B♭ ($\hat{4}$) over the subdominant at R210+1 and A is substituted for G ($\hat{2}$) at R210+6. Although these substitutions weaken the fundamental line, they strengthen the connection between the structural levels, creating a middleground composing-out of the F major arpeggiation that opens the duet.

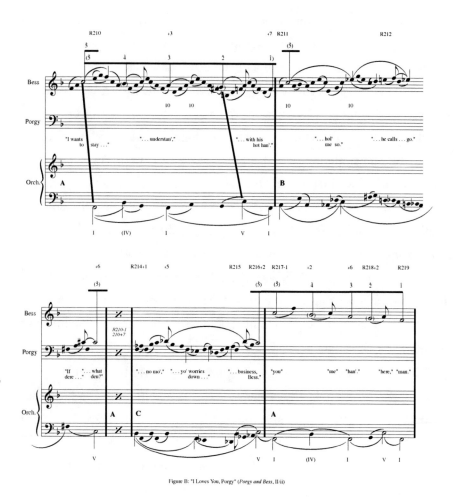

Figure B: "I Loves You, Porgy" (*Porgy and Bess*, II/ii)

Figure 11 "I Loves You Porgy," voice leading

Though the intervening harmonies stray far from the home key, the contrasting sections of the rondo outline fairly simple melodic and harmonic progressions. The B section prolongs $\hat{5}$ with a skip up to E♭, supported by the C minor sequential repetition of the harmony and the primary tone is reinstated over the dominant at the end of the section. In the C section, D♭ is the focus of the melodic progression, and is resolved as an upper neighbor to the primary tone at R216+2. With the final return of the A section, the primary tone is reaffirmed over the tonic and the fundamental line closes on the tonic over a perfect authentic cadence at R219.

Based on the conclusions that were derived from the structure of "Bess You Is My Woman Now," it is safe to say that rondo forms are no longer a guaranteed sign of confidence and stability. Rather, it seems that in the interest of revealing their underlying anxiety about the future, Gershwin has his characters singing A sections one *too many* times, as if by sheer force of will they could convince themselves that nothing untoward will befall them. Obviously, this strategy was not greatly successful when Porgy and Bess employed it in their first duet (Crown snatched Bess in the next scene), and they had no reason to believe that mere willpower would prevail here. Yet, despite their misgivings, each of the characters achieves their main objective in the scene: Bess convinces Porgy to take her back and protect her from Crown, and Porgy reassures Bess and calms her fears. It is also worth noting that, although Porgy guides the return to the home key in both numbers, it is Bess who closes the fundamental line, demonstrating that the attainment of Porgy's main objectives depends entirely on her.

The first of Porgy's two E major numbers that form the closing section of the opera, "Bess, Oh Where's My Bess?" is also the third in the series of simple rondos that Porgy sings in Act II and III (see Figure 12). As in "Bess, You Is My Woman Now," this number combines the coda with the final refrain, leaving the return of the main theme to the orchestra while the vocal line develops new melodic material. Unlike most of the other numbers in the opera, the main theme does not conform to either a sentential or a periodic phrase structure. Instead, it ends with a comparatively weak imperfect authentic cadence (supporting an added sixth in the melody) that permits a seamless segue into the contrasting sections. These sound at first like they will be continuations of the main theme, but soon break new harmonic ground of their own.

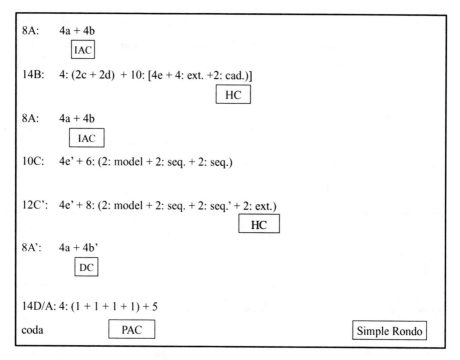

Figure 10 "I Loves You Porgy," form

The distinguishing characteristic of this number is its large amount of sequential material. In the C section (R160+1), after restating the four-bar theme from the second half of the B section, Gershwin uses a descending minor third (E♭–C) as a model (R161–3) and twice sequences it down chromatically by half step (D–B, D♭–B♭). He then sequences the entire C section up chromatically by whole step (R161+4), producing another set of descending minor thirds (F–D, E–C♯, E♭–C) at R162+2. In the final sequence, however, he replaces C with A♭ (R163–2), in order to be able to reinterpret the final pitch enharmonically as an added sixth over a B⁹ chord, the dominant of the home key.

There are three foreground harmonic events that warrant a brief discussion. At R156+1, Gershwin outlines the pitches of a Neapolitan ♭II chord (F major) in the lower voices of the accompaniment, superimposing a $[V^{M7}] \rightarrow V$ in the upper voices. This juxtaposition, which combines elements of both modal mixture and tonicization, is strongly reminiscent of the chromatic harmonies of Sporting Life's musical numbers, and serves as a poignant reminder of the reason for Bess's absence. The skewed secondary dominant resolves to a V^7_{sub6} on the third beat of R156+1.

Another harmonic conundrum may be found at R157+6. Here Gershwin superimposes a ii^7 over a G♯ pedal tone in the bass, subsequently adding a B♯ (decorated by a neighbor tone) in an inner voice. The resulting harmonic configuration (G♯–F♯–A–B♯–E) sounds like a cross between a half-diminished ii^7 and a I^6. Because it is immediately followed by a $[V^7_{sub6}] \rightarrow ii$, this harmony can also be interpreted as a secondary dominant ($[V^9_{sub6}] \rightarrow vi$), part of the descending-fifths progression of applied chords that leads to the perfect authentic cadence at R159.[55]

Finally, instead of setting Porgy's final climactic high E at R165–2 with a tonic triad, Gershwin uses a collection of pitches completely foreign to the key of E major, building an eleventh chord on ♭$\hat{5}$ and chromatically altering some of the chord members. The ensuing chord (B♭–D–F–G♯–C–E) is never resolved to the dominant, but moves directly to the tonic instead at R165+1.

The sequential C section and C^1 section melodies (described above) are both harmonized by sequences of descending chromatic fifths: E♭–A♭, D–G, D♭–G♭, and F–B♭, E–A, E♭–A♭, respectively. Taken as a whole, they form a harmonic double-neighbor that embellishes the key of A♭ major, which can be understood enharmonically as ♯III (G♯ major) in the home key of E major.

The primary tone, B ($\hat{5}$ in E major), is initiated at R156, and is subsequently prolonged by a middleground 5–6 motion to an upper neighbor C♯ at R156+5 (see Figure 13). In the B section, a middleground voice exchange prolongs E in the melody, a consonant skip from the primary tone. At R158+4, the primary tone returns by implication over the dominant. In the C section, the upper-neighbor C♯ ($\hat{6}$) from the refrain is enharmonically respelled as D♭ and is used as the controlling melodic tone of the first sequential passage; E♭, likewise, controls the C^1 section, and may be respelled as D♯. Acting as $\hat{7}$, supported by a respelled ♯II, this pitch forms an important registral link with the end of the number, where it connects to Porgy's final high E. This connection is strengthened by the return of $\hat{7}$ immediately prior to the final E, now properly spelled as D♯.

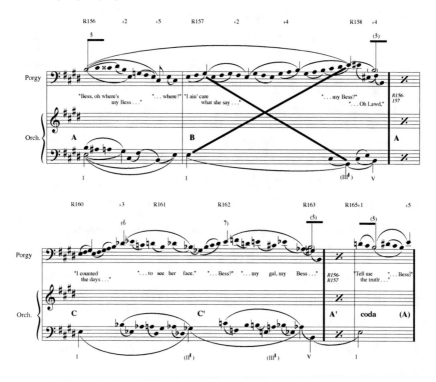

Figure 13 "Oh, Bess, Oh Where's My Bess?" voice leading

The middleground $\hat{5}$–$\hat{6}$–$\hat{7}$ ascent, ending as it does on the leading tone, is a poignant reminder of Porgy's unfulfilled longing for Bess. This motive is established at the foreground level in the opening measures of the number, when it asks the question "Bess, oh where's my Bess?" Though it stops short of the tonic, the ascending contour of Porgy's opening melodic gesture is interrogative and hopeful.[56] In contrast to this opening gesture, the subsequent descending thirds, the first of which is emphasized by the "blue note" G♮, indicate Porgy's despair.

All of the foreground harmonic anomalies discussed above occur at significant dramatic moments in the number. The augmented-sixth chord at R156+1 occurs on the word "where" in the phrase "Bess, oh *where's* my

Bess?" emphasizing the source of Porgy's distress. The hybrid chord at R157+6 occurs on the word "Bess" in the same phrase, replacing the tonic that would have typically supported $\hat{1}$ in Porgy's line, as does the chromatic chord built on $\flat\hat{5}$ at R 165–2 ("show me de *way*!"). These harmonic signs of Porgy's distress, combined with the lack of a stable phrase structure, lend a sense of desperation to Porgy's questioning of his friends. The chromatically descending sequences, which evoke the lament, hint at Porgy's flagging courage.

Porgy's main objective (to force his friends to reveal Bess's whereabouts) is not achieved during the song. Though Serena and Maria let Porgy know that Bess has fallen in with Sporting Life, taken up drugs again, and gone far away, it is not until after the number that Porgy learns she has gone to New York. The combination of the ascending $\hat{5}$–$\hat{6}$–$\hat{7}$ middleground motion in his vocal line and the failure of the fundamental line to descend from the primary tone simultaneously project Porgy's yearning for closure and his lack of fulfillment.

Very little need be said about Porgy's final number, because it is a continuation of "Bess, Oh Where's My Bess?" From a formal standpoint, it is the simplest of Porgy's numbers, consisting of nothing more than a single expanded phrase: a 32-bar period that is actually a 16-bar period in 4/2 hypermeter (see Figure 14). As we have seen in his other numbers, most readily observed in "I Got Plenty O' Nuttin'," Porgy often uses periodic phrase structure to project his confidence and self-assurance, and that is certainly the case in the final number.[57]

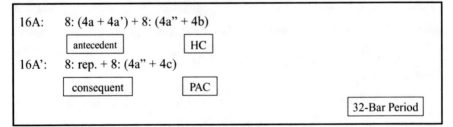

Figure 14 "Oh Lawd, I'm On My Way," form

The song is harmonically straightforward, employing only a few added sixth chords and an occasional secondary dominant, but its fundamental structure is unique because it offers one of the few glimpses of a "gapped" linear progression in *Porgy and Bess* (see Figure 15). After establishing the primary tone (B, $\hat{5}$ in E major) with a first-order arpeggiation at R177, Porgy prolongs it throughout the A section with a series of consonant skips and a middleground $\hat{5}$–$\hat{6}$–$\hat{7}$ motion that recalls "Bess, Oh Where's My Bess?" After repeating the first half of the antecedent, Gershwin alters Porgy's vocal line so that it descends to the tonic. Rather than descending through $\hat{4}$ (supported by V^7) to $\hat{3}$ (supported by I), prolonging $\hat{3}$ temporarily, and then moving to the final $\hat{2}$–$\hat{1}$ over a perfect authentic cadence, Gershwin waits until the last possible moment to introduce $\hat{4}$ (supported by ii) and then moves directly to $\hat{2}$ in the same measure (R180+6). The omission of $\hat{3}$ creates a gapped fundamental line, which has important ramifications for the interpretation of this final song.

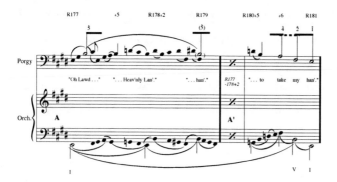

Figure 15 "Oh Lawd, I'm On My Way," voice leading

Even while Porgy puts on a brave face for his friends and finishes the opera in heroic triumph with what seems to be the most straightforward of musical numbers, two features of the fundamental structure of "Oh Lawd, I'm On My Way" reveal the fact that the outcome of Porgy's quest is far from certain. First, the yearning chromatic motion from the primary tone up to the leading tone (B–C#–D–D#), a reference to the main theme of the previous number, communicates Porgy's desire to be reunited with Bess, but leaves that desire unfulfilled by refusing a complete ascent to the tonic. It is a middleground "cliffhanger" of compound melody, dangling the leading tone as the apex of a steady ascent in the tessitura of Porgy's vocal line. Second, the gapped fundamental line seems to imply that Porgy is, quite literally, jumping to conclusions. Porgy assumes that because his is a righteous cause he will prevail; the music begs to differ.

Porgy's role presents a difficult challenge, comprising a total of eight numbers. As Figure 16 shows, these numbers may be grouped together as components of a background 3-line in A minor. The first three numbers, "They Pass By Singin'," "Oh, Little Stars," and "I Got Plenty O' Nuttin'," form an *Anstieg* up to the primary tone C, which is initiated in "Buzzard Song." As mentioned previously, this is consistent with Porgy's growing confidence, in that the first two numbers are formally vague and it is not until "Buzzard Song" that Porgy ventures away from the home key into atonal dissonance within a number. The primary tone is then prolonged through a neighbor motion to $\flat\hat{2}$ (enharmonically respelled as $\sharp\hat{1}$ and supported by $\sharp$VI) in the duet "Bess, You Is My Woman Now." After the reinstatement of the primary tone over the submediant in "I Loves You, Porgy," the fundamental line moves to $\hat{2}$ over the dominant in "Bess, Oh Where's My Bess?" and is prolonged through Porgy's final number, "Oh Lawd, I'm On My Way."

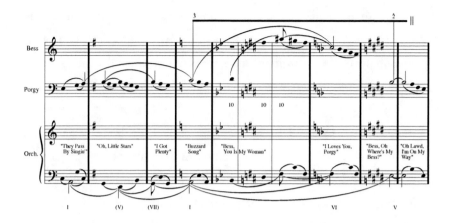

Figure 16 Porgy (background)

Summary

Porgy and Bess serves as an admirable introduction to the multi-movement permanent interruption. By declaring that any piece that reaches a final tonic gives "the effect of incompleteness,"[58] Schenker intended to demote such pieces to the level of second-class citizens; yet, the interruption of Porgy's line on $\hat{2}$ structurally reinforces the ambiguity built into the plot's ending by DuBose Heyward. Though Porgy announces his intention to go to New York City in search of Bess, the audience is left with many unanswered questions as the curtain falls: Will he reach New York safely? Will he be able to find Bess? Will she agree to return with him to Catfish Row? Will Sporting Life permit Porgy to take her back? Will she even be alive when he finds her? Rather than resolve all of these questions, Heyward creates a cinematic ending. Porgy rides off into the sunset on his goat cart as the curtain falls and the orchestra plays on—the theatrical equivalent of a fade-out. A return to Porgy's original key of A minor, especially with the inclusion of a Picardy third in the tonic at the final cadence, would indicate a level of conclusiveness that is literally "out of character" with the story told by the libretto.

From a theoretical perspective, analyzing the multi-movement background structure of Porgy's role raises three new questions. First, how should the analyst select a primary tone for songs or arias that do not have a complete background structure of their own? In "They Pass By Singin'," for example, Porgy's melody emphasizes E as $\hat{3}$ of C major at the opening of the number, only to conclude by focusing on A after the song has spent time both in C major and A minor. In the absence of a conventional primary tone (i.e., one that initiates a descent toward a tonic or supports other linear prolongations), the next logical choice is the tonic itself, since it is the most stable and consonant melodic tone in any given tonal piece. For this reason, the background graph of Porgy's role (refer again to Figure 16) selects A as the "static primary tone" of the song, prolonged by a consonant skip from the opening E and by a lower-neighbor G.

The second issue involves "Bess, You Is My Woman." How should the analyst select a primary tone for numbers that begin and end in different keys? Most Schenkerian analysts assign priority to the latter key, reading the first closely related key as an auxiliary cadence that delays the arrival of the primary tone through large-scale harmonic substitution.[59] In the case of "Bess, You Is My Woman," however, this is more difficult to do because the duet modulates chromatically by major third from B♭ major through D major to F♯ major; B♭ major must be read as a consonant skip to a consonant skip, placing greater emphasis on D major as the intermediary key. This interpretation is fortuitously supported by the formal design of the duet, in which D occurs twice and occupies twice as much space of B♭ major. Nonetheless, the concluding key of F♯ major must be enharmonically reinterpreted as G♭ major, the distantly related key of ♭VII in A minor, supporting ♭$\hat{2}$ (Bess's climactic high A♯, respelled as B♭), creating a middleground harmonic dissonance similar to those discuss in the background of *Treemonisha*.

Finally, what is the best interpretation of the pentatonic "gapped line" in "Oh Lawd, I'm On My Way"? Given that it includes four five pitches of a 5-line, that it is stable in E major throughout, and that it concludes with a descent to the tonic over a perfect authentic cadence, this song is best understood as a folk "inflection" of a 5-line that initiates B as its primary tone and skips over $\hat{3}$ due to the nature of its basic melodic material. [60] Therefore, "Oh Lawd, I'm On My Way" prolongs the background interruption of the previous number by repeating B ($\hat{2}$) as a common primary tone between the two numbers.

ENDNOTES

[1] David Ewen, *American Composers: A Biographical Dictionary* (London: Robert Hale, 1982), 252.

[2] Edward Jablonski, *Gershwin* (New York: Doubleday, 1987), x.

[3] Ibid., xiv.

[4] Edward Jablonski and Lawrence D. Stewart, *The Gershwin Years* (New York: Doubleday, 1973), 15–16.

[5] Jablonski, *Gershwin*, xii.

[6] Ibid., xv.

[7] Jablonski and Stewart, *The Gershwin Years*, 189. Gershwin himself rejected a subject involving the American Indian, which he discussed with the Metropolitan Opera in 1929. See Jablonski, *Gershwin*, xiii.

[8] Deena Rosenberg, *Fascinating Rhythm: The Collaboration of George and Ira Gershwin* (New York: Dutton, 1991), 265.

[9] Ibid.

[10] Ibid., 263.

[11] John Andrew Johnson, "Gershwin's *Blue Monday* (1922) and the Promise of Success," in *The Gershwin Style: New Looks at the Music of George Gershwin*, ed. Wayne Schneider (Oxford: Oxford University Press, 1999), 116.

[12] Jablonski, *Gershwin*, 165–6.

[13] Ibid. Gershwin also met Kurt Weill in Berlin and Alban Berg in Vienna during this trip. See Jablonski, *Gershwin*, 165, 167.

[14] Ibid., 195.

[15] Jablonski and Stewart, *The Gershwin Years*, 112.

[16] Ibid., 113.

[17] Hollis Alpert, *The Life and Times of "Porgy and Bess": The Story of an American Classic* (New York: Alfred A. Knopf, 1990), 51.

[18] Jablonski and Stewart, *The Gershwin Years*, 190–1.

[19] Ibid., 192. Heyward released the rights to Jolson on October 17, 1932.

[20] Ibid., 187, 202.

[21] Jablonski, *Gershwin*, 265.

[22] Ibid., 264.

[23] Jablonski and Stewart, *The Gershwin Years*, 203.

[24] Ibid., 211.

[25] Ibid., 212.

[26] Ibid., 233.

[27] Jablonski, *Gershwin*, 232–33.

28 The extent of Schillinger's influence on *Porgy and Bess* is discussed in detail in Wayne D. Shirley, "'Rotating' *Porgy and Bess*," in Schneider, *The Gershwin Style*, 21–34.

29 Jablonski and Stewart, *The Gershwin Years*, 229.

30 Jablonski, *Gershwin*, 288.

31 Jablonski and Stewart, *The Gershwin Years*, 231. Musicologist Charles Hamm argues that it was never Gershwin's intent for *Porgy and Bess* to be considered an opera. See Charles Hamm, "Towards a New Reading of Gershwin," in Schneider, *The Gershwin Style*, 3–18, and "The Theatre Guild Production of *Porgy and Bess*," *Journal of the American Musicological Society* 40 (1987): 495–532.

32 Jablonski, *Gershwin*, 289.

33 Ibid.

34 Alpert, *Porgy and Bess*, 115.

35 Ibid., 116.

36 Ibid., 118. Thomson's rancor may have been motivated by his perception that Gershwin had capitalized on the inroads Thomson had made with *Four Saints in Three Acts*, from which Gershwin hired his musical director (Alexander Smallens), his choir (the Eva Jessye Choir) and one of his cast members (Edward Matthews, who played Jake in *Porgy*). See Jablonski, *Gershwin*, 268, and Alpert, *Porgy and Bess*, 101.

37 Alpert, *Porgy and Bess*, 118.

38 Ibid., 181–2.

39 Ibid., 179.

40 Ibid., 292.

41 Ibid., 293, 303.

42 Ibid., 298.

43 To date, *Porgy and Bess* has received scant attention from music analysts. One important exception that is particularly relevant to the present study is Steven E. Gilbert, *The Music of Gershwin* (New Haven: Yale University Press, 1995), 16–23 and 182–207.

44 Both the melody and the harmonic progression of the E major section are identical to the parallel passage in "I Got Plenty O' Nuttin'."

45 He also adds in the main theme from "I Got Plenty O' Nuttin'" at R121–1, where Porgy makes a successful roll of the dice and takes in the pot, establishing this melody as a leitmotivic symbol of Porgy's elation.

46 The harmonic motion, in half notes, from a B minor chord to a C♯ minor chord is also reminiscent of the opening progression of "Summertime" (see R17).

47 The inner-voice descent from G to E creates parallel octaves at the middleground level with the bass. Such voice-leading "errors" are by no means anomalous in the opera, and are typically broken up by foreground harmonic motion—in this case a move to ♯II in the middle of R118+4.

[48] On ascending linear structures, see David Neumeyer, "The Ascending *Urlinie*," *Journal of Music Theory* 31/2 (1987): 275–304.

[49] One of the songs in Schubert's song cycle *Winterreise* is entitled "*Die Krähe*." It features a crow that serves as a prophet of death and doom (Müller's wanderer asks, "Do you intend soon to grasp my body for your prey?"), much like the buzzard that Porgy drives away in "Buzzard Song."

[50] The introduction to the aria (R72–73) also features an octatonic embellishment of the dominant, created by the juxtaposition of tritone-related triads built on E and B♭.

[51] This passage contains a pitch-specific reference to the head motive of "It Ain't Necessarily So," D–D♭–C–C♭–B♭.

[52] When Sporting Life reappears in Act 3 and tempts Bess with cocaine again, she angrily refers to him as a "buzzard" (R73) making an explicit connection with "Buzzard Song."

[53] Here and in the two analyses that follow, the designation "rondo" is meant simply to suggest a form consisting of a series of repetitions of a main theme, interspersed with contrasting material.

[54] The modulation to F♯ major thus serves both the aesthetic purpose of distancing Porgy and Bess from their troubled past, and the practical purpose of showcasing Bess's upper tessitura.

[55] In atonal terms, this chord is an instance of 6-34 [0, 2, 4, 6, 8, 9], Scriabin's "mystic" chord. Another transposition of the chord occurs at R157+6.

[56] In a general sense, it is also an inversion of the chromatic descent in "It Ain't Necessarily So," providing yet another reminder of Bess's misfortune.

[57] The confident attitude of the number is also fueled by its lively Charleston rhythm and brisk tempo.

[58] Schenker, *Free Composition*, 126 n6.

[59] For a discussion of pieces that begin and end in different keys, see Loeb, "Dual-Key Movements."

[60] For another example of a piece that can be read as a pentatonic, "gapped" line (from 8̂!), and also as a permanent interruption, see Rachmaninoff, *Rhapsody on a Theme of Paganini*, Variation 18.

CHAPTER 6

The Multi-Movement Initial Arpeggiation: Kurt Weill's "Broadway Opera" *Street Scene* (1947)

The Nazi persecution of European Jews brought a wave of emigrants to America's shores in the 1930s and 1940s. Among the composers that fled Europe to escape the Nazis, Kurt Weill, Igor Stravinsky (1882–1971), and Ernst Krenek (1900–1991) all made important contributions to the operatic genre after relocating to the United States.[1] While Krenek chose to continue working primarily with German-language libretti (e.g., *Pallas Athena weint* in 1950 and *Der goldene Bock* in 1963–4), Stravinsky, and especially Weill, made a conscious effort to produce English-language operas that reflected aspects of their adopted homeland. In Weill's *Street Scene* (1947), the world-weary yet increasingly multicultural character of post-war American life was placed in sharp relief, while Stravinsky's *The Rake's Progress* (1951) represented another chapter in the synthesis of European musical forms and idioms with an American libretto (by W. H. Auden).

Like Schoenberg, Weill left Germany for Paris in 1933, relocating again to America in 1935, in time to attend the premiere of *Porgy and Bess*.[2] He became a United States citizen in 1943. Though he maintained some contact with colleagues in Germany after his departure, Weill lost all of the full scores to his German works when the Gestapo seized them from the offices of Universal Edition during the war.[3] Writing in response to a review of *Street Scene*, Weill declared that, from 1935 on, he considered himself an American composer, not a German one. In letters to his former German colleagues, however, his wording was more cautious: he talked of his work "over here," albeit enthusiastically, as belonging to one of two worlds.[4]

Disagreement among Weill's biographers on how best to portray the output of a composer whose artistic career spanned two continents and a number of different musical genres can be traced back to the writings of Virgil Thomson and David Drew in the 1950s. Thomson, on one hand, divided Weill's oeuvre geographically, praising the German works as "pure" and decrying the American works as "commercial."[5] On the other hand, Drew argued for the legitimacy of Weill's entire output, and advocated a unified approach to his work. As Douglas Jarman noted in his biography of Weill, Drew "almost alone among musicologists … championed Weill's cause for many years and [provided] the most perceptive and often the only source of scholarly information about Weill's output."[6]

Despite Drew's efforts, Thomson's divided view of Weill proved influential for subsequent biographers. Kim Kowalke, who was appointed president of the Kurt Weill Foundation for Music by Weill's wife, Lotte Lenya, just before her death, focused exclusively on the "European Weill" in his 1979 study.[7] Thereafter, biographers attempted to be more comprehensive, but retained the division between Weill's compositional personae. Ronald Sanders, in his 1980 "popular biography" of Weill, epitomizes this trend in claiming that the "real Weill" was a "chameleon" with no less than eight separate compositional profiles.[8] His characterization is refined in Jarman's more scholarly 1982 study, where Weill's output is divided into three categories (German instrumental music, German theatrical music, and American theatrical music),[9] yet Jarman continues to demote the American music and uses Weill's reaction to the trauma of emigration as a justification for its "anonymous" character.[10] Ronald Taylor's 1991 "literary-historical"[11] biography provides the most recent example of this strain of Weill scholarship. Following Sanders, Taylor again characterizes Weill as a "musical chameleon," lamenting the loss of "the old, the inimitable Weill," and accusing him of selling out.[12]

In the eyes of many of his biographers, Weill's success or failure as an American composer seems to be determined largely by the contemporaries against whom he is measured. Sanders, in a bid to cement Weill's reputation as a twentieth-century opera composer, compares him favorably with Hindemith and Puccini, both in terms of lyricism and sensitivity to issues of text-setting, citing with approval Andrew Porter's pronouncement in the *New Yorker* that Weill and Händel were America's and England's greatest opera composers, respectively.[13] Jarman, on the other hand, measures Weill against "the giants of twentieth-century music," including Schoenberg and Stravinsky, and declares Weill only "a minor master."[14] Taylor, for his part, judges Weill by the standards of American musical theater, comparing him to Cole Porter, Irving Berlin, Jerome Kern, George Gershwin, and Richard Rodgers, and again finds Weill's music wanting.[15]

In the past decade, however, a resurgence of interest in Weill's American works has prompted a revisionist approach on the part of biographers, resulting in a more complete and unified portrait of Weill as a serious, but successful, composer. Inspired by the publication of David Drew's handbook on Weill, the culmination of three decades of research into bridging the gap between the German and American Weill, recent biographers have rejected the "two-Weill theory" and celebrated the German and American works each on its own terms.[16] Jürgen Schebera's 1995 biography, the only major German-language biography of Weill to appear in translation, astutely compares Weill with innovators such as Marc Blitzstein, George Antheil, and Virgil Thomson, in addition to Gershwin.[17] David Farneth's 2000 survey in pictures and documents highlights Weill's efforts to create a uniquely American fusion of the Broadway and opera genres.[18] Most recently, Foster Hirsch, in a study of Weill as a composer for the stage, uses the words "hybrid " and "*chiaroscuoro*" to describe Weill's blending of serious and light elements, and hails him as heir to Gershwin's musical legacy and precursor to Stephen Sondheim and Leonard Bernstein.[19]

Like Joplin's *Treemonisha* and Gershwin's *Porgy and Bess*, Weill's American theatrical works, particularly *Street Scene*, ought rightfully to be celebrated for the ways in which they achieve a synthesis of musical theater and opera, rather than being disparaged for the ways in which they fail to measure up when evaluated solely in either category. As will be demonstrated in the remainder of this chapter, Weill was able to incorporate many of the idioms and techniques of American musical theater into *Street Scene* without sacrificing the thematic development and large-scale musico-dramatic organization that are hallmarks of opera.

The connection between *Street Scene* and *Porgy and Bess* as "Broadway operas" has been established by many writers on Weill, and is supported by numerous first-hand accounts. Reminiscing in 1979 on the dress rehearsal for *Porgy*, to which Weill was invited by Gershwin, Lotte Lenya remarked that "he listened very closely and he said 'you know, it is possible to write an opera for Broadway.'" From that point forward, Weill was "always consciously working towards an opera."[20] Weill was particularly influenced by the commercial success of Cheryl Crawford's 1942 revival of *Porgy* in which the recitatives were excised, "a strategy that Weill proposed and about which, indeed, he offered Crawford some professional advice."[21]

Indeed, the influence of Gershwin on Weill cannot be overestimated. He attended the concert given by Paul Whiteman and his orchestra at the Grosses Schauspielhaus in Berlin in 1926 and was fascinated by Gershwin's performance of *The Rhapsody in Blue*.[22] Morever, as Hirsch notes, *Porgy and Bess* was one of the first American productions Weill saw and it "remained for [him] at once a model of the kind of American opera he wanted to create and a reminder of the Broadway musical's flexible boundaries,"[23] creating in him a "keen desire to write his own *Porgy and Bess*."[24] Under pressure both from Broadway's Richard Rodgers, who claimed that his musicals *Oklahoma!* (1943) and *Carousel* (1945) had sparked a new interest in the integration of music, text, and dance,[25] and Gian-Carlo Menotti, whose one-act operas *The Telephone* and *The Medium* were double-billed at New York's Metropolitan

Opera in 1947, Weill found in Gershwin a model for the kind of synthesis he hoped would set him apart and help to establish his compositional legacy.[26]

In preparation for the composition of *Street Scene*, Weill studied Verdi scores and American folk songs.[27] In a letter to his wife dated May 1, 1945, Weill wrote, "I feel more and more like writing opera again—opera for Broadway, of course."[28] As he explained to Rouben Mamoulian, the director of *Porgy and Bess*, he planned to "avoid the conventional musical comedy technique and to work it out as a kind of popular Broadway opera."[29] In fact, Weill was so excited about the direction in which the work was headed that he wrote to his parents, Emma and Albert Weill, declaring that *Street Scene* "is the biggest and most daring project I have undertaken over here so far, because this time I'm writing a real opera for the Broadway theatre."[30]

Weill began working on the opera in November 1945, three months after the end of the war, and continued to develop it throughout 1946, under the auspices of the Playwright's Company.[31] To facilitate the musical continuity required for an opera, Weill and Elmer Rice—co-librettist and author of both the book for the opera and the play upon which it was based—"decided to have the numbers grow out of action and to have the dialogue underscored— to avoid the break between spoken word and sung word."[32] Though Weill was not entirely satisfied with the results of the experiment—he remarked, "in some parts, especially in the first act, we have not succeeded yet in blending the elements of the show. In some places we try to be too legitimate, in other places, too musical comedy"[33]—he nonetheless regarded *Street Scene* as the personal culmination of a series of steps he had taken throughout his career (both in Europe and in America) toward the unity of music and drama.[34] In the liner notes for the original cast recording, Weill speaks of two "dreams" or compositional goals: first, to write an opera in which "the spoken word as well as the dramatic action are embedded in overall musical structure," and second, to write an American opera that "could only take place on Broadway, because Broadway represents the living theatre in this country, and an American opera, as I imagined it, should be a part of the living theatre."[35]

To perform the leading roles in his Broadway opera, Weill and his director, Charles Friedman, cast singer-actors from the world of opera. Only Anne Jeffreys, who played the role of Rose Maurrant, was untested as an opera singer at the time of casting, but she was still a classically trained soprano.[36] As a counterbalance to this operatic emphasis, Weill and Friedman chose Broadway dancers for many of the supporting roles, and Weill gave over the orchestration for their dance numbers to jazz bandleader and arranger Ted Royal.[37] The numbers employing Royal's "hot" or jazzy orchestrations, however, including those for "Moon-Faced, Starry-Eyed" and "Wrapped in a Ribbon and Tied With a Bow," were not included in the original cast recording. Danny Daniels, the dancer who played Dick McGann, speculated that Weill resented having to include the jazz numbers in the production, and noted that the dancers were isolated from the rest of the cast during rehearsals.[38]

Weill's grand experiment, like Gershwin's "folk opera" only twelve years before, was met with profoundly mixed reactions, though on the whole it garnered more positive reviews than *Porgy and Bess*.[39] When it opened for a tryout in Philadelphia on December 16, 1946, however, *Street Scene* was a disaster.[40] Elmer Rice and the great Broadway director Moss Hart, who visited the tryout, advised cutting the elements of the production that were most deeply indebted to musical comedy, which Weill did, though he left some Broadway elements intact.[41] Billed as a "dramatic musical," the production opened at the Adelphi Theatre in New York on January 9, 1947, under the direction of Charles Friedman and the musical direction of Maurice Abravanel, and ran for one hundred forty-eight performances. While the generic ambiguity of *Street Scene* might have been a factor in its early exit from Broadway, the production's short run was due primarily to the fact that it opened at the same time as the enormously popular musicals *Finian's Rainbow* and *Brigadoon*.[42]

Though *Street Scene* opened on Broadway, critics including Brooks Atkinson and Olin Downes of the *New York Times* immediately identified it as an opera.[43] Downes called it "the most important step toward significantly American opera that the writer has yet encountered in the musical theater,"[44] while Atkinson praised it as "a sidewalk opera" that established Weill as "the foremost music maker in the American theater."[45] John Chapman, of the *New York Daily News*, hailed it as "a moving, remarkable opera—a work of great individuality that makes no compromise with Broadway formula."[46] Later productions of the opera, however, did not fare as well. When Julius Rudel, general director and principal conductor of the New York City Opera, mounted *Street Scene* in 1959, one reviewer dubbed it a "Broadway-slick musical ... wrapped in an operatic ribbon and tied with a Broadway bow."[47]

This ambivalence toward Weill's incorporation of musical theater idioms into his compositions was reflected even more acutely among his contemporaries. In America, Douglas Moore, the composer of *The Devil and Daniel Webster* (1939) and *The Ballad of Baby Doe* (1956), despised both *Street Scene* and Weill's music in general, while Aaron Copland supported him, helping to get him nominated for membership in the American Academy of Arts and Letters.[48] Elliott Carter praised Weill's workmanlike technique, but missed the spontaneity and freshness apparent in Weill's German works.[49] In Europe, Weill's teacher, Ferrucio Busoni, warned him that other composers' fear of triviality was pushing music toward esotericism, and encouraged him to be true to his material, particularly in theatrical works.[50] Ernst Krenek and Otto Klemperer, on the other hand, criticized Weill for courting success and catering to popular taste,[51] and Theodor Adorno dismissed him altogether.[52]

Synopsis

Street Scene is set in and around a Depression-era New York tenement in the sweltering heat of summer. Sam Kaplan, who lives with his family on the first floor, is in love with Rose Maurrant, who lives above him with her family. Rose's mother, tired of her abusive and suffocating relationship with Frank Maurrant, has begun an affair with Mr. Sankey, the milkman, which is met with disapproval by her gossipy neighbors (No. 3). Alone in his room, Sam expresses feelings of isolation, even in the midst of the city, and longs for affection and friendship (No. 10). Later, coming home from a date, Rose avoids the unwelcome advances of her boss, Mr. Easter (No. 11), and declares herself more interested in true love than wealth (No. 12). As Act 1 concludes, she and Sam sing together of their frustration and their dreams of happiness (No. 14).

In the opening of Act 2, Mrs. Maurrant arranges a meeting with her lover while her husband, an actor, is in New Haven for the weekend for the tryout of his new show. Before her husband leaves, he warns her darkly not to forget her obligations to her family (No. 16). Rose and Sam meet again in front of the tenement and impulsively plan to run off together to escape their troubled lives in the city (No. 18). When Frank arrives home early and catches his wife with Mr. Sankey, he fatally shoots both of them and flees the scene. When Rose finds out what has happened, she decides to leave the city and set out on her own. She bids goodbye to Sam and to her father, who has been apprehended by the police. Despite Sam's plea for Rose to take him with her, she leaves on her own, reassuring him that they will perhaps meet again some day (No. 22).

Scoring and Analyzing the Roles of Sam and Rose

Like Porgy and Bess, Sam Kaplan and Rose Maurrant eventually join forces to attempt the attainment of their respective superobjectives. Sam wants to find a cure for his loneliness, but throughout Acts 1 and 2 he is unable to escape from the depressing realities of life in his neighborhood (see Table 1). He tries to come to grips with his feelings of isolation and when that fails he attempts to convince Rose to come away with him, out of the city, to start a new life together (another "inverted" reference to *Porgy and Bess*).

	Y/N	KEY	CADENCE	LINE
SO: *to find a cure for his loneliness*	n	E♭	HC	$\hat{3}\text{-}\hat{2}^{\parallel}$
MO₁ (I/10): to understand and come to grips with his feelings of isolation ("Lonely House")	n	E♭	PAC	$\hat{8}\text{-}\hat{5}^{\parallel}$
MO₂ (I/14): to escape from the depressing reality of life in the city ("A Sprig With Its Flower We Break")	n	C	IAC	$(\hat{5})$
MO₃ (II/17): to convince Rose to leave New York and start a new life together with him ("We'll Go Away Together")	n	E♭	IAC	(5-line)
MO₄ (II/22): to persuade Rose to allow him to come with her when she leaves town ("There's No Hope For Us")	n	B♭	—	$(\hat{5})$

Table 1 The Score of Sam's Role

Rose, for her part, wants to find a true soulmate (see Table 2). She begins well, establishing her personal credo in her opening aria, but like Sam she wishes she could escape the anxiety and sadness in her life, and is unable to do so. Moreover, when she finally decides to put her dreams of a life together with Sam behind her in their final duet, she nonetheless leaves open the possibility of seeing him and returning home.

	Y/N	KEY	CADENCE	LINE
SO: *to find a true soulmate*	n	E♭	HC	3̂–2̂
MO₁ (I/12): to reject fame and fortune in favor of true love; to establish a credo ("What Good Would the Moon Be?")	y	E♭	PAC	5-line
MO₂ (I/14): to escape from the depressing reality of life in the city ("A Sprig With Its Flower We Break")	n	C	IAC	(5̂)
MO₃ (II/18): to resolve to leave the city and start a new life with Sam ("We'll Go Away Together")	n	E♭	IAC	(5-line)
MO₄ (II/22): to put her dreams for a life with Sam behind her ("There's No Hope For Us")	n	B♭	—	(5̂)

Table 2 The Score of Rose's Role

Sam and Rose have been selected for analysis here not only because they are the protagonists of the drama but also because their music represents the best example of the stylistic synthesis Weill sought to achieve in *Street Scene*. If "Moon-Faced, Starry-Eyed," a jitterbug, and "Wouldn't You Like to Be On Broadway," a soft-shoe number, are pure musical theater,[53] then the Act 1 arias for Mr. and Mrs. Maurrant are pure grand opera. Mrs. Maurrant's aria, "Somehow I Never Could Believe," is over six minutes long, and Lotte Lenya recalled Weill saying, "if this aria goes over [with the audience], it will prove to me that I have written the opera that I wanted to write."[54] Sam and Rose's music falls somewhere between these two extremes. As Anne Jeffreys noted, Rose's aria, "What Good Would the Moon Be," was "more or less in the popular range," but its difficult intervals and wide leaps made it atypical for popular music, though not for Weill.[55]

"Lonely House," the E♭ major aria[56] that musically reveals Sam's deepest longing—to find a cure for his loneliness—begins with an extended introduction (mm. 1–20) that prolongs the tonic harmony by means of a continuous E♭ pedal tone in the bass, punctuated periodically by dominant-over-tonic harmonies and several evocative musical gestures (e.g., the minor-second "taxi horns" in mm. 1–9 and the cacophonous telephone "conversation" in m. 16). When the 16-bar double period that comprises the A section begins at m. 21, $\hat{1}$ in the melody is harmonized by a recurrence of the tonic, but this time the familiar harmony is destabilized by the addition of C and D♭, lending it the sound of a dominant seventh with added sixth, or $[V^{\natural 3}_{\flat 7}] \rightarrow IV$. Though the altered chord fits seamlessly into the jazz-inflected harmonic vocabulary established by Weill at the outset of the opera, it nonetheless creates the effect of restlessness, driving the music forward and creating a fitting musical symbol of Sam's longing. This restlessness is compounded by the absence of dominant harmony at the end of the antecedent's first half, where a chain of applied dominants[57]—$[V^9_7] \rightarrow [V^9_7] \rightarrow [V^{\flat 9}_7] \rightarrow V$—sets up a half cadence that never occurs (mm. 23–24): the "missing" dominant, which does appear in the corresponding place in the consequent phrase (m. 32, fourth beat), is replaced by a whole-tone chord built on E [E, A♭, D, G♭] that functions enharmonically as an inverted linear augmented-sixth chord.[58]

The lack of fulfillment projected by the first four bars of the main theme is maintained throughout the aria, not only in its form (rounded binary, with extensive variation/concealment of repeated A section material, as shown in Figure 1), but also in its cadential plan. Of the seven possible cadence points, not including the "abandoned" cadence in mm. 24–25 discussed above, only two end in authentic cadences (mm. 36 and 52), and the closure inherent in each of these is poignantly undercut by harmonic substitutions (I^{sub6} at m. 36 and $V^{\flat 9}_3$ at m. 51) as well as Weill's use of the blue note ♭3 in the melody over each cadential dominant (mm. 35 and 51).[59] The remaining cadences are either half cadences (mm. 28, 32, 44, 48) if one chooses to focus on the phrase structure and the melodic line and accept as idiomatic the ninths and/or sevenths routinely added by Weill to the dominant throughout the opera, or "evaded cadences" if one chooses to emphasize the pull of the dominant seventh in the orchestra toward an elided tonic at the beginning of each subsequent phrase.[60] In this latter interpretation, an authentic cadence is evaded either through the re-emergence of $\hat{7}$ or ♭$\hat{7}$ over the tonic harmony (m. 29, 33 and 45) or through the use of a chordal substitution for the tonic that lacks the simple triadic stability of a deceptive cadential goal. For example, compare the deceptive cadence to vi in A♭ major, mm. 39–40, with the evasion to ♭VI$^{♭9}_{♮7}$ in E♭ major, mm. 48–49.[61]

20 intro.	4 + 8:[4:(2a + 2b) + 4:(2a' + 2a)] + 8:[4:(2a + 2a') + 4:(2a + 2a")]
	(HC) (HC) (HC)
16 AA1	8A:[4:(2c+ 2d) + 4:(2e + 2f)] + 8A1:[4:(2c+ 2d) + 4:(2e' + 2g)]
	parallel period HC→EC PAC
18 BA2	8B:[4:(2h+ 2i) + 4:(2h' + 2i')] + 10A2:[4:(2j+ 2j') + 6:(2k + 4k')]
	period HC→EC PAC
Rounded Binary	

Figure 1 "Lonely House," form

The linear structure of "Lonely House" reinforces the lack of closure projected by its formal and cadential plan (see Figure 2). After a four-bar instrumental introduction, Sam enters on $\hat{5}$ and initiates an ascending middleground sixth-progression that culminates at m. 16 with the recurrence of ♭3. Despite this salient pitch's enharmonic relationship to the F♯ of the "taxi horn" figure in m. 2, and its lower-neighbor connection to the head note of the solo violin motive of m. 3, it is ultimately left "hanging": Sam's vocal line returns directly to B♭, decorated by an upper-neighbor C, to conclude the aria's introduction.

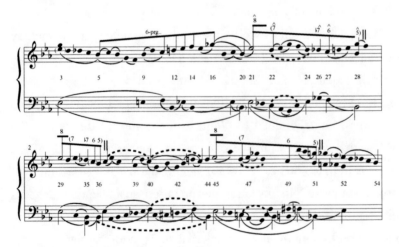

Figure 2 "Lonely House," voice leading

In place of G ($\hat{3}$), Weill installs E♭ ($\hat{8}$) as the primary tone of the aria on the downbeat of m. 21 ("Lonely house") and initiates a middleground descent to $\hat{5}$ (mm. 21–28), embellished by the chromatic passing-tone D♭ in m. 26. The goal of this descent—B♭ ($\hat{5}$)—is obscured by a reaching over in which G♭–F (♭$\hat{3}$–$\hat{2}$) serves as a substitution for the implied B♭ in m. 28, reinstating the upper-register connection to the blue-note G♭ of the introduction (cf. m. 16). Both registral strands (G♭–F, and E♭–D–D♭–C– [B♭]) suggest a middleground interruption at m. 28, an event that is subsequently repeated at m. 36, where $\hat{5}$ (B♭) is re-contextualized as $\hat{1}$ of B♭ major, the dominant key.

The idiomatic blues gesture that occurs in Sam's melody at m. 35—namely the substitution of ♭$\hat{3}$ for $\hat{2}$ over the dominant—makes a poignant return at the close of the aria (m. 51), this time in the home key of E♭ major, where it becomes G♭, the pitch that has come to epitomize loneliness and longing, as evidenced by its ubiquitous presence in the aria. This longing remains ultimately unfulfilled in the aria's linear structure, as the fundamental descent from E♭ is permanently interrupted at $\hat{5}$, while the upper line that covers it is denied true linear closure through the chromatic substitution outlined above (m. 52).

Like "Lonely House," Rose's aria "What Good Would the Moon Be" reveals her superobjective: to find a true soulmate. Her immediate and impassioned rejection of Mr. Easter's unwelcome advances prior to the aria ("Wouldn't You Like to Be on Broadway?") stand in sharp contrast to Bess's mute capitulation to Sporting Life in *Porgy and Bess*, following "There's a Boat That's Leavin' Soon for New York." Set in E♭ major, the key of "Lonely House," her aria begins with two poignant foreground pitch motives, both in m. 4: the melodic leap to the goal tone ($\hat{1}$, E♭), suggesting her desire to pursue beauty in her life, and the use of ♭3 (G♭) on the word "cold," portraying her disillusionment. As shown in Figure 3, the primary tone ($\hat{5}$, B♭) is initiated at m. 6, and a middleground descent to $\hat{2}$, one that is strongly reminiscent of the descent in "Lonely House," ensues. This descent includes both the prolongation of a chromatic passing tone (♯$\hat{4}$, vs. ♭$\hat{7}$ in "Lonely House") in mm. 7–9 and a reaching over that obscures the interruption itself (mm. 10–11). As in "Lonely House," this interruption is subsequently repeated, and treated to a substantial expansion (mm. 23–27).

Figure 3 "What Good Would the Moon Be," voice-leading graph

Unlike Sam's aria, "What Good Would the Moon Be" does not contain periodic phrase structure. Instead, Weill demonstrates Mr. Easter's limited effect on Rose through his expansion of the quasi-sentential structure used by Easter in "Wouldn't You Like to be on Broadway?" [62] Rose adopts the suggestive, forward-looking quality of the sentence, but takes it in a new direction, using it as a platform for her extended, rhapsodic self-dedication to "someone who'll love just me." Again, in contrast to the numbers sung by both Sam and Easter, Rose's aria is also set in varied strophic form, as outlined in Figure 4.

12 intro.	2: intro. + 10:[4:(2a + 2b) + 6:(1c + 1d + 1d' + 3*e)]
	HC
16 AB	8A:[4:(2f + 2g) + 4:(2f + 2h)] + 8B:[4:(2i + 2j) + 4k]
	(IAC) HC
20 AB'	8A rep.+ 12B':[4:(2i'+ 2j') + 8:(2l + 2l' + 4l'')]
	PAC
Varied Strophic	

Figure 4 "What Good Would the Moon Be," formal chart

The lack of a contrasting formal section emphasizes Rose's naïveté, and highlights the only departure from A section material: the ascent that couples G4 ($\hat{3}$) to G5 (mm. 37–46), after which the fundamental line concludes its descent to the tonic in the fifth register. The resulting disruption of the aria's obligatory register, which was established as the fourth register by the initiation of the primary tone as Bb4 in m. 6, prevents Rose's vocal line from linking directly to the register of Sam's aria, the A section of which begins on Eb4, which is the putative goal tone of Rose's melody. Her conviction that she will find someone "to have and to hold" is therefore placed in the realm of fantasy, with the implication that she is not talking about the flesh-and-blood Sam, but rather an idealized vision of the future. [63]

The first duet between Rose and Sam, "A Sprig With Its Flower We Break," is brief, consisting of just twenty-nine measures (pv165–7) and only gradually takes harmonic and formal shape.[64] C major, the key in which the duet concludes, is not permanently installed until m. 18, and the final imperfect authentic cadence (m. 24) is the only real cadence contained within it.[65] The majority of the duet is given over to a series of extended two-measure tonicizations of other scale-steps: it begins in IV (F major, mm. 1–2, varied in mm. 3–4) and subsequently fills in the tonal space thus created with an ascending-step sequence from I (C major, mm. 5–6) through ii (D minor, mm. 7–8) to iii (E minor, mm. 9–10). Each of these tonicizations is melodically embellished with dissonant ninths; the latter three featuring transferred 9–(8) suspensions with delayed resolutions. Before the duet can regain IV, however, the sequence is broken, and the harmonic pattern is converted into a descending-fifths progression that eventually brings the music back to the key of C major, beginning in m. 18.

The linear structure of the duet brings out a rather unusual aspect of its text. Although this is the first time that Rose and Sam sing together, the text is more reminiscent of a farewell than a greeting. Three bars before the beginning of the duet (*meno mosso*, pv 165-3), Rose foreshadows their eventual parting, hinting that they will be together only "in our dreams," and at the *tranquillo*

(m. 13ff.) they urge each other "And when you see the lilac bush bright in the morning air, remember, always remember, remember that I care!" While the doomed nature of their relationship is reinforced by the formal and tonal structure of the duet—its lack of formal repetition contributes to a sense of instability and transience, and its C major tonal setting prevents arrival on E♭, the goal tone of both characters' previous arias—it is the linear structure that most poignantly foreshadows the relationship's ultimate failure.

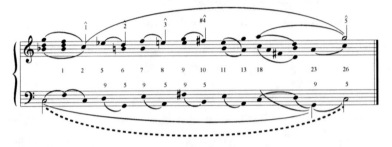

Figure 5 "A Sprig With its Flower We Break," voice-leading graph

Using an 8-5 linear intervallic pattern embellished by the ninths discussed above, Weill constructs a middleground ascent from C to F♯ in mm. 2–10 (see Figure 5). Though this ascent is suddenly reversed at m. 11, returning by step to an implied C at m. 24, the true goal of the initial ascent is G, which occurs as the final pitch in both vocal parts, mm. 26–29. Ironically, this G is present from the outset in various contexts, but always as a dissonant non-harmonic tone, or a member of a dissonant chord (see Figure 6). In mm. 1 and 3, G opens the duet as a ninth against F in the bass. It clashes even more strongly with F♯ in m. 9, and returns as a seventh above A in m. 16. When the proper harmonic support for G (I) arrives at m. 17, the melody instead moves to an upper-neighbor A, settling on G only in m. 26, where the presence of an added sixth in the tonic harmony implies a voice exchange, under which the upper-neighbor is retained in an inner voice.

Figure 6 "A Sprig With its Flower We Break," harmonic support for $\hat{5}$

The repeated use of G as a dissonance at the foreground level, coupled with the obvious evasion of it as goal for the middleground linear fifth-progression begun in m. 2, mark its appearance as an important structural event. The inability of Sam and Rose to attain this salient pitch within a stable harmonic context until the final measures of the duet mirrors their inability to find a stable foundation upon which to build a future together. The fact that they ultimately attain stability only in the key of C major, VI with respect to their home key of E♭ major, indicates that any aspirations they have for such a future exist only in the realm of fantasy. Moreover, although they do attain G at m. 26, it does not serve as the primary tone of a fundamental line descending to C ($\hat{1}$), but rather as the conclusion of an ascending linear progression that prolongs G throughout the duet.

For Sam and Rose's second duet, Weill deftly blends elements of each character's earlier aria, combining the rounded binary form of "Lonely House" with the sentential phrase structure used in "What Good Would the Moon Be?" Despite this formal allusion to the deepening ties between Sam and Rose, who begin here to make definite plans for their future, this duet supercedes "Lonely House" in its use of cadential evasion (see Figure 7).

24 intro.	3 + 8:[4:(2a + 2a¹) + 4:(2a2 + 2b)] + 13:[4:(2a3 + 2c) + 9:(3b' + 6d)] HC→EC
16 AA	8A:[4:(2e + 2f) + 4:(2e2 + 2f')] + 8A':[4:(2e + 2f) + 4:(2e³ + 2g)] HC→EC HC→DC
21 BA¹	9B:[4:(2h + 2h') + 5:(¹ᐟ² + ¹ᐟ² + ¹ᐟ² + ¹ᐟ² + 3cad.)] + sentence HC→EC
	12A¹:[4:(2e+ 2f) + 4:(2i + 4e⁴) + 4:(1j + 1j' + 2)] DC EC
16 AA	rep. (instrumental)
22 BA2	8B:[4:(2h + 2h') + 4:(1/2 + 1/2 + 1/2 + 1/2 + 2cad.)] + sentence HC→EC
	14A²:[4:(2e+ 2f) + 4:(2i + 4e⁴) + 6:(1j + 1j' + 4)] DC IAC

Double Rounded Binary

Figure 7 "We'll Go Away Together," formal chart

As in Sam's aria, a number of the cadential moments in the duet can be interpreted either as half cadences, if preference is given to the phrase structure and the melodic line, or evaded/deceptive cadences, if emphasis is placed on the pull of the cadential dominant (because of the ubiquitous added ninth and/or seventh) toward the downbeat of the subsequent measure (mm. 7–9, 15–17, 24–26). In addition to these cadentially ambiguous moments, however, Weill includes a more conventional deceptive cadence, V($\frac{9}{7}$)–[vii°⁷]→vi, mm. 32–33, and a true elided cadential evasion: V($\frac{9}{7}$)– [vii°⁷]/V$_{pedal}$→V$^{13}_{7}$/vi–IV, mm. 34–36.

The irony of the A¹ section's final cadence, which is elided with an orchestral restatement of the opening theme, is that it sets the pitches that would have concluded Sam and Rose's fundamental line, G–F–E♭ (mm. 35–36). That Sam sings these pitches indicates the strength of his belief in the possibilities for the couple, yet Rose does not sing this final phrase with him, and the orchestra refuses to provide cadential support. Sam is too starry-eyed to see what Rose and the orchestra already know: the wistful dreaming of the two would-be lovers is just a temporary escape from the harsh realities of their lives, not a viable plan for the future. In the final cadence of the duet (m. 70), the same G–F–E♭ ($\hat{3}$–$\hat{2}$–$\hat{1}$) descent is conspicuously absent: Rose sings $\hat{7}$–$\hat{3}$ instead, while Sam sings $\hat{3}$ (an added sixth above the dominant) before moving to $\hat{5}$.[66]

Like "What Good Would the Moon Be." the middleground linear structure of the duet consists of a series of interrupted 5-lines, strengthening the connection between the two numbers as unrealized fantasies (see Figure 8). Sam's opening phrase in the A section (mm. 1–4) circles around the primary tone in a manner that is strongly reminiscent of the opening of "I Loves You Porgy," embellishing B♭ with neighbor tones before finally reaching it only on the last beat of m. 4. His vocal line then descends to $\hat{2}$ over the dominant at m. 8 and is interrupted, whereupon it is repeated by Rose with a substitution of the leading tone for the implied $\hat{2}$ over the cadential dominant at m. 16. The B section also contains a middleground reference to the main theme of "Lonely House" in its linear progression from $\hat{8}$ back to $\hat{5}$, embellished by ♭$\hat{7}$ (mm. 17-21). The only true descent from $\hat{5}$ to $\hat{1}$ in the duet occurs in the A¹ and A² sections, but each arrival on $\hat{1}$ is harmonized deceptively by the submediant, preventing true closure to the tonic and driving the music forward once more.

Figure 8 "We'll Go Away Together," voice leading

Sam and Rose's final duet begins as one of the most dissonant and formally indistinct moments in the opera. Consisting primarily of a string of diminished and half-diminished seventh chords, the opening recitative-like *moderato* section (mm. 1–53) passes fleetingly through F minor (mm. 10–14) and C minor (mm. 38–40). In the second section (*allegro non troppo*, mm.54–65, and *agitato*, mm, 66–73), Weill abandons tonality altogether, concluding the section with a sequence of half-diminished seventh chords descending by half-step from G to A (mm. 69–73), set against a chromatic orchestral line that ascends a thirteenth, from G to E♭.

At the second *allegro non troppo* (m. 74), Weill suddenly brings back E♭ major, the key of "Lonely House," "What Good Would the Moon Be," and "We'll Go Away Together," along with the main theme of the latter in the orchestra, creating a tonal and melodic connection to the couple's earlier sentiments that is startlingly incongruous now that the murder of Rose's mother, Mrs. Maurrant, has been revealed. The irreparably fractured nature of the couple's relationship is accented by Sam's melody; whereas in "We'll Go Away Together" he began with the upper-neighbor C and continued with a strong stepwise descent from B♭ to F ($\hat{5}$ to $\hat{2}$), here he huddles miserably around C (mm. 74–80), leaping desperately to $\hat{2}$ at the last minute (m. 81).

Rose's reply is even more telling: she begins by singing the main theme of "We'll Go Away Together," (mm. 81–85) but just at the moment when she would have initiated the primary tone B♭ (m. 85), resolving the double-neighbor A–C above the tonic, she breaks off the melody (see Figure 9). In its place, she sings another variation of the "Lonely House" theme that leaves the melody on B♭ ($\hat{5}$) for the *tranquillo* section (mm. 91–105), one that is harmonized by an E half-diminished seventh chord. The duet concludes with an *andantino* section (mm. 106–130) that recalls the *tranquillo* section of "A Sprig With Its Flower We Break" as it moves through G minor (mm. 117–121) to B♭ major (mm. 121–130). Here, however, the music has been transposed down a whole step (the original keys were A minor and C major), and therefore Rose's melody concludes on F, not on G. The failure of the couple to achieve their goal is complete: because the key of E♭ major does not return, Rose's F (m. 130) is not permitted to continue down to E♭. A large-scale interruption takes place, similar to the one shown for Porgy's role in the previous chapter. Like Porgy, Rose leaves to seek her fortune elsewhere, and the audience never learns what becomes of her.

Figure 9: "There's No Hope For Us," voice-leading graph

Summary

Kurt Weill's "Broadway opera" is a masterful blend of elements of opera and American musical theater, in the mold of *Porgy and Bess*. Despite the occasional nod to Broadway convention ("Moon-Faced, Starry-Eyed," "Wrapped in a Ribbon and Tied With a Bow"), Weill manages to create a compelling musical drama in which the forms, keys, themes, and even harmonic progressions he employs are intimately linked to dramatic fulfillment or failure. Nowhere is this more evident than in his treatment of Sam and Rose. As shown in the above analyses, Weill strategically manipulates both the linear and harmonic aspects of tonal closure, withholding cadences and particular scale-degrees for dramatic effect in a manner that is strikingly similar, particularly on the background level, to Gershwin's treatment of Porgy and Bess. A summary of the background structure of Sam and Rose's music is given in Figure 10.

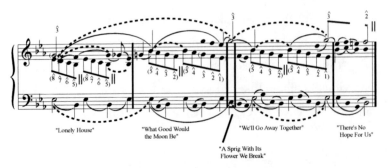

Figure 10 Street Scene (Sam and Rose), Background Structure

Beginning with "Lonely House," in which the two interrupted descents from $\hat{8}$–$\hat{5}$ in Sam's vocal line are shadowed by the presence of the higher G–G♭ in the upper tessitura, a full arpeggiation of the E♭ major tonic triad couples G1 to G2. When G2 arrives over C major (the "wrong key" major submediant) in "A Sprig With Its Flower We Break," it serves as a reminder that Sam and Rose's dreams are unattainable. G2 then reappears in "We'll Go Away Together," but only at the end of the duet, where it signifies the couple's longing to escape, but not the escape itself. When "There's No Hope For Us," rather than concluding a 5-line from its primary tone B♭, ends with F2 over B♭, the dominant of the home key, the connection to the previous statements of G2 is very clear: a life together for the couple is now impossible, and resolution to the E♭ major tonic will not be forthcoming.

The background analysis of Sam and Rose's roles in Figure 10 engages the important Schenkerian issue of "obligatory register," the primary register of the fundamental line. Sam's opening aria initiates the primary tone an octave below the obligatory register (in the tenor range); it is then "coupled" to the higher G when Rose joins him in their duets. As with Porgy's final number, the couple's final duet does not contain an "active" primary tone, but instead prolongs F as its final pitch via a large-scale lower-neighbor.

ENDNOTES

1. Czech-born composer Hugo Weisgall (1912–1997) also wrote important operas after moving to America for separate reasons in 1920, most notably *Six Characters in Search of an Author* (1959).

2. David Farneth, *Kurt Weill,* 272. For more on the connection between Weill and Schoenberg as Jewish composers, see Foster Hirsch, *Kurt Weill on Stage: From Berlin to Broadway* (New York: Alfred A. Knopf, 2002), 260.

3. Farneth, *Kurt Weill*, 251.

4. Ibid.

5. Ronald Sanders, *The Days Grow Short: The Life and Music of Kurt Weill* (New York: Holt, Rinehart, and Winston, 1980), 399.

6. Douglas Jarman, *Kurt Weill: An Illustrated Biography* (Bloomington: Indiana University Press, 1982), 9.

7. Kim H. Kowalke, *Kurt Weill in Europe* (Ann Arbor, MI: UMI Research Press, 1979).

8. Sanders portrays Weill variously as a German, French, English, American, and Jewish composer, and as an opera composer, show composer, and concert hall composer. See Sanders, *The Days Grow Short*, 4–5.

9. Jarman, *Kurt Weill*, 7. Jarman's categories comprise the years 1919–1925, 1926–1934, and 1935–1949, respectively.

10. Ibid., 139–41. Jarman argues that Weill cultivated an "anonymous" American style as part of a conscious rejection of German intellectualism. See also Sanders, *The Days Grow Short*, 397.

11. Jürgen Schebera, *Kurt Weill: An Illustrated Life*, trans. Caroline Murphy (New Haven: Yale University Press, 1995), ix.

12. Ronald Taylor, *Kurt Weill: Composer in a Divided World* (New York: Simon and Schuster, 1991), 304–6.

13. Sanders, *The Days Grow Short*, 354–7 and 403.

14. Jarman, *Kurt Weill*, 9.

15. Taylor, *Kurt Weill*, 304.

16. David Drew, *Kurt Weill: A Handbook* (London: Faber and Faber, 1987)

17. Schebera, *Kurt Weill*, 311–16.

18. Farneth, *Kurt Weill*, 238–73.

19. Hirsch, *Kurt Weill on Stage*, 6.

20. Lotte Lenya to Joseph Horowitz, 26 October 1979 interview in the *New York Times*. Quoted in Jarman, *Kurt Weill*, 136.

21. Drew, *Kurt Weill*, 354. See also Hirsch, *Kurt Weill on Stage*, 209, and Lys Symonette and Kim H. Kowalke, *Speak Low (When You Speak Love): The Letters of Kurt Weill and Lotte Lenya* (Berkeley: University of California Press, 1996), 282 and 287.

[22] Hirsch, *Kurt Weill on Stage*, 18.

[23] Ibid., 135.

[24] Ibid., 178

[25] Taylor, *Kurt Weill*, 300–2. On Weill's competitiveness toward Rodgers, see Kurt Weill to Lotte Lenya, January 5, 1945, quoted in Farneth, *Kurt Weill*, 240.

[26] Weill cites *Carousel* as an important precursor of *Street Scene* in the liner notes to the original cast recording (Columbia M-MM-6831), reproduced in Farneth, *Kurt Weill*, Plate 19. See also Lotte Lenya's bitter July 7, 1944, letter to Weill regarding the success of *Oklahoma!* in Symonette and Kowalke, *Speak Low,* 382.

[27] Schebera, *Kurt Weill*, 315.

[28] Kurt Weill to Lotte Lenya, May 1, 1945. Quoted in Farneth, *Kurt Weill*, 240.

[29] Kurt Weill to Rouben Mamoulian, January 22, 1946. Quoted in Farneth, *Kurt Weill*, 243.

[30] Kurt Weill to Emma and Albert Weill, September 9, 1946. Quoted in Farneth, *Kurt Weill*, 245.

[31] Weill was the first new member of the Playwright's Company since its inception in 1938, and the only composer. Other members included playwrights Elmer Rice, Maxwell Anderson, and Robert E. Sherwood.

[32] Kurt Weill to Dwight Deere Wiman (producer), Langston Hughes (librettist), Charles Friedman (director), and Elmer Rice, December 21, 1946. Quoted in Farneth, *Kurt Weill*, 247.

[33] Ibid.

[34] Sanders, *Kurt Weill*, 359.

[35] Farneth, *Kurt Weill*, Plate 19.

[36] Hirsch, *Kurt Weill on Stage*, 261.

[37] Farneth, *Kurt Weill*, 249.

[38] Hirsch, *Kurt Weill on Stage*, 266.

[39] Ibid., 275.

[40] Ibid., 250.

[41] Taylor, *Kurt Weill*, 301.

[42] Schebera, *Kurt Weill*, 319.

[43] Ibid., 318.

[44] Olin Downes, January 26, 1947, review in *New York Times*, quoted in Farneth, *Kurt Weill*, 248.

[45] Farneth, *Kurt Weill*, 250.

[46] Ibid.

[47] Hirsch, *Kurt Weill on Stage*, 336–37. The reviewer is alluding to one of the show's signature musical-theatre numbers, "Wrapped in a Ribbon and Tied With a Bow."

[48] Farneth, *Kurt Weill*, 251.

[49] Jarman, *Kurt Weill*, 79.

[50] Farneth, *Kurt Weill*, 257.

[51] Taylor, *Kurt Weill*, 305. Krenek's objection is ironic, given his own predilection for using elements of jazz style in his own works, most notably in *Jonny spielt auf*. For a fascinating comparison of Krenek and Weill and their respective agendas, see Susan C. Cook, *Opera for a New Republic: The* Zeitopern *of Krenek, Weill, and Hindemith* (Ann Arbor: UMI Research Press, 1988).

[52] Hirsch, *Kurt Weill on Stage*, 344–45. For an alternative perspective on Weill's compositional style that situates both his German and American works within the *neue Sachlichkeit* (New Objectivity) movement of Weimar-era Berlin, see Cook, *Opera for a New Republic*.

[53] Foster Hirsch, *Kurt Weill on Stage*, 264.

[54] Lotte Lenya, 1960 interview with unidentified man. Quoted in Hirsch, *Kurt Weill on Stage*, 272.

[55] Hirsch, *Kurt Weill on Stage*, 270.

[56] Hirsch calls "Lonely House" a "blues song," akin to "A Marble and a Star." This designation is somewhat misleading, however, since it is likely based on surface harmonic features, rather than on the use of the blues form. See Hirsch, *Kurt Weill on Stage*, 264.

[57] Weill makes striking use of another chain of applied chords in the B section. See mm. 41–42: [vii°$^6_5$]→ [vii°$^6_5$]→ [vii°$^6_5$]→ vi^6.

[58] Weill's use of a chord built on E to replace the dominant built on B♭ can also be interpreted as a form of the "tritone substitution," a technique common in the jazz repertory.

[59] Caplin discusses the abandoned cadence in detail in *Classical Form*, 107.

[60] For a thorough and erudite discussion of the evaded cadence, see Schmalfeldt, "Cadential Processes" and Caplin, *Classical Form*, 101–9.

[61] The aria in general is full of harmonic substitutions, particularly via simple and secondary mixture. See mm. 21 (♭VII$^{13}_{♭7}$), 22 (VI$^9_7$), 23 (IV$^9_{♭7}$), 26 (♭III$^9_7$), 27 (II^7–ii$^{°7}_{♭5}$), and especially m. 49 (♭VI$^{♯9}_{♯7}$)

[62] Easter sings an 8-bar sentence [4pres:(2a + 2a^1) + 4cont:(2a^2 + 2b)], while Rose sings a 16-bar double sentence. Neither theme, however, contains the typical melodic fragmentation and acceleration of harmonic rhythm in the continuation.

[63] The terms "fifth register" and "fourth register" are meant to refer to the octaves C4–C5 and C5–C6, respectively. Acoustical Society of America designations are used here as a matter of convenience, to facilitate comparison of the obligatory register to the one that replaces it.

[64] The abbreviation "pv" is used in reference to pages in the piano-vocal score. The duet's measures are numbered beginning with the *poco piu mosso* on pv165 as m. 1, and will subsequently be cited by measure number.

[65] Other candidates, including F major: V^7–$vi^{\natural 9}_7$, mm. 4-5, and E minor: V^9_7–$i^{\sharp 7}$, mm. 10–11, occur in the midst of sequential material, and are further weakened by the presence of unresolved non-harmonic tones.

[66] Weill marks the final B♭ in Sam's vocal line as optional, and gives E♭ as an alternative, probably because Broadway singers often do not have the vocal technique required to sustain the higher pitch.

CHAPTER 7

The Prolonged Permanent Interruption:
Aaron Copland's "Operatic Tone Poem"
The Tender Land (1954)

"In the United States opera has held an uncertain and precarious position but is now meeting an unprecedented and revolutionary tide of awareness from composers, performers and laymen."[1]

Although this frank and optimistic assessment was made more recently, it also accurately captures the rising stock of American opera in the 1950s. American composers took a new interest in opera after World War II, both because of the success of opera composers like Gian-Carlo Menotti and Benjamin Britten and because of the increasing number of venues capable of mounting full-scale productions for a fraction of the cost, including university theaters and regional companies.[2] With this expansion of venues came an intensification of the search for uniquely American operas, manifested in a consistent focus on the question of musical materials and their relationship to genre. Although Joplin preferred to call *Treemonisha* a "grand opera," his wife Lottie referred to it as a "ragtime opera," and its characteristic ragtime rhythms have helped to foster its return from obscurity. Gershwin, for his part, wanted *Porgy and Bess* to be known as a "folk opera," yet many persisted in calling it a "jazz opera," and it is permanently linked in the minds of many with his popular songs of the same period.[3] Weill, the most brazen of the three, perhaps because as an immigrant he did not inherit the same obsession with genre, referred unabashedly to *Street Scene* as a "Broadway opera"—for him, a term of endearment, rather than a derogatory epithet.

Copland himself claimed that he wanted to produce something suitable for an opera workshop (i.e., at one of the new university theaters springing up all around the country), with "very plain" music, "closer to musical comedy than grand opera."[4] He accepted a commission in early 1952 from the League of Composers (funded by a $1,000 grant from the famed musical theatre team of Richard Rodgers and Oscar Hammerstein II)[5] to write an "opera for television"—another obsession of 1950s America. He intended to write a small-scale work, suitable for a college production, and chose his former lover, the dancer Erik Johns, to write a libretto based on James Agee's 1941 book *Let Us Now Praise Famous Men*, with photographs by Walker Evans.[6] Writing under the pen name Horace Everett, Johns quickly completed the libretto and the opera was finished by April 1954.

The early 1950s were a trying time in Copland's life. Called to testify before Senator Joseph McCarthy's infamous House Committee on Un-American Activities regarding his alleged involvement with communist organizations, he was later bitterly disappointed when a performance of his *Lincoln Portrait* was cut from the inaugural program for President Dwight D. Eisenhower.[7] His romantic relationship with Johns had ended in 1952 as they commenced work on *The Tender Land*, and he was later shaken by the death of both his mentor, the conductor Serge Koussevitsky, and his close friend pianist William Kapell.[8] Musicologist Christopher Patton has detected a sense of loss in Copland's music from this period, particularly in the Emily Dickinson songs and *The Tender Land*; he cites "time and the inevitability of loss" as the central themes of the opera.[9] Prominent Copland scholar Elizabeth B. Crist takes a slightly more optimistic view, seeing the opera as a portrayal of "disappointment and hope" that shows the simple and secure world of Act I to be "an unattainable ideal." She reads a critique of McCarthyism into Johns and Copland's portrayal of the suspicious and unforgiving Grandpa Moss, who accuses Martin and Top and later refuses to recant, angrily declaring that they are "guilty all the same."[10]

Paired with another television opera, Menotti's *Amahl and the Night Visitors*, *The Tender Land* was by most accounts a critical flop in its New York premiere.[11] Although Wilfrid Mellers, one of Copland's favorite reviewers, remained benignly neutral in his later review of the published score, calling the opera "the homiest of all his regional works: an American Vaughan Williams,"[12] the rest of the reviewers were not as positive. As usual, the main problem was the problem of the work's genre. Copland described opera as "*la forme fatale*," and it certainly proved to be so for him in 1954.[13] Harriet Johnson of the *New York Post* found it "not entirely successful as an opera per se,"[14] and influential critic Olin Downes of *The New York Times* declared the ending "inconclusive and unsatisfying." Edward Mattos, reviewing a revised version of the work premiered at Oberlin College in 1955, declared it "a very puzzling work … it is certainly not grand opera, and yet it is clearly not of the Menotti-Broadway genre."[15] A young Joseph Kerman even got in on the act, blaming the opera's "folksy musical-comedy book," and Copland's reliance on "musical theater" idioms and harmonic progressions "in the rather facile Hollywood manner."[16]

In a letter to fellow American composer Carlos Chávez immediately following the premiere, Copland cites "criticism of the libretto and the usual complaint about few melodies" as the causes for the negative critical reaction.[17] Downes scoffed that the libretto did not offer "much that is of character, or motivation, or consequence,"[18] and recent commentators have tended to agree with him. Eric Roseberry, in a review of the recent Plymouth Music Series recording of the complete opera, notes that the libretto contains "a fundamental lack of dramatic 'tension.'"[19] Patton, arguing for a reconsideration of the opera's dramatic premise, asserts that "there is no conflict-driven, event-filled plot … it lacks the traditional, dramatically satisfying tragic or happy ending that ties up all loose ends and sends the audience out of the opera house feeling that a complete story has been told."[20] In his own defense, Johns did not consider the opera "a big dramatic number"; in fact, he referred to it an "operatic tone poem."[21]

Several recent authors, noted Copland biographer Howard Pollack first among them, have offered a fresh appraisal of the opera, based on a reinterpretation of the "inconclusive" ending that rankled its original critics. Pollack compares the ending favorably to *Porgy and Bess*, noting that both operas end with "a particularly sober optimism," and that "both composers opted against defeat or death for their two protagonists, similarly abandoned by their lovers, but rather for a poised, courageous departure from their provincial communities."[22] His eloquent evaluation of these two operas and their place in American cultural history is worth quoting in its entirety:

> [These two operas] epitomize the American lyric stage at its
> most representative. For many of the twentieth century's most
> successful mid-century American operas and musicals—
> from *The Mother of Us All*, *Regina*, *Susannah* and *The
> Ballad of Baby Doe* to *Show Boat*, *Carousel* and *Fiddler
> on the Roof*—conclude with individuals departing from or
> triumphing over a repressive community. These endings are
> neither tragic nor comic, but stoic, resolute, optimistic, and
> deeply reflective of the industrial and immigrant society
> from which they arose.[23]

Daniel Mathers offers an alternative interpretation of the opera's ending informed by an examination of Copland's status as a gay man in 1950s America. He sees Laurie as a symbol of difference because she does what girls at the time were not supposed to do—she strikes out on her own and forges her own way, in the face of resistance from her repressive community. For Mathers, Laurie's departure from the fenced-in yard of her mother's farm is, in a sense, her private "coming out" party.[24] This reading is echoed by Howard Pollack, who notes, "many of Copland's dramatic and texted works— including the operas, the ballets, the films, and the large Emily Dickinson song cycle—depict an outsider's struggle for self-realization through a dialectical exploration of isolation and engagement."[25] Although the analysis offered below does not approach *The Tender Land* as an explicitly queer text, it will supplement these and other readings by suggesting that Copland's musical response to Johns' libretto, whatever its subtext, constitutes a sensitive and compelling depiction of musical incompleteness or longing.

Synopsis

The opera opens with Laurie's little sister, Beth, and her mother in front of their farmhouse on the day before Laurie's graduation from high school. Mr. Splinters, the postman, arrives to deliver Laurie's graduation dress and is invited to her party that evening. He warns Ma Moss that the neighbors' daughter encountered two strange men in the fields the night before, and that it might be the same pair that had raped another girl two months before. Laurie comes home from school and lingers outside the house, thinking about her future ("Once I Thought I'd Never Grow"). Ma Moss comes onto the porch and the two quarrel about Laurie's obligations to her family, particularly her grandfather. Ma promises Laurie more independence after graduation, but strikes her when Laurie scoffs at her promise, then pleads with her to avoid confrontation until after graduation.

Martin and Top, two itinerant farmhands, arrive at Laurie's house and introduce themselves ("We've Been North, We've Been South"). Grandpa Moss returns home, overcomes his initial skepticism, and agrees to hire them to help bring in the harvest ("A Stranger May Seem Strange, That's True"). Ma Moss remains suspicious of them, thinking they might be the two men mentioned by Mr. Splinters, but nonetheless allows Laurie to invite them to her graduation party. Both men are smitten by Laurie's beauty and Top urges Martin to distract Grandpa Moss at the party that night, so that he can he can try his luck with Laurie; Martin urges caution and warns him not to cost them their new jobs.[26] The act concludes with a hymn of thanksgiving, led by Martin and sung by all the leading characters ("The Promise of Living").

Act 2 opens at the party, with the guests seated at the dinner table eating and drinking. Grandpa Moss toasts Laurie, and she rises to thank everyone, yet expresses profoundly mixed emotions about this important moment of her life ("Thank You, Thank You All"). The dancing begins ("Stomp Your Foot Upon the Floor"), and Top urges Martin to dance with Laurie while he gets Grandpa Moss drunk, reminding him that they will switch roles later. Ma Moss, her suspicion growing, takes Mr. Splinters aside and asks him to fetch the sheriff to question the two men.

As Top entertains the guests with tall tales, Martin waltzes with Laurie, her head spinning with possibilities for the future ("You Dance Real Well"), then takes her onto the front porch and kisses her. He professes his love for her and asks if she feels the same way, wondering if she wants to settle down with him ("I'm Gettin' Tired of Travelin' Through"). Laurie shyly acknowledges that she does love him, and begs him to stay with her ("In Love? In Love? Yes, Yes I Do Love You"). Grandpa Moss, now quite drunk, discovers the couple on the porch and tries to attack Martin. The other guests arrive and restrain him, but Ma Moss announces that Martin and Top are the two wanted men, only to have Mr. Splinters return with the news that the two actual culprits are already in custody. Grandpa Moss, disgraced, orders them to leave the next morning anyway and harshly condemns Laurie for her behavior. Defiant, she declares herself innocent of any wrongdoing and asserts her independence. The act concludes with the guests dispersing, leaving Grandpa Moss alone with his head in his hands.

Act 3 takes place later the same night. Martin, restless and unable to sleep, leaves the shed where he and Top are sleeping and calls to Laurie from beneath her window ("Laurie, Laurie, is there someone in there that's called Laurie, Laurie"). She hears him and answers softly, rushing out of the house to meet him. She asks for and receives a declaration of love from Martin, and when he tells her he must leave in the morning she begs him to take her with him, as his wife. They plan to leave at dawn, but after Laurie goes back to her room Martin begins to have misgivings. Top wakes up and convinces him to abandon the plan for Laurie's own good ("That's Crazy! Hoppin' the Freight, After It's Late"). The two men leave abruptly, and Laurie, heartbroken when she discovers Martin's betrayal, decides to leave as well. Though Ma Moss pleads with her to stay, she remains resolute and, becoming a stranger to her own mother and sister, leaves the farm to seek her future. Ma Moss is left to turn her attention to Beth and think about her own future.

Scoring and Analyzing the Roles of Martin and Laurie

Both Laurie and Martin experience dramatic success throughout *The Tender Land*, although Copland's decision to forego the use of traditional authentic cadences and fundamental lines focuses the musical realization of that success solely at the background level through the prolongation of primary tones in each scene rather than through structural descents. The score of Laurie's role, shown in Table 1, reveals that her opening scene, in which she tries to overcome her anxiety about the future, is the only scene in which she fails to achieve her main objective. Once she meets Martin, her confidence grows and she is able to adopt his optimistic vision of the future, charm him with her dancing and conversation, and convince him to take her away with him. Nonetheless, she is unable to attain her superobjective by the end of Act 3, since the opera ends like *Treemonisha*, *Porgy and Bess*, and *Street Scene*—with the female lead beginning a journey or taking on a new role, the implications of which have yet to be determined.

	Y/N	KEY	CADENCE	LINE
SO: *to discover the joys of adulthood*	?	G	HC	$\hat{5}$-$\hat{2}\|\|$
MO_1 (I/R45): to overcome her fears about leaving home and facing the future ("Once I Thought I'd Never Grow")	n	G	DC	5-line
MO_2 (I/R97): to adopt Martin's optimistic vision of the future ("The Promise of Living")	y	F	(PC)	($\hat{4}$)
MO_3 (II/R56): to charm Martin ("You Dance Real Well")	y	G	—	($\hat{3}$)
MO_4 (III/R7): to convince Martin to take her away from the farm ("Yes, Yes, I Do Love You!")	y	D	—	($\hat{2}$)
MO_5 (III/R19): to maintain her faith in Martin ("Is There Someone in There")	y	D	—	($\hat{2}$)

Table 1 The Score of Laurie's Role

Though Martin is almost as successful as Laurie at achieving his main objectives, his superobjective is more clearly delineated during his Act 2 aria ("I'm Gettin' Tired of Travelin' Through"), as is his failure to attain it (see Table 2). He is able to convince Grandpa Moss to hire him and Top to bring in the harvest, and he wins Laurie over with his honesty and integrity, but he struggles to reconcile his wanderlust with his desire to find stability. When he abandons Laurie at Top's urging in Act 3, he forfeits his goal of finding a wife, settling down, making a home and earning respectability. He leaves the stage with no more stability or prospects for his future than when he began.

	Y/N	KEY	CADENCE	LINE
SO: *to find stability and build a better future*	n	G	HC	$\hat{5}$-$\hat{2}$‖
to hold a steady job	n			
to find a wife and settle down	n			
to have a home and earn respectability	n			
MO_1 (I/R78): to convince Grandpa Moss to hire him and Top to work the fields ("A Stranger May Seem Strange")	y	D	—	$\hat{8}$-$\hat{5}$‖
MO_2 (I/R97): to spread an optimistic vision of the future ("The Promise of Living")	y	F	(PC)	($\hat{4}$)
MO_3 (II/R57): to charm Laurie with his honesty				
$\quad BO_1$ (II/57): to sweep Laurie off her feet ("You Dance Real Well")	y	G	—	($\hat{3}$)
$\quad$ BO2 (II/62): to reconcile his wanderlust with his desire to settle down ("I'm Gettin' Tired of Travelin'")	n	D	—	($\hat{2}$)
MO_4 (III/R7): to prove his integrity				
$\quad$ BO1 (III/R7): to force Laurie to face reality ("Yes, Yes, I Do Love You!")	y	D	—	($\hat{2}$)
$\quad$ BO2 (III/R19): to test Laurie's resolve ("Is There Someone in There")	y	D	—	($\hat{2}$)

Table 2 The Score of Martin's Role

Laurie's opening aria, "Once I Thought I'd Never Grow," establishes both her superobjective and the primary obstacle she must overcome to achieve it: in order to discover what the future holds for her, she must overcome her fear of the unknown. Although in the musically adventurous B section of the aria she boldly asks, "What makes me think I'd like to try to go down all those roads beyond that line above the earth and 'neath the sky?" (I/R48), she concludes the aria hesitantly, declaring "Oh it's so strange, I'm strange inside. The time has grown so short, the world so wide!" (I/R50+2).[27] Laurie sings this aria to try to come to grips with her desire to leave home, and what that might mean for her future.

The musical structure of the aria mirrors both Laurie's temporary uncertainty and her overarching desire to find her own way into the future, a future she is sure lies beyond the restrictive confines of home and family. Although Copland notates a key signature of two sharps, C♯ is cancelled by naturals throughout the aria and the prevailing tonal context is that of G major. The most striking aspect of the aria's harmonic structure is the way in which G major is defined: wholly without reference to the tonic triad (present only by implication) and with only an occasional passing reference to the dominant until the final deceptive cadence to the subdominant at m. 42.[28]

The lack of tonic and dominant support lends the aria a naïve but restless quality reinforced by the absence of conventional cadential closure. Of the twelve possible cadence points, only two end on tonic or dominant, and both of those are in foreign keys: a weak half cadence in D major, the dominant key (m. 20), and an elided plagal cadence in F♯ major, the double-mixed key of the leading tone (m. 28).[29] The rest of the phrases end on either the mediant or the subdominant, raising the question of whether a new cadential typology is required for this music.[30] Should closure to the mediant, for example, when preceded by a pre-dominant chord, be considered a "deceptive half cadence" with the mediant substituting for the cadential dominant, or is it better described as a "deceptive plagal cadence," in which the mediant substitutes for the tonic resolution of the pre-dominant harmony? Likewise, should phrase endings that conclude on the subdominant be considered "plagal half cadences," because they do not resolve the subdominant to the tonic?

Although it is possible to answer each of these questions affirmatively, the use of such hybrid categorizations is somewhat beside the point in this aria. Copland intends the music to be harmonically indecisive, either to reflect Laurie's indecision about whether she is indeed ready to become more independent, or to indicate the uncertainty of her future. Nowhere is the bittersweet nature of this uncertainty, indicative of both her reluctance and anticipation, more apparent than in the "Laurie chord" itself, a hexachordal summary of the aria's unconventional harmonic motion comprised of superimposed C major (IV) and B minor (iii) triads. The Laurie chord, which could also be classified as a C major seventh chord with added ninth and raised eleventh, is arpeggiated six times in succession before the aria begins (R44) and is repeated throughout the aria (mm. 8, 12, 16, 34 and 38).

With its abundant use of motivic patterns and clear stepwise progressions, Laurie's melody stands in sharp contrast to the tonal ambiguity created by Copland's nearly ubiquitous use of alternating mediant and subdominant triads in the orchestra. As shown in Figure 1a, the melody begins with a three-note initial ascent to the primary tone (D, $\hat{5}$ in G major), and this three-note figure becomes the alpha motive for the aria, while the arpeggiation up to $\hat{4}$ that concludes m. 1 forms a complementary beta motive. An octave coupling, filled in with a retrograde statement of the alpha motive (D–C–B), and a registrally-transferred upper neighbor (E) prolongs the primary tone.

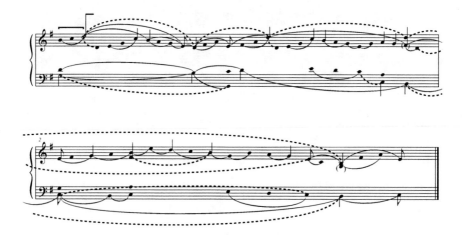

Figure 1a Voice leading, "Once I Thought I'd Never Grow"

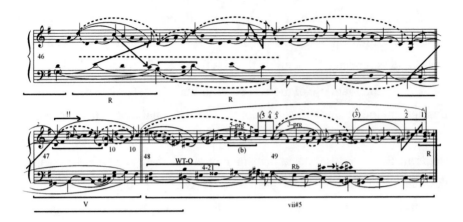

Figure 1b Voice leading, "Once I Thought I'd Never Grow" (cont.)

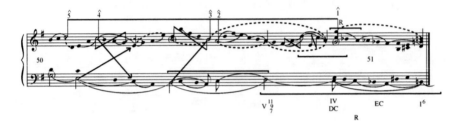

Figure 1c Voice leading, "Once I Thought I'd Never Grow" (cont.)

In this first section of the aria (mm. 1–8), Laurie introduces two central ideas: her curiosity about the future, and her experience of maturation. The questioning, open-ended nature of the alpha motive, with its ascent to $\hat{5}$, is an appropriate symbol of Laurie's curiosity and longing to know what sort of future lies in store for her. This motive is highlighted in numerous ways in the aria, especially through its isolated presentation in bare octaves in the measure before the aria begins and in an orchestral interlude at m. 35. The beta motive, on the other hand, is bolder and more expansive than alpha, spanning a minor sixth via arpeggiation. In its original form, it reaches up to $\hat{4}$, suggesting a descent from alpha's primary tone ($\hat{5}$) toward a melodic conclusion on $\hat{1}$ (G), which is accentuated by the semitonal relationship between $\hat{4}$ and $\hat{3}$. Such an interpretation suggests that the beta motive represents growth and progress—the suggestion of a goal and an initial step toward reaching it—a fitting symbol of Laurie's maturation.

As she describes her youth in the opening section, however, Laurie's world remains circumscribed by the comparatively modest octave from D4 to D5, the only exception being her ascent to F♯5 in m. 6 on the word "grew" as she describes growing both in stature and in wisdom. The limited range of mm. 1–8 is also significant in that it lies below the first passagio of the soprano voice, in a less brilliant (and more technically secure) range for the young singers Copland had in mind when he wrote the opera. In a technical sense then, the lower range represents the safety and security of home for Laurie.

Although Laurie's music in the A section (mm. 1–16), comprised entirely of octave couplings and neighbor tones at the middleground level, does not achieve any real linear progress, it does serve to elaborate her two primary motives. The bass line of the orchestral accompaniment, in particular, contains many statements of the prime and retrograde forms of the alpha motive, bracketed and labeled in Figure 1b. Combined with the use of middleground upper neighbor tones in the melody, the alternation of the ascending and descending forms of the motive lends the music a cyclical quality, hinting at not only the passing of the seasons as Laurie grows older, but also hinting at the mundane routine from which she hopes one day to free herself.

With its abrupt modulations and abundant chromaticism, the B section of the aria (mm. 17–33) represents both Laurie's eagerness to expand her horizons and the anxiety she feels about the future. A middleground enlargement of the alpha motive, varied through the substitution of C♯4 for C4, governs the section. Copland's use of $\sharp\hat{4}$ at the deep middleground level, with its tendency to resolve up to $\hat{5}$ by semitone, intensifies the yearning, questioning nature of the alpha motive and also provides a strong tonal contrast to the home key: $\sharp\hat{4}$ is related to the home key tonic by tritone and is harmonized as $\hat{5}$ of F♯ major (mm. 26-27), the second-most distant relative of G major. Laurie's uncertainty ("Why Am I Strange Inside?"), heard in the static melody and harmonically ambiguous hand-wringing of mm. 17-23, gives way to an emotional outburst ("What makes me think I'd like to try") over a jubilant F♯ major tonic at m. 24, punctuated by an orchestral tutti. This is the first moment where Copland allows Laurie to transcend the tessitura of the A section and rise above the first *passagio*: mm. 24–28 comprise a motion from E♯5 ($\hat{7}$) to F♯5.

Despite the registral, tonal, and motivic evidence to the contrary, Laurie is not yet ready to leave home. Her vision of the future is a naïve, idealistic fantasy, untempered by the harsh lessons of reality. For this reason, Copland does not allow her to complete a middleground 5-line in F♯ major. After descending to $\hat{3}$ (mm. 23–29), her melodic descent is temporarily interrupted by a lower-neighbor prolongation. When the descent resumes (mm. 31–33), the arrival of $\hat{2}$ is harmonized by the minor dominant, and Laurie is not allowed to complete the descent to the tonic. Harmonically, the B section ends with a weak deceptive cadence from v to iv⁶ (m. 33), the ambitious C♯4 settles back to C4, and Laurie returns to G major, the key of her unfulfilled dreams and desires.

After the chromatic adventures of the B section, the restatement of the diatonic alpha motive in the orchestra at m. 35 projects a sense of wistful, but determined pragmatism that is heightened by the return of linear descending motion from the primary tone in the A¹ section (mm. 33–43). When the background descent culminates at m. 42, it is not on the expected G4 over tonic harmony but rather with a registrally transferred G5 over a deceptive subdominant that disrupts the aria's obligatory register (*obligate Lage*). With this descent, Copland sends a clear signal that Laurie will have to wait for the opportunity to turn her dreams into reality.[31] During the subsequent dialogue between Laurie and Ma Moss (R51–R51o), Copland destabilizes the G major tonic by placing it in a variety of inversions and tonal contexts, returning to the primary tone at 51a and 51o only over the same first-inversion tonic that concluded the brief postlude to the aria itself (m. 47).

Although it introduces Martin and his friend Top to Grandpa Moss and earns Martin the privilege of staying "in a place for a while," the trio "A Stranger May Seem Strange That's True" does not move Martin any closer to his superobjective: to build a better life for himself through the acquisition of a steady job, a family, and a place to call home. The work Grandpa Moss offers him and Top is the sort of seasonal labor to which he is already accustomed, and though he is attracted to Laurie, it is clear from the outset that her family would not look favorably on any advances he might make toward her.

The trio's D major key is closely related to Laurie's home key of G major ("Once I thought I'd never grow"), and Martin, as shown in Figure 2, adopts Laurie's primary tone D ($\hat{8}$) as his own, strengthening the musical connection between the two numbers. As in Laurie's aria, the primary tone is prolonged via an essentially static octave coupling before the melodic line begins its descent toward the tonic. Because the trio does not move him any closer to achieving his superobjective, however, Copland does not permit Martin to close an 8-line in this number, opting instead for a middleground interruption on $\hat{5}$ (A) over V^6 at m. 7 that is repeated throughout the number.[32] The pentatonic opening of the number's main theme also raises the possibility of a gapped line ($\hat{8}$–$\hat{6}$–$\hat{5}$), but Copland's use of the non-pentatonic C♮ at m. 6 provides a Mixolydian inflection instead.

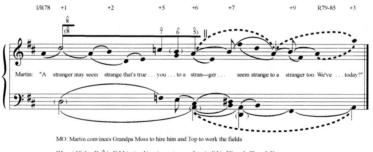

Martin: "A stranger may seem strange that's true . . . you . . . to a stran---ger . . . seem strange to a stranger too. We've . . . today?"

MO: Martin convinces Grandpa Moss to hire him and Top to work the fields

[He establishes D ($\hat{8}$ in D Major) as his primary tone, as Laurie did in "Once I Thought"]

Figure 2 Voice leading, "A Stranger May Seem Strange That's True"

Both the use of an incomplete background structure and a chromatic C♮ further recall Laurie's aria which, like this trio, is notated in D major with repeated C♮ accidentals and does not provide tonic-supported closure to 1̂ at its conclusion. Though Laurie and Martin have not yet established a relationship with one another, Copland establishes the possibility of one by tonally linking the two characters yet denying each one individual closure. They are both searching for something, but are their goals compatible? Moreover, the reharmonization of the couple's background primary tone (D) in the key of the dominant and its middleground prolongation via interruption foreshadows the couple's failure to achieve musical closure later in Act 3 of the opera.

Martin begins the F major ensemble number that closes the first act of the opera, "The Promise of Living." Like Laurie's aria, it begins on 5̂ (C), prominently features 8̂ (F), and lacks linear-harmonic closure to the tonic, as shown in Figure 3. Copland's choice of F major for this number is important for two reasons. First, it helps to move the G major background structure of the couple one step closer to its goal by harmonizing C (4̂ of G major) as its local primary tone. Second, it reinforces at the background level the Mixolydian inflection used in Martin's earlier duet with Top, given that F major is the lowered subtonic (♭VII) of G major. This inflection, which weakens the drive toward the tonic by removing the leading tone, represents Martin's inability to reconcile his dreams and ambitions for the future with the harsh reality of his present situation, culminating in his Act 2 aria.

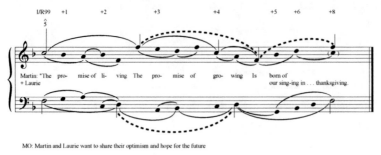

Figure 3 Voice leading, "The Promise of Living"

The word "promise" in the title has two potential meanings. When sung by Ma Moss and the rest of the ensemble later in the number (R99ff.), it connotes a divine covenant made with a thankful people, as in this lyric from R103–104: "the promise of ending in right understanding is peace in our own hearts and peace with our neighbour." When sung by Martin and Laurie at the opening of the number, however, it indicates hope for the future, as in R98–99: "the promise of growing with faith and with knowing is born of our sharing our love with our neighbour."

It is appropriate that as Martin and Laurie look forward to a future filled with promise (R97–99) Copland chooses to withhold harmonic support for their melodic lines, opting instead for a solo orchestral line acting as a functional pedal point: the promise they are singing of is not yet realized. When Ma Moss enters at R99, Copland supplies a complete diatonic accompaniment in F major that, like Laurie's aria, prominently features the mediant and subdominant triads, concluding with a plagal cadence at m. 32.[33] The addition of the chordal accompaniment and the fact that Copland borrowed the melody of the number from a popular Protestant hymn tune makes its conclusion a jubilant song of praise and thanksgiving for the harvest, mentioned specifically in the B section of the number (R100–102), that is extended in Ma Moss's augmentation of the main theme at R103.

The ambiguous key of Martin and Laurie's first duet, "You Dance Real Well," brings the modal inflection used in Martin's previous numbers to the fore. Though Copland scores the duet using a key signature of two sharps, the absence of tonic and dominant harmonies from either D major or B minor weakens the sense of tonality. Copland uses E minor, F♯ minor and G major harmonies in mm. 1–23 that imply repeated motion to the submediant in B minor (B Aeolian or the natural minor), but that motion is never confirmed by a corresponding move from dominant to tonic.[34] In the final measures (mm. 26–29), the orchestral melody substitutes C♮ for C♯ and outlines a V[7], indicating the possibility that G major is no longer the submediant but the tonic.

Whether it is being used as submediant or tonic, the G major triad in mm. 3–6 and 10–15 is the focal harmony of the duet and it supports B in both Laurie and Martin's melodic line, as shown in Figure 4. As the putative primary tone of the duet, despite the absence of tonic support, B is prolonged in both the vocal lines and the orchestral melody by successive repetitions of the middleground upper-neighbor C♯. Copland's choice of B as primary tone for the duet is ironic in that it continues the progression of Martin and Laurie's fundamental line toward closure on the tonic of G major and is supported by a G major triad, yet that triad's failure to act as a tonic calls the linear-harmonic progress it suggests into question. This combination of linear progress and harmonic reticence reflects the current dramatic situation in the opera: Martin and Laurie have met in what should be a sanguine romantic encounter, yet Martin quashes Laurie's languorous daydreaming ("Isn't there a place where dancing never stops?") with a terse reply ("It always stops"). Copland refuses to allow the duet to settle in G major, even while he extends the tantalizing possibility of future closure in that key through both melodic and harmonic means.[35]

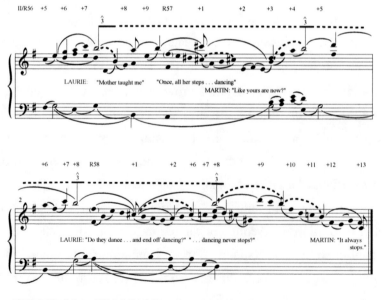

Figure 4 Voice leading, "You Dance Real Well"

The continuation of the duet (mm. 30–51) is comprised of a descending Phrygian octave line in the orchestra from G to G that foreshadows the chromaticism of Martin's upcoming aria. By setting each note of the linear progression with a transposed member or subset of set-class 5–35 (the pentatonic scale), Copland purposefully avoids implying G major as the key of the continuation. Moreover, because he chromatically alters the descent by borrowing tones from a modal minor scale (G Phrygian duplicates G natural minor, with the addition of $\flat\hat{2}$), and harmonizes the final G with an E♭ major triad (a deceptive ♭VI in G major), Copland is able to allude harmonically to the pessimism that Martin expresses in his reply to Laurie's wistful question and suggest how it might ultimately prevent closure in G major for the couple in the opera.

Martin's aria "I'm Gettin' Tired of Travelin' Through," a *de facto* proposal to Laurie, begins by moving the couple's fundamental line to $\hat{2}$ (A) over a D major tonic (V in G major), raising the possibility that Martin will overcome his cynicism and the couple will be successful in their search for a better life together (see Figure 5). As the aria progresses, however, Martin's love for Laurie comes into conflict with his love of the land and his desire to be free. At m. 12, Martin's focus begins to shift away from Laurie as he talks of wanting to "see a seedling grow" and of his desire to know "special skies, special rain, and snow."[36] The middleground descent in his vocal line bypasses diatonic $\hat{7}$ (C♯), moving instead to C♮ and destabilizing D major, and Copland soon uses C♮ as a new leading tone and modulates to D♭ major (m. 14). This modulation to an extremely distant key (VII♭$^5_3$, spelled enharmonically as ♭I!) creates the effect of a chromatic "slippage." Martin has become distracted by thoughts of working the land ("A man must take a handful of earth and work it for his own"), and the aria's brief B section remains in D♭ major as his vocal line descends from C to B♭ over the submediant (mm. 17-22), concluding on A♭ over the local tonic in m. 23. It is particularly telling that, in mm. 15-16 as he foreshadows the notes of Laurie's "love" motive (played by the orchestra as Laurie declares her love at R68, and sung by Laurie herself at R72), he is singing of his love for the land, not for Laurie.

Figure 5 Voice leading, "I'm Gettin' Tired of Travelin' Through"

As a result of the modulation to D♭ major, the middleground linear progression that began on D at m. 8, rather than prolonging the primary tone A via a diatonic fourth-progression from 8̂ (D) to 5̂ (A), winds up descending instead by whole step to A♭, outlining a member of set-class 4–21 [8t02], a whole-tone tetrachord. This "overshooting" of the original primary tone (A, 5̂ in D major) underscores the difficulty Martin faces in trying to reconcile his need to roam freely with his desire to be with Laurie. Earlier, he mused that he would like to "stay in a place *for a while*" (m. 10, emphasis added), and he echoes the same carefree sentiment at m. 26, declaring that he would like to "have a wife for a while" as his thoughts return to Laurie and the key shifts back to D major.

Although Martin's music is firmly rooted in D major throughout much of the A¹ section (mm. 26–39), thoughts of the land once again cause him to roam away from the tonic, this time into B major, the major submediant (VI♯), as he speaks of his desire to "walk out on the land" (mm. 36–39). He remains in B major through the conclusion of the aria's final C section (mm. 40–54), and when Laurie's "love" theme returns again in the orchestra (mm. 50-53), he does not echo it in the vocal line, concluding instead with the hesitant question "Do you *feel in love* the way I do?" (mm. 52–54, emphasis added). In contrast, Laurie responds with the bold declaration "Yes, yes, I do love you" as the scene continues at R68.

Once again, Martin's modulation away from the tonic, re-established in the A^1 section, causes him to "overshoot" a return to the aria's primary tone (A). This time however, his melody descends diatonically from $\hat{8}$ to $\hat{6}$ (D-C♯-B), before the modulation to B major prompts him to move to A♯ rather than A, leading to a conclusion on G♯. In place of a whole-tone descent, the resultant linear progression outlines 5–31 [8te12], a subset of octatonic collection III. The enharmonically equivalent linear trajectories in the B and C sections from $\hat{8}$ to ♭$\hat{6}$ (B♭/A♯) and ♭$\hat{5}$ (A♭/G♯) reveal a man that is divided between two passions and is unable to reconcile them.

The duet that serves as the conclusion of Martin and Laurie's pivotal three-part scene, "In Love? In Love? Yes, Yes, I Do Love You," returns to the key of D♭ major as Laurie enharmonically reinterprets the final G♯ of Martin's aria as A♭ ($\hat{5}$) and transfers it up two octaves (see Figure 6). This prolongation of A♭ precludes a return to A and a continuation of the background descent to the tonic (G). Instead, the couple affirms their love for one another only in a wistful D♭ major, the furthest possible key from their original home key of G major, and that affirmation is immediately followed by the intrusion of Grandpa Moss, who denounces Laurie and orders Martin and Top to leave town the next morning.

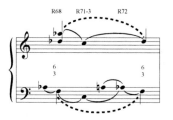

Figure 6 Voice leading, "In Love? In Love? Yes, Yes, I Do Love You"

Act III opens with Martin beneath Laurie's window, calling up to her ("Laurie! Laurie! Is there someone in there that's called Laurie, Laurie?").

Musically, he picks up where the couple left off at the conclusion of their duet in Act II, re-establishing A♭ as the primary melodic tone within a D♭ Lydian context (Figure 7). Both the modally inflected tonality and the return of A♭ (♭2̂ in G major) suggest that Martin is waiting in vain for a reply. When Laurie appears at the window, however, Copland shifts the key to D major, allowing her to return to A in the vocal line and rekindling hope that her grandfather's stern reprieve has not diminished her love for Martin. After several brief tonal excursions, the duet returns to D major at R19, concluding over an extended dominant chord at R22 with A prolonged in the melody. Despite offering this last opportunity for the continuation of progress toward background tonal closure, Copland never permits Martin or Laurie to return to G major and close a 5-line to the tonic. Instead, he prolongs the permanent interruption first reached in Martin's aria throughout Act III, occasionally returning to the "spoiler" key of D♭ major to further discourage any lingering association with the couple's G major tonic.

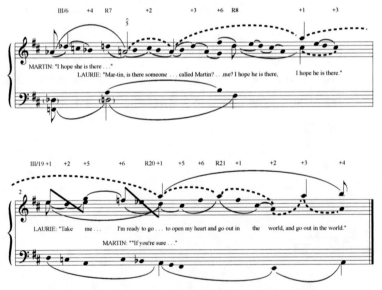

Figure 7 Voice leading, "Laurie! Laurie!"

Summary

Unlike the first three operas studied in this book, *The Tender Land* does not make extensive use of linear-harmonic tonality in individual numbers. Laurie's Act I aria, "Once I Thought I'd Never Grow" is the most tonal of the arias and duets examined in this chapter, and even its closure of a 5-line to the tonic is supported only by a deceptive cadence to IV. Instead Copland focuses the tonal drama at the background level, as shown in Figure 8. Like Sam and Rose, Martin and Laurie share a common primary tone, established even earlier here than it was in *Street Scene*. Copland then prolongs a single primary tone in each scene that the lovers share together, foregoing local descent but occasionally re-harmonizing a common tone to avoid parallel voice leading (as in the re-harmonization of D as $\hat{8}$ in D major in Martin's first appearance). Like all three of the previous operas, *The Tender Land* concludes with a weakening of tonality (the register transfer of A, supported only by an arpeggiation from the dominant), as Martin and Laurie struggle to reconcile their different needs and desires

SO: Martin and Laurie are looking for opposite things; he wants stability and she wants adventure; they try to find them in each other.

[United by a common primary tone (D as $\hat{5}$ of G Major), the two attempt to close a 5-line to the tonic, reaching $\hat{2}$/V]

Figure 8 Background structure, Martin and Laurie

However, the most unusual number in Copland's opera is Martin's aria, which introduces the possibility of linear-dramatic analysis in a post-tonal context. "Linear analysis" is the name given by renowned music theorist Allen Forte to analyses that appropriate Schenkerian techniques for the examination of twentieth-century music.[37] While some authors have criticized the use of Schenkerian tools or symbols for post-tonal repertoire, on the grounds that without diatonic tonality the system is rendered ineffective at best, misleading at worst,[38] Copland's music offers a middleground. Diatonic tonality is present at the background of each number, and thus can suggest a tonic and a primary tone, even if there is no subsequent descent to a tonic. Since the present study seeks to illuminate multi-movement structure, a single primary tone and tonic pitch are the only requirements for each number to be related one to the other. The study of "linearity as drama," however, will have to wait for a second volume; it is my fond hope that the present one has made such a volume both worthwhile and feasible.

ENDNOTES

[1] Howard Pollack, *Aaron Copland: The Life and Work of an Uncommon Man* (New York: Henry Holt, 1999), 470 n6.

[2] Ibid., 469–70.

[3] "Summertime," Clara's Act I aria from the opera, is a particular favorite with jazz players even today.

[4] Copland, notes to the Plymouth Music Series recording of *The Tender Land*, dir. Philip Brunelle, 1992 Virgin B000002RZP. Quoted in Larry Starr, "Review: Copland on Compact Disc III: Opera and Songs," *American Music* 11/2 (1993): 256–61.

[5] Hammerstein preferred the label "musical play" for his own works. See Oscar Hammerstein II, *Lyrics* (New York, 1949).

[6] James Agee, *Let Us Know Praise Famous Men* (Boston, 1941). Reprinted by Houghton Mifflin, 1960.

[7] Christopher W. Patton, "Discovering 'The Tender Land': A New Look at Aaron Copland's Opera," *American Music* 20/3 (2002): 331.

[8] Patton notes that the end of their relationship seems not to have affected or been instigated by their work on the opera. See Patton, "Discovering 'The Tender Land,'" 322.

[9] Ibid., 331–32.

[10] Elizabeth B. Crist, *Music for the Common Man: Aaron Copland During the Depression and War* (Oxford: Oxford University Press, 2005).

[11] Ironically, Menotti's opera, a Christmas favorite about the journey of the magi to Bethlehem to see the Christ child, has enjoyed continued popular success since its premiere and is regularly staged by local companies across the United States during the Christmas season.

[12] Wilfrid Mellers, "Review of *The Tender Land* (Abridged) by Copland," *The Musical Times* 107/1483 (1966): 784.

[13] Pollack, *Aaron Copland*, 470.

[14] Harriett Johnson, "Copland's *Tender Land* at Center," *New York Post*, April 2, 1954, 60; Olin Downes, "Music: One-Act Opera Has Premiere," *New York Times*, April 2, 1954, 24.

[15] Edward Mattos, "*Tender Land* Absorbing: Mattos," *Oberlin Review* 83/57 (1955): 1.

[16] Joseph Kerman, "Review of *The Tender Land*. Opera in Three Acts by Aaron Copland; Horace Everett." *Notes* 14/1 (1956): 57.

[17] Aaron Copland to Carlos Chávez, 5 April 1954, in *The Selected Correspondence of Aaron Copland*, ed. Elizabeth B. Crist, Wayne Shirley (New Haven: Yale University Press, 2006), 211–12.

[18] Downes, "One-Act Opera Has Premiere," 24.

[19] Roseberry, Eric. "Review of Copland: *The Tender Land* by Plymouth Music Series, Minnesota," *Tempo* 175 (1990): 41.

[20] Patton, "Discovering *The Tender Land*," 318.

[21] Erik Johns, letter to Aaron Copland. Not dated. Aaron Copland Collection, Music Division, Library of Congress, Washington, D.C. Cited in Patton, "Discovering 'The Tender Land'," 318.

[22] Howard Pollack, "Copland, Gershwin and the American Landscape," in *Copland Connotations*, ed. Peter Dickinson (Woodbridge: The Boydell Press, 2002), 66–72.

[23] Ibid.

[24] Daniel E. Mathers, "Expanding Horizons: Sexuality and the Re-zoning of *The Tender Land*," in *Copland Connotations*, ed. Peter Dickinson (Woodbridge: The Boydell Press, 2002), 118–35.

[25] Howard Pollack, "The Dean of Gay American Composers," *American Music* 18/1 (2000): 39–49.

[26] Top's plan is strongly reminiscent of the one designed by Don Giovanni to seduce Zerlina in Mozart's *Don Giovanni*.

[27] Here and throughout the chapter, locations in the piano-vocal score will be given by act and rehearsal number. The rehearsal numbers are taken from Aaron Copland, *The Tender Land: An Opera in Three Acts* (New York: Boosey and Hawkes, 1956).

[28] Measures are numbered beginning at rehearsal 45 (Copland, *The Tender Land*, 26).

[29] "Double mixture" is a term used by Edward Aldwell and Carl Schachter to describe a two-step process of modal mixture whereby one borrows from the parallel mode then changes the mode of the chord again, usually by altering the third of the new chord. See Edward Aldwell and Carl Schachter, *Harmony and Voice Leading*, 4th ed. (New York: Wadsworth, 2008).

[30] For a recent discussion of alternative cadences, see the smt-list archives.

[31] For an extended discussion of the importance of obligatory register to the interpretation of linear structure, see Ernst Oster, "Register and the Large-Scale Connection," *Journal of Music Theory* 5/1 (1961): 54–71. An alternative reading of the aria's background structure as a Neumeyerian ascent from $\hat{5}$ (D5) to $\hat{8}$ (G5) would emphasize the sense of Laurie's dreams as an idealized fantasy. See David Neumeyer, "The Ascending *Urlinie*."

[32] Measures are numbered from I/R78. Schenker defines interruption at $\hat{5}$ as the normative form of an interrupted 8-line. See Schenker, *Free Composition*.

[33] Measures are numbered from R97.

[34] Measures are numbered from R57–7.

[35] Copland marks F♯ as an alternative to the C♯ that closes Martin's vocal line at m. 29, probably for registral reasons (a lighter tenor voice cannot reliably project C♯). Read in B minor, the given C♯ would suggest a permanent interruption on $\hat{2}$ (implying a

3-line), while the alternate F♯ would privilege an interruption on $\hat{5}$ (implying an 8-line). Though both readings support the pessimistic tone of the duet's conclusion, they are each hindered by the lack of B minor tonal confirmation in the duet.

[36] Measures are numbered from R62–2.

[37] Allen Forte, "New Approaches to Linear Analysis," *Journal of the American Musicological Society* 41/2 (1988): 315–48.

[38] Joseph N. Straus, "The Problem of Prolongation in Post-Tonal Music," *Journal of Music Theory* 31/1 (Spring 1987): 1–22.

BIBLIOGRAPHY

BOOKS

Abbate, Carolyn and Roger Parker, eds. *Analyzing Opera: Verdi and Wagner*. Berkeley: University of California Press, 1989.

————. *In Search of Opera*. Princeton: Princeton University Press, 2001.

Adler, Samuel. *The Study of Orchestration*. 2nd ed. New York: Norton, 1989.

Adler, Stella. *The Technique of Acting*. Toronto: Bantam Books, 1988.

Almén, Byron and Edward R. Pearsall, eds. *Approaches to Meaning in Music*. Bloomington: Indiana University Press, 2006.

Alpert, Hollis. *The Life and Times of* Porgy and Bess: *The Story of an American Classic*. New York: Alfred A. Knopf, 1990.

Arseniy, G. *Teatr i iskusstvo* 22 (1899).

Beach, David, ed. *Aspects of Schenkerian Theory*. New Haven: Yale University Press, 1983.

Beckerman, Bernard. *Dynamics of Drama*. New York: Knopf, 1970.

Benedetti, Jean, ed. and trans. *The Moscow Art Theatre Letters*. London: Methuen Drama, 1991.

Benedetti, Robert L. *Seeming, Being and Becoming: Acting in Our Century*. New York: Drama Book Specialists, 1976.

————. *The Actor at Work*. 4th ed. Englewood Cliffs, NJ: PrenticeHall, 1986.

————. *Stanislavski*. New York: Routledge, 1988.

Bent, Ian, ed. *Music Analysis in the Nineteenth Century*. Cambridge: Cambridge University Press, 1994.

Berlin, Edward A. *King of Ragtime: Scott Joplin and his Era*. Oxford: Oxford University Press, 1994.

Berry, David Carson. *A Topical Guide to Schenkerian Literature: An Annotated Bibliography With Indices*. Hillsdale, NY: Pendragon, 2004.

Berry, Wallace. *Musical Structure and Performance*. New Haven: Yale University Press, 1989.

Blackmer, Corinne E. and Patricia Juliana Smith, eds. *En Travesti: Women, Gender Subversion, Opera*. New York: Columbia University Press, 1995.

Boleslavsky, Richard. *Acting: The First Six Lessons*. New York: Theatre Arts Books, 1933.

Boykan, Martin. *Silence and Slow Time: Studies in Musical Narrative*. Oxford: Scarecrow Press, 2004.

Brown, Matthew. *Explaining Tonality: Schenkerian Theory and Beyond*. Rochester: University of Rochester Press, 2005.

Burstein, L. Poundie and David Gagné, ed. *Structure and Meaning in Tonal Music: Festschrift in Honor of Carl Schachter*. Hillsdale: Pendragon, 2006.

Cadwallader, Allen and David Gagné. *Analysis of Tonal Music: A Schenkerian Approach*, second edition. Oxford: Oxford University Press, 2007.

Cadwallader, Allen, ed. *Trends in Schenkerian Research*. New York: Schirmer, 1990.

Caplin, William. *Classical Form: A Theory of Formal Functions for the Instrumental Music of Haydn, Mozart, and Beethoven*. New York: Oxford University Press, 1997.

Carlson, Marvin. *Theories of the Theatre: A Historical and Critical Survey, from the Greeks to the Present*, expanded ed. Ithaca: Cornell University Press, 1993.

Chekhov, Michael. *On the Technique of Acting*. Edited by Mel Gordon. New York: HarperCollins Publishers, 1991.

Chua, Daniel K.L. *Absolute Music and the Construction of Meaning*. Cambridge: Cambridge University Press, 1999.

Clurman, Harold. *On Directing*. New York: Macmillan, 1972.

Cone, Edward T. *Musical Form and Musical Performance*. New York: W. W. Norton, 1968.

———. *The Composer's Voice*. Berkeley: University of California Press, 1974.

Copland, Aaron and Vivian Perlis. *Copland: Since 1943*. New York: St. Martin's Press, 1989.

Crist, Elizabeth B. and Wayne Shirley, eds. *The Selected Correspondence of Aaron Copland*. New Haven: Yale University Press, 2006.

Crist, Elizabeth B. *Music for the Common Man: Aaron Copland During the Depression and War*. Oxford: Oxford University Press, 2005.

Curtis, Susan. *Dancing to a Black Man's Tune: A Life of Scott Joplin*. Columbia, MO: University of Missouri Press, 1994.

d'Alembert, Jean le Rond. *Élémens de musique, suivant les principes de M. Rameau*. Lyon: Bruyset, Père, et Fils, 1779.

Damschroder, David. *Music Theory From Zarlino to Schenker: A Bibliography and Guide*. New York: Pendragon Press, 1990.

Dent, Edward J. *Mozart's Operas: A Critical Study*. London: Chatto and Windus, 1913.

Dickinson, Peter, ed. *Copland Connotations: Studies and Interviews*. Woodbridge: The Boydell Press, 2002.

Drew, David. *Kurt Weill: A Handbook*. London: Faber and Faber, 1987.

Edwards, Christine. *The Stanislavsky Heritage: Its Contribution to the Russian and American Theatre*. New York: New York University Press, 1965.

Ewen, David. *American Composers: A Biographical Dictionary*. London: Robert Hale, 1982.

Farneth, David. *Kurt Weill: A Life in Pictures and Documents*. Woodstock, NY: Overlook Press, 2000.

Forte, Allen and Steven E. Gilbert. *Introduction to Schenkerian Analysis*. New York: Norton, 1982.

———. *The American Popular Ballad of the Golden Era, 1924–1950*. Princeton: Princeton University Press, 1995.

Gammond, Peter. *Scott Joplin and the Ragtime Era*. New York: St. Martin's Press, 1975.

Gilbert, Steven E. *The Music of Gershwin*. New Haven: Yale University Press, 1995.

Gorchakov, Nikolai M. *Stanislavsky Directs*. Translated by Miriam Goldina. New York: Funk & Wagnalls, 1954.

Gordon, Mel. *The Stanislavsky Technique: Russia: A Workbook for Actors*. New York: Applause Theatre Book Publishers, 1988.

Hagen, Uta. *A Challenge for the Actor*. New York: Charles Scribner's Sons, 1991.

Haskins, James. *Scott Joplin: The Man Who Made Ragtime*. New York: Scarborough, 1980.

Hatten, Robert S. *Interpreting Musical Gestures, Topics, and Tropes: Mozart, Beethoven, Schubert*. Bloomington: Indiana University Press, 2004.

———. *Musical Meaning in Beethoven: Markedness, Correlation, and Interpretation*. Bloomington: Indiana University Press, 1994.

Hirsch, Foster. *Kurt Weill on Stage: From Berlin to Broadway*. New York: Alfred A. Knopf, 2002.

Hoover, Marjorie L. *Meyerhold: The Art of Conscious Theater*. Amherst: University of Massachusetts Press, 1974.

Hull, S. Loraine. *Strasberg's Method as Taught by Lorrie Hull: A Practical Guide for Actors, Teachers, and Directors*. Woodbridge, CT: Ox Bow Publishing, 1985.

Jablonski, Edward and Lawrence D. Stewart. *The Gershwin Years*. New York: Doubleday, 1973. First edition published in 1958.

Jablonski, Edward, *Gershwin*. New York: Doubleday, 1987.

Jarman, Douglas. *Kurt Weill: An Illustrated Biography*. Bloomington: Indiana University Press, 1982.

Katz, Adele T. *Challenge to Musical Tradition: A New Concept of Tonality*. New York: Alfred A. Knopf, 1945.

Klein, Michael L. *Intertextuality in Western Art Music*. Bloomington: Indiana University Press, 2004.

Komar, Arthur, ed. *Robert Schumann:* Dichterliebe. New York: Norton, 1971.

Kommisarzhevsky, Theodore. *Myself and the Theatre.* London: William Heinemann Ltd., 1929.

Kowalke, Kim H., ed. *A New Orpheus: Essays on Kurt Weill.* New Haven: Yale University Press, 1986.

Kugel', Aleksandr. *Teatr i iskusstvo* 8 (1899).

Laskowski, Larry. *Heinrich Schenker: An Annotated Index to His Analyses of Musical Works.* New York: Pendragon Press, 1978.

Leach, Robert. *A History of Russian Theatre.* Cambridge: Cambridge University Press, 1999.

———. *Makers of Modern Theatre: An Introduction.* New York: Routledge Press, 2004.

———. *Stanislavsky and Meyerhold.* New York: Peter Lang, 2003.

Leafstedt, Carl S. *Inside* Bluebeard's Castle: *Music and Drama in Béla Bartók's Opera.* Oxford: Oxford University Press, 1999.

Levarie, Siegmund. *Mozart's* Le Nozze di Figaro: *A Critical Analysis.* Chicago: University of Chicago Press, 1952.

Levin, Irina and Igor Levin. *Working on the Play and the Role: The Stanislavsky Method for Analyzing the Characters in a Drama.* Chicago: Ivan R. Doe, 1992.

———. *The Stanislavsky Secret: Not a System, Not a Method, But a Way of Thinking.* New York: Meriweather Publishers, 2002.

Lewis, Robert. *Advice to the Players.* New York: Harper & Row, 1980.

Lorenz, Alfred O. *Das Geheimnis der Form bei Richard Wagner*, 4 vols. Berlin: M. Hesse, 1924–33.

Magarshack, David. *Stanislavski: A Life.* New York: Chanticleer Press, 1951.

Meisel, Martin. *How Plays Work: Reading and Performance.* Oxford: Oxford University Press, 2007.

Merlin, Bella. *Beyond Stanislavsky: The Psycho-Physical Approach to Actor Training.* New York: Routledge Press, 2001.

———. *Konstantin Stanislavsky.* New York: Routledge Press, 2003.

———. *The Complete Stanislavsky Toolkit*. New York: Drama Publishers, 2007.

Meyerhold, Vsevolod. *Perepiska 1896–1939*. Moscow: Iskusstvo, 1976.

Miller, Richard. *The Structure of Singing: System and Art in Vocal Technique*. New York: Schirmer, 1986.

———. *Training Tenor Voices*. New York: Schirmer, 1993.

Moore, Sonia, ed. and trans. *Stanislavski Today: Commentaries on K.S. Stanislavski*. New York: American Center for Stanislavski Theatre Art, 1973.

———. *The Stanislavski System: The Professional Training of an Actor*. 2nd ed. New York: Penguin, 1984.

Nattiez, Jean-Jacques. *Music and Discourse*. Translated by Carolyn Abbate. Princeton: Princeton University Press, 1990.

Nemirovitch-Dantchenko, Vladimir. *My Life in the Russian Theatre*. Translated by John Cournos. New York: Theatre Arts Books, 1968.

Nichols, David, ed. *Cambridge History of American Music*. Cambridge: Cambridge University Press, 1995.

Noske, Frits. *The Signifier and the Signified: Studies in the Operas of Mozart and Verdi*. The Hague: Nijhoff, 1977.

Perle, George. *The Operas of Alban Berg*. 2 vols. Berkeley: University of California Press, 1980.

Perry, John. *Encyclopedia of Acting Techniques*. Cincinnati: Betterway Books, 1997.

Petty, Jonathan Christian. *Wagner's Lexical Tonality*. Lewiston: Mellen Press, 2005.

Pitches, Jonathan. *Science and the Stanislavsky Tradition of Acting*. New York: Routledge Press, 2006.

Pollack, Howard. *Aaron Copland: The Life and Work of an Uncommon Man*. New York: Henry Holt, 1999.

Rink, John S., ed. *The Practice of Performance: Studies in Musical Interpretation*. Cambridge, England: Cambridge University Press, 1995.

Rosenberg, Deena. *Fascinating Rhythm: The Collaboration of George and Ira Gershwin*. New York: Dutton, 1991.

Salzer, Felix. *Structural Hearing: Tonal Coherence in Music*. 2 vols. New York: C. Boni, 1952.

Samith, Peter H. *Expressive Forms in Brahms's Instrumental Music: Structure and Meaning in His Werther Quartet*. Bloomington: Indiana University Press, 2005.

Sanders, Ronald. *The Days Grow Short: The Life and Music of Kurt Weill*. New York: Holt, Rinehart, and Winston, 1980.

Sayler, Oliver M. *Inside the Moscow Art Theatre*. New York: Brentano's, 1925.

Schachter, Carl and Hedi Siegel, eds. *Schenker Studies 2*. Cambridge: Cambridge University Press, 1999.

————. *Unfoldings: Essays in Schenkerian Theory and Analysis*. Edited by Joseph N. Straus. Oxford: Oxford University Press, 1999.

Schebera, Jürgen. *Kurt Weill: An Illustrated Life*. Translated by Caroline Murphy. New Haven: Yale University Press, 1995.

Schenker, Heinrich. *Free Composition: Volume III of "New Musical Theories and Fantasies."* 2 vols. Edited and translated by Ernst Oster. New York: Longman, 1979. Originally published as *Der Freie Satz*. Vienna: Universal Edition, 1935.

————. *The Art of Performance*. Edited by Heribert Esser and translated by Irene Scott Schreier. Oxford: Oxford University Press, 2000.

Schmalfeldt, Janet. *Berg's* Wozzeck: *Harmonic Language and Dramatic Design*. New Haven: Yale University Press, 1983.

Schneider, Wayne, ed. *The Gershwin Style: New Looks at the Music of George Gershwin*. Oxford: Oxford University Press, 1999.

Shchepkin, Mikhail. *Zhizn i tvorchestvo*. Moscow: Iskusstvo, 1984.

Sheean, Vincent. *First and Last Love*. New York: Random House, 1956.

Siegel, Hedi, ed. *Schenker Studies*. Cambridge: Cambridge University Press, 1990.

Simonov, Ruben. *Stanislavsky's Protégé: Eugene Vakhtangov*. Translated and adapted by Miriam Goldina. New York: DBS Publications, 1969.

Stanislavsky, Konstantin. *An Actor Prepares*. Translated by Elizabeth Reynolds Hapgood. New York: Theatre Arts Books, 1936.

————. *Building a Character*. Translated by Elizabeth Reynolds Hapgood. New York: Theatre Arts Books, 1949.

————. *Creating a Role*. Edited by Hermine I. Popper and translated by Elizabeth Reynolds Hapgood. New York: Theatre Arts Books, 1961.

————. *My Life in Art*. Translated by J. J. Robbins. Boston: Little, Brown, and Company, 1924.

————. *Sobranie Sochineii*. 8 vols. Moscow: Iskusstvo, 1988–94.

————. *Stanislavsky on the Art of the Stage*. Translated by David Magarshack. New York: Hill and Wang, 1961.

————. *Stanislavsky Produces* Othello. Translated by Helen Nowak. New York: Theatre Arts Books, 1963.

————. *Stanislavsky's Legacy: A Collection of Comments on a Variety of Aspects of an Actor's Art and Life*. Edited and translated by Elizabeth Reynolds Hapgood. New York: Theatre Arts Books, 1968.

Stanislavsky, Konstantin. *"The Seagull" Produced by Stanislavsky*. Edited by S. D. Balukhaty and translated by David Magarshack. New York: Theatre Arts Books, 1984. Originally published by D. Dobson (London, 1952).

Stanislavsky, Konstantin and Pavel Rumyantsev. *Stanislavsky on Opera*. Edited and translated by Elizabeth Reynolds Hapgood. New York: Theatre Arts Books, 1975.

Starr, Larry. *The Dickinson Songs of Aaron Copland*. Hillsdale, NY: Pendragon Press, 2002.

Strasberg, Lee. *A Dream of Passion: The Development of the Method*. Edited by Evangeline Morphos. Boston: Little, Brown, and Company, 1987.

Symonette, Lys and Kim H. Kowalke. *Speak Low (When You Speak Love): The Letters of Kurt Weill and Lotte Lenya*. Berkeley: University of California Press, 1996.

Taylor, Ronald. *Kurt Weill: Composer in a Divided World*. New York: Simon and Schuster, 1991.

Treitler, Leo. *Music and the Historical Imagination*. Cambridge: Harvard University Press, 1989.

Vineberg, Steve. *Method Actors: Three Generations of an American Acting Style.* New York: Schirmer, 1991.

Whyman, Rose. *The Stanislavsky System of Acting: Legacy and Influence in Modern Performance.* Cambridge: Cambridge University Press, 2008.

Worrall, Nick. *The Moscow Art Theatre.* London: Routledge, 1996.

Wyatt, Robert and John Andrew Johnson, eds. *The George Gershwin Reader.* Oxford: Oxford University Press, 2004.

Yeston, Maury, ed. *Readings in Schenker Analysis and Other Approaches.* New Haven: Yale University Press, 1977.

———. *The Stratification of Musical Rhythm.* New Haven: Yale University Press, 1976.

ARTICLES

Agawu, Kofi. "Theory and Practice in the Analysis of the Nineteenth-Century Lied." *Music Analysis* 11/1 (1992): 3–36.

Baker, James M. "Schenkerian Analysis and Post-Tonal Music." In Beach, *Aspects of Schenkerian Theory*, 153–88.

Beach, David, ed. "The Cadential Six-Four as Support for Scale-Degree Three of the Fundamental Line." *JMT* 34/1 (1990): 81–100.

———. "The Current State of Schenkerian Research." *Acta Musicologica* 57/2 (1985): 275–307.

———. "A Schenker Bibliography." *JMT* 13/1 (1969): 2–37.

———. "A Schenker Bibliography: 1969–1979." *JMT* 23/2 (1979): 275–86.

———. "More on the Six-Four." *JMT* 34/1 (1990): 281–90.

———. "Schenkerian Theory." *Music Theory Spectrum* 11/1 (1989): 3–14.

———. "The Functions of the Six-Four Chord in Tonal Music." *JMT* 11/1 (1967): 2–31.

Berlioz, Hector. "*Les Huguenots:* The Score." In Bent, *Music Analysis in the Nineteenth Century*, 39–57.

Bernard, Jonathan. "On *Density 21.5:* A Response to Nattiez." *Music Analysis* 5/2–3 (1986): 207–32.

Berry, Wallace. "Formal Process and Performance in the *Eroica* Introduction." *Music Theory Spectrum* 10 (1988): 3–18.

———. "Review of Edward T. Cone, *Musical Form and Musical Performance*." *Perspectives of New Music* 9/2 and 10/1 (1971): 271–90.

Brown, Matthew. "Isolde's Narrative: From *Hauptmotiv* to Tonal Model." In Abbate and Parker, *Analyzing Opera: Verdi and Wagner*, 180–201.

Burkhart, Charles. "Schenker's 'Motivic Parallelisms'." *JMT* 22/2 (1978): 145–76.

Burr, Jessica. "Copland, the West and American Identity." In Dickinson, *Copland Connotations*, 22–28.

Cadwallader, Allen. "More on Scale Degree Three and the Cadential Six-Four." *JMT* 36/1 (1992): 187–98.

Carnicke, Sharon Marie. "Stanislavsky: Uncensored and Unabridged." *TDR* 37/1 (1993): 22–37.

Chinoy, Helen Krich. "The Emergence of the Director." In *Directors on Directing: A Source Book of the Modern Theatre*, edited by Toby Cole and Helen Krich Chinoy. New York: Bobbs-Merrill, 1963.

Clurman, Harold. "In the USA." *World Theatre* 8/1 (1959): 30–7. Originally published in Harold Clurman, *Lies Like Truth*. New York: Macmillan, 1958.

Cohn, Richard and Douglas Dempster. "Hierarchical Unity, Plural Unities: Toward a Reconciliation." In *Disciplining Music: Musicology and its Canons*, edited by Katherine Bergeron and Philip V. Bohlman, 156–81. Chicago: University of Chicago Press, 1992.

Cohn, Richard L. "Uncanny Resemblances: Tonal Signification in the Freudian Age." *JAMS* 57/2 (2004): 285–323.

Cone, Edward T. "*Musical Form and Musical Performance* Reconsidered." *Music Theory Spectrum* 7 (1985): 149–58.

Conner, Ted. "Cherubino Rediscovered: Text, Music, and Narrative in Mozart's Trio." *Theory and Practice* 25 (2000): 27–64.

Cooper, Leslie Irene. "Stanislavsky Changes His Mind." *TDR* 9/1 (Fall 1964): 63–8.

Crist, Elizabeth B. "Aaron Copland and the Popular Front." *JAMS* 56/2 (2003): 409–65.

Davis, Andrew C. "On Schachter, Schenker, and the Reading of Musical Expressivity." *Indiana Theory Review* 20/2 (1999): 1–17.

Downes, Olin. "Music: One-Act Opera Has Premiere." *New York Times*, April 2, 1954, 24.

Drabkin, William. "Characters, Key Relations and Tonal Structure in *Il Trovatore.*" *Music Analysis* 1/2 (1982): 143–54.

Dunsby, Jonathan. "Guest Editorial: Performance and Analysis of Music." *Music Analysis* 8/1–2 (1989): 5–20.

———. "Recent Schenker: The Poetic Power of Intelligent Calculation (Or, the Emperor's Second Set of New Clothes)." *Music Analysis* 18/2 (1999): 263–73.

Everett, Horace (Erik Johns) and Aaron Copland. "*The Tender Land:* An Opera in Two Acts: Synopsis." *Tempo* 31 (1954): 10, 12–16.

Everett, Walter. "Deep-Level Portrayals of Directed and Misdirected Motions in Nineteenth-Century Lyric Song." *JMT* 48/1 (2004): 25–68.

Fisher, George and Judy Lochhead. "Analysis, Hearing, and Performance." *Indiana Theory Review* 14/1 (1993): 1–36.

———. "The Performer as Theorist: Preparing a Performance of Daria Semegen's *Three Pieces For Clarinet and Piano* (1968)." *In Theory Only* 6/7 (1982): 23–39.

Forte, Allen. "A Schenkerian Reading (of an Excerpt from *Tristan und Isolde*)." *Musicae Scientiae* (1998): 15–26.

———. "New Approaches to Linear Analysis." *JAMS* 41/2 (1988): 315–48.

———. "Reflections upon the Gershwin-Berg Connection." *The Musical Quarterly* 83/2 (1999): 150–68.

———. "Schenker's Conception of Musical Structure." *JMT* 3/1 (1959): 1–30.

———. "Tonality, Symbol, and Structural Levels in Berg's *Wozzeck.*" *The Musical Quarterly* 71/4 (1985): 474–99.

Hadreas, Peter. "Deconstruction and the Meaning of Music." *Perspectives of New Music* 37/2 (1999): 5–28.

Haimo, Ethan. "Atonality, Analysis, and the Intentional Fallacy." *Music Theory Spectrum* 18/2 (1996): 167–99.

Hamm, Charles. "The Theatre Guild Production of *Porgy and Bess.*" *JAMS* 40 (Fall 1987): 495–532.

———. "Towards a New Reading of Gershwin." In Schneider, *The Gershwin Style: New Looks at the Music of George Gershwin*, 3–18.

Herz, Joachim. "Wozzeck: *Musikalische Struktur und Dramaturgie* [*Wozzeck: Musical Structure and Dramaturgy*]." In *Alban Bergs* Wozzeck *und die Zwanziger Jahre*, edited by Jürgen Kühnel, Ulrich Müller, Oswald Panagl, Franz Viktor Spechtler, Peter Csobádi, and Gernot Gruber, 199–217. Anif-Salzburg: Mueller-Speiser, 1999.

Hubbs, Nadine. "Schenker's Organicism." *Theory and Practice* 16 (1991): 143–62.

Johns, Erik. Interview with Christopher W. Patton, April 5, 2000. Cited in Christopher W. Patton, "Discovering *The Tender Land:* A New Look at Aaron Copland's Opera." *American Music* 20/3 (2002): 317–40.

Johnson, Harriett. "Copland's *Tender Land* at Center." *New York Post*, April 2, 1954, 60.

Johnson, John Andrew. "Gershwin's *Blue Monday* (1922) and the Promise of Success." In Schneider, *The Gershwin Style: New Looks at the Music of George Gershwin*, 111–41.

Kaminsky, Peter. "How to do Things with Words and Music: Towards an Analysis of Selected Ensembles in Mozart's *Don Giovanni.*" *Theory and Practice* 21 (1996): 55–78.

Kerman, Joseph. "Review of *The Tender Land*. Opera in Three Acts by Aaron Copland; Horace Everett." *Notes* 14/1 (1956): 56–57.

Kleppinger, Stanley V. "On the Influence of Jazz Rhythm in the Music of Aaron Copland." *American Music* 21/1 (2003): 74–111.

Korsyn, Kevin. "Schenker's Organicism Reexamined." *Intégral* 7 (1993): 82–118.

Kristi, Grigori V. "The Training of an Actor in the Stanislavski School of Acting." In Moore, *Stanislavski Today: Commentaries on K.S. Stanislavski*, 22–33. Langham Smith, Richard.

"The Play and its Playwright." In *Claude Debussy:* Pelléas et Mélisande, edited by Roger Nichols and Richard Langham Smith, 1–29. Cambridge: Cambridge University Press, 1989.

Latham, Edward D. "Analysis and Performance Studies: A Summary of Current Research." *Jahrbuch der Gesellschaft für Musiktheorie* (2006). Originally published in *Zeitschrift der Gesellschaft für Musiktheorie* 2/2 (2005), http://www.gmth.de/www/zeitschrift.php?option=show&ausgabe=7&archiv=1.

———. "Britten's Strategic Use of Tonality: A Review-Essay on Philip Rupprecht's *Britten's Musical Language* (2001)." *Theory and Practice* 28 (2003): 137–46.

———. "It Ain't Necessarily So: Sporting Life's Triumph in Gershwin's *Porgy and Bess*." *Indiana Theory Review* 25 (Fall 2005): 29–45.

———. "Reuniting the Muses: Cross-Disciplinary Analysis of Debussy's *Pelléas* and *Prelude à l'après-midi d'un faune*." *Ex Tempore* (Fall 2006).

———. "Review of Ethan Haimo's 'Atonality, Analysis and the Intentional Fallacy'" *Music Theory Spectrum* 18/2 (Fall, 1996)." *Music Theory Online* 3.2 (1997), http://mto.societymusictheory.org/issues/mto.97.3.2/mto.97.3.2.latham.html.

———. "The Prophet and the Pitchman: Dramatic Structure and its Musical Elucidation in *Moses und Aron*, Act 1, Scene 2." In *Religious and Political Ideas in Schoenberg's Works*, edited by Russell Berman and Charlotte Cross. New York: Garland Press, 2000.

Lawton, David. "On the 'Bacio' Theme in *Othello*." *Nineteenth-Century Music* 1/3 (1978): 211–20.

Lester, Joel. "Reply to David Beach." *JMT* 36/1 (1992): 199–206.

Levarie, Siegmund. "Tonal Relations in Verdi's *Un Ballo in Maschera*." *Nineteenth-Century Music* 2/2 (1978): 143–7.

Locke, Ralph P. "What Are These Women Doing in Opera?" In Blackmer and Smith, *En Travesti: Women, Gender Subversion, Opera*, 74.

Loeb, David. "Dual-Key Movements." In *Schenker Studies*, edited by Hedi Siegel. Cambridge: Cambridge University Press, 1990.

Logan, Joshua. "Rehearsal with Stanislavsky." *Vogue* (June 1949): 134–8.

Maisel, Arthur. "Voice Leading as Drama in *Wozzeck*." In Schachter and Hedi Siegel, *Schenker Studies 2*, 160–91.

Major, Leon. Interview with Christopher W. Patton. April 5, 2000. Cited in Christopher W. Patton, "Discovering *The Tender Land:* A New Look at Aaron Copland's Opera." *American Music* 20/3 (2002): 317–40.

Mathers, Daniel E. "Expanding Horizons: Sexuality and the Re-zoning of *The Tender Land*." In Dickinson, *Copland Connotations*, 118–35.

Mattos, Edward. "*Tender Land* Absorbing: Mattos." *Oberlin Review* 83/57 (1955): 1.

McCreless, Patrick. "Schenker and Chromatic Tonicization: A Reappraisal." In Siegel, *Schenker Studies*, 125–45. Mellers, Wilfrid. "Review of *The Tender Land* (Abridged) by Copland." *The Musical Times* 107/1483 (1966): 784.

Merriman, James D. "The Parallel of the Arts: Some Misgivings and a Faint Affirmation." *The Journal of Aesthetics and Art Criticism* 31 (1972–3): 155–61.

Meyerhold, Vsevolod. "The Isolation of Stanislavsky." In Vsevolod Meyerhold, *Meyerhold on Theatre*, edited and translated by Edward Braun. New York: Hill and Wang, 1969.

Morgan, Robert P. "Dissonant Prolongations: Theoretical and Compositional Precedents." *JMT* 20/1 (1976): 49–92.

Nattiez, Jean-Jacques. "Varèse's *Density 21.5:* A Study in Semiological Analysis." *Music Analysis* 1/3 (1982): 243–340.

Neumeyer, David. "Organic Structure and the Song Cycle: Another Look at Schumann's *Dichterliebe*." *Music Theory Spectrum* 4 (1982): 92–105.

———. "The Ascending *Urlinie*." *JMT* 31/2 (1987): 275–304.

Northcott, Bayan et al. "Open Forum Discussion." In Dickinson, *Copland Connotations*, 175–84.

Novack, Saul. "The Analysis of Pre-Baroque Music." In Beach, *Aspects of Schenkerian Theory*, 113–34

Oster, Ernst. "Register and the Large-Scale Connection." *JMT* 5/1 (1961): 54–71.

Parker, Roger and Matthew Brown. "*Ancora un bacio*: Three Scenes from Verdi's *Otello*." *Nineteenth-Century Music* 9/1 (1985): 50–61.

———. "Motivic and Tonal Interaction in Verdi's *Un Ballo in Maschera*." *JAMS* 36/2 (1983): 243–65.

Patton, Christopher W. "Discovering *The Tender Land:* A New Look at Aaron Copland's Opera." *American Music* 20/3 (2002): 317–40.

Perlis, Vivian. "A New Chance for *Tender Land.*" *New York Times*, April 26, 1987, sec. 2, 28 and 32.

Pollack, Howard. "Copland, Gershwin and the American Landscape." In Dickinson, *Copland Connotations*, 66–73.

Pollack, Howard. "The Dean of Gay American Composers." *American Music* 18/1 (2000): 39–49.

Priore, Irna. "Further Considerations of the Continuous $\hat{5}$ With an Introduction and Explanation of Schenker's Five Interruption Models." *Indiana Theory Review* 25 (2004): 115–38.

Rast, Nicholas. "A Checklist of Essays and Reviews by Heinrich Schenker." *Music Analysis* 7/2 (1988): 121–32.

Roseberry, Eric. "Review of Copland: *The Tender Land* by Plymouth Music Series, Minnesota." *Tempo* 175 (1990): 41–2.

Rothgeb, John. "Design as a Key to Structure in Tonal Music." *JMT* 15/1–2 (1971): 230–53.

Rothstein, William. "The Americanization of Heinrich Schenker." *In Theory Only* 9/1 (1986): 5–17. Reprinted in *Schenker Studies*, edited by Hedi Siegel, 193–203. Cambridge: Cambridge University Press, 1990.

Samarotto, Frank. "Sublimating Sharp $\hat{4}$: An Exercise in Schenkerian Energetics." *Music Theory Online* 10/3 (2004), http://mto.societymusictheory.org/issues/mto.04.10.3/mto.04.10.3.samarotto.html.

Sanguinetti, Giorgio. "La carta e il sentiero: Interpretazione e analisi in una prospettiva schenkeriana [The Map and the Path: Interpretation and Analysis from a Schenkerian Perspective]." In Giorgio Sanguinetti, *Intersezioni: Quattro studi di teoria e analisi musicale*, 9–36. Cosenza: Università della Calabria, 1999.

———. "*La funzione drammatica del campo tonale: Il duetto tra Carlo ed Elisabetta nel secondo atto del* Don Carlo [The Dramatic Function of the Tonal Field: The Duet between Carlo and Elisabetta in the Second Act of

Don Carlo].” In Giorgio Sanguinetti, *Intersezioni: Quattro studi di teoria e analisi musicale*, 109–36. Cosenza: Università della Calabria, 1999.

———. “*L'opera italiana nella critica musicale di Heinrich Schenker* [Italian Opera in Heinrich Schenker's Music Criticism].” *Nuova rivista musicale italiana* 29/3 (1995): 431–67.

Schiff, David. “Who Was That Masked Composer?” *The Atlantic Monthly* 285/1 (2000): 116–21.

Schmalfeldt, Janet. “On the Relation of Analysis to Performance: Beethoven's *Bagatelles* Op. 126, Nos. 2 and 6.” *JMT* 29/1 (1985): 1–32.

———. “Cadential Processes: The Evaded Cadence and the ‘One More Time’ Technique.” *Journal of Musicological Research* 12/1–2 (1992): 1–52.

———. “In Search of Dido.” *The Journal of Musicology* 18/4 (2001): 584–615.

———. “On Performance, Analysis, and Schubert.” *Per musi: Revista de performance musical* 5–6 (2002): 38–54.

———. “Towards a Reconciliation of Schenkerian Concepts with Traditional and Recent Theories of Form.” *Music Analysis* 10/3 (1991): 233–87.

Shirley, Wayne D. “‘Rotating’ *Porgy and Bess*.” In Schneider, *The Gershwin Style: New Looks at the Music of George Gershwin*, 21–34.

Sidlin, Murray. Interview with Christopher W. Patton, April 5, 2000. Cited in Christopher W. Patton, “Discovering *The Tender Land*: A New Look at Aaron Copland's Opera.” *American Music* 20/3 (2002): 317–40.

Siegel, Hedi, ed. *Schenker Studies*. Cambridge: Cambridge University Press, 1990.

Simonov, P.V. *The Method of Konstantin Stanislavski and the Physiology of Emotion*. Moscow: Iskusstvo, 1962. Excerpted in Moore, *Stanislavski Today: Commentaries on K.S. Stanislavski*, , 34–43.

Smyth, David H. “‘Balanced Interruption’ and the Formal Repeat.” *Music Theory Spectrum* 15/1 (1993): 76–88.

Starr, Larry. “Copland, Ives and Gambling with the Future.” In Dickinson, *Copland Connotations*, 74–82. Starr, Larry. “Review: *Copland on Compact Disc III: Opera and Songs*.” *American Music* 11/2 (1993): 256–61.

———. “Tonal Traditions in Art Music from 1920 to 1960.” In Nichols, *Cambridge History of American Music*, 471–81.

Stempel, Larry. "*Street Scene* and the Enigma of Broadway Opera." In Kowalke, *A New Orpheus: Essays on Kurt Weill*, 321–42.

Tovstonogov, Georgi A. "The Profession of a Director." In Moore, *Stanislavski Today: Commentaries on K.S. Stanislavski*, 57–62.

Wolzogen, Hans von. "Prelude, Act I [*Parsifal*]." In Bent, *Music Analysis in the Nineteenth Century*, 88–105.

UNPUBLISHED MATERIALS

Alegant, Brian and Don McLean. "Motivic Enlargement." Paper presented at the annual meeting for the Society for Music Theory, New York City, New York, October 1995.

Cook, Susan C. Opera for a New Republic: The Zeitopern of Krenek, Weill, and Hindemith. Ann Arbor: UMI Research Press, 1988.

Davis, Andrew C. "Structural Implications of Stylistic Plurality in Puccini's *Turandot*." PhD diss., Indiana University, 2003.

DeLapp, Jennifer. "Copland in the Fifties: Music and Ideology in the McCarthy Era." PhD diss., University of Michigan, Ann Arbor, 1997.

Everett, Walter. "Singing About the Fundamental Line: Vocal Portrayals of Directed and Misdirected Motions." Paper presented at the annual meeting for the Society for Music Theory, Phoenix, Arizona, October 30, 1997.

Flannery, James William. "Nemirovich-Danchenko, Stanislavsky and the Singer-Actor." MFA thesis, Yale University, 1961.

Gaillard, Ottofritz. *The German Stanislawski Book*. Translated by Evelyn Hoffman. MFA diss., Yale University, 1957. Originally published as *Das Deutsche Stanislawski Buch*. Berlin: Aufbau-Verlag, 1946.

Hebert, Rubye Nell. "A Study of the Composition and Performance of Scott Joplin's Opera *Treemonisha*." DMA thesis, Ohio State University, 1976.

Johns, Erik. "More Notes on *The Tender Land*." Program for the Bronx Opera Company production, December 1994.

Johns, Erik. Letters to Aaron Copland. Not dated. Aaron Copland Collection, Music Division, Library of Congress, Washington, D.C.

Johnson, John Andrew. "Gershwin's 'American Folk Opera': The Genesis, Style and Reputation of *Porgy and Bess* (1935)." PhD diss., Harvard University, 1996.

Jones, Ryan Patrick. "*The Tender Land:* Aaron Copland's American Narrative." PhD diss., Brandeis University, 2005.

Kilroy, David Michael. "Kurt Weill on Broadway: The Postwar Years (1946–1950)." PhD diss., Harvard University, 1992.

Lawton, David. "Tonality and Drama in Verdi's Early Operas." PhD diss., University of California, Berkeley, 1973.

Marcozzi, Rudy. "The Construction of Large-Scale Harmonic and Dramatic Structure in the Verdi Operas Adapted from Shakespeare." PhD diss., Indiana University, 1992.

Petty, Wayne. "Imagining Drama as an Aid to Musical Performance." Paper presented at the annual meeting for the New England Conference of Music Theorists, Wellesley College, Wellesley, Massachusetts, April 1995.

Proire, Irna. "The Case for a Continuous $\hat{5}$: Expanding the Schenkerian Interruption Concept—With Analytical Interpretations of Beethoven Opp. 101, 109, and 111." PhD diss., University of Iowa, 2004.

Smith, Peter H. "Formal Ambiguity and Large-Scale Tonal Structure in Brahms's Sonata-Form Recapitulations." PhD diss., Yale University, 1992.

Stanislavsky, Konstantin. Notes to *The Blue Bird* cast, January/February 1908. Taken down by Sulerzhitsky. Konstantin Stanislavsky Archive, No. 1392.

Thornhill, William Robert. "Kurt Weill's Street Scene." PhD diss., University of North Carolina, Chapel Hill, 1990.

Warrick, Kimberley J. "A Stylistic Analysis of Aaron Copland's Two Operas." PhD diss., University of Northern Colorado, Greeley, 1996.

Werley, Matthew M. "From Alienation to Abnegation: Jenufa and the Metaphysics of Dramatic and Musical Discourse at the Turn of Century." Paper presented at the annual meeting for the Music Theory Society of the Mid-Atlantic, Baltimore, Maryland, April 4–5, 2003.